HILDEGARD VON BINGEN'S
PHYSICA

HILDEGARD VON BINGEN'S
PHYSICA

The Complete English Translation of
Her Classic Work on Health and Healing

Translated from the Latin by
PRISCILLA THROOP

Illustrations by
MARY ELDER JACOBSEN

Healing Arts Press
Rochester, VT 05767

Healing Arts Press
One Park Street
Rochester, Vermont 05767
www.gotoit.com

Note to the reader: This book is intended as an informational guide. The remedies, approaches, and techniques described herein are meant to supplement, and not to be a substitute for, professional medical care or treatment. They should not be used to treat a serious ailment without prior consultation with a qualified health-care professional.

Library of Congress Cataloging-in-Publication Data

Hildegard, Saint, 1098–1179.
   [Physica. English]
   Hildegard von Bingen's Physica : the complete translation
of her classic work on health and healing / translated from the
Latin by Priscilla Throop ; illustrations by Mary Elder Jacobsen.
     p.   cm.
   ISBN 978-0-89281-661-3 (hardcover)
   1. Medicine, Medieval. I. Throop, Priscilla, 1946–
   R128.H5313   1998   98-1811
   610—dc21   CIP

Printed and bound in India

10　9　8

Text design and layout by Kristin Camp
This book was typeset in Bembo

Healing Arts Press is a division of Inner Traditions International

Contents

*To Irene Horbar and Andrea Salgado
for their help and encouragement*

Translator's Introduction

VISIONARY, MYSTIC, HEALER, LINGUIST, POET, artist, musician, playwright, biographer, theologian, preacher, and spiritual counselor—the multi-faceted Hildegard von Bingen (1098–1179), twelfth-century Benedictine abbess of the Rhineland, outshines others from her period, and indeed from any period.

Hildegard led a relatively normal life for a child of the nobility, having been given at the age of eight to an anchoress for education. The anchoress, Jutta of Spanheim, also of the local nobility, was attached to the Benedictine monastery of Disibodenberg, which had been founded by a seventh-century Irish monk, Disibod. By the time Hildegard took her vows as a nun and received the veil from Bishop Otto of Bamberg, the enclosure had expanded and become a convent. At the death of Jutta in 1136 Hildegard was elected abbess.

Perhaps what distinguishes the work of Hildegard von Bingen are her visionary experiences, which she began having at a very young age. She had been keeping them to herself until one of these visions compelled her to write,

> When I was forty-two years and seven months old, a burning light of tremendous brightness coming from heaven poured into my entire mind. Like a flame that does not burn but enkindles, it enflamed my whole heart and breast, just like the sun that warms an object with its rays. . . . A voice from heaven was saying, *O weak person, you who are ash of ash and decaying of*

decaying, speak and write what you see and hear. Since you are timid about speaking, and simple in your explanation, and unskilled in writing about these things, speak and write . . . as one who hears and understands the words of a teacher and explains them in his own way.

At this, she started on her major visionary work, *Scivias,* or "Know the Ways (of God)," which depicts each vision with beautiful illuminations and elaborative text. Pope Eugenius III read some of this work at a synod in Trier (winter of 1147–48) and authorized Hildegard to continue. Hildegard had previously exchanged letters with Bernard of Clairvaux, who was instrumental in bringing her work to the pope's attention. Now recognized as an agent through whom God's will might be known, she received letters fom popes, emperors, kings, queens, and bishops, as well as from people of lesser degree—all asking for her prayers and advice. She did not hesitate to scold the highest among these, if need be.

In 1150, in an unusual move for a woman and against the will of the abbot (who would miss the dowries the women brought as their entry fee to the monastery), Hildegard took eighteen or twenty nuns from Disibodenberg—which had continued to expand, as had Hildegard's fame—to establish a new convent at Rupertsberg, a day's journey away. Fifteen years later she founded another community at Eibingen, which she visited often.

Upon finishing *Scivias,* she turned to her medical works, known today as *Physica* ("Medicine," or "Book of Medicinal Simples") and *Causae et curae* ("Causes and Cures," or "Book of Compound Medicine"), on which she worked between 1151 and 1158.* The distinction between the "medical" and "visionary" works is not as clear-cut as we might like to think. Her medical and physiological ideas make up a great deal of her *Liber divinorum operum simplicis hominis,* or "Book of Divine Works," and the so-called medical works were revealed by direct transmission from the Divine, in the same way her more theologically based visions were. Renown for her healing ability overwhelmed appreciation for her many other talents during her lifetime, and all ranks of people visited her for healing, exorcism, and counsel.

---

*Causae et curae, of which there is one extant manuscript, has been reagrded as a separate work by Hildegard. Much of it correlates word for word with the material in *Physica,* leading me to wonder if it may have been compiled at a later time, synthesizing Hildegard's work.

Hildegard's musical works took shape before 1158, although she would make later additions. Included in these is what has been called the first known mystery play, *Ordo virtutum* or "The Play of the Virtues," written as a finale to *Scivias*. The central character, the Soul, is torn between opposing arguments of the Devil and a choir of Virtues. We do not know if this play was intended for any specific liturgical occasion, but we do know that Hildegard composed her own sequences for masses. Here too she overstepped the usual confines of women. For example, when Héloise wanted music for her convent, the Paraclete, she did not venture to compose it, but asked Abelard to write it for her.

Then followed Hildegard's second visionary work, *Liber vitae meritorum,* "Book of Life's Merits," in which the Virtues answer words spoken by Vices. In this work, Hildegard recommends a variety of penitential activities to aid in throwing off the Vices.

During the five years she was engaged in the composition of *Liber vitae meritorum* she made three preaching tours—another highly irregular activity for a woman; in fact it was debated at that time whether even monks or canons had the right to preach. These tours, for which she had been "stirred up by the Spirit of the Lord to teach the true heaven," took her along nearby rivers. The first was along the Main River, the second along the Moselle and Saar, and the third along the Rhine. Seven or eight years later she made yet another tour which took her to the Danube. During this period of extensive travel she preached to monks, nuns, secular clergy, and the public.

Her third visionary work, *Liber divinorum operum simplicis hominis,* "Book of Divine Works," completed around 1173, deals with the world of humanity—the origin of life, foundation of the world, human nature, the physiology of the body, the kingdom of the hereafter, and the history of salvation.

Among her minor works are biographies of Disibod and Rupert and commentaries on the Gospels, the Athanasian Creed, and the Benedictine Rule. She also invented a unique language and alphabet for the use of her nuns.

HILDEGARD'S MEDICINE

When he wrote his *Rule* in the sixth century, Benedict of Nursia listed care of the sick as one of the instruments of good works. At that time the monks cultivated gardens with healing herbs and were the doctors of their day. In the ninth century, another precursor of Hildegard was Liutbirg, East Saxony's first recluse, who restored paupers to a healthy condition and devoted herself to the care of the sick.

In her biography of the saint who first cultivated the area later called Disibodenberg, Hildegard describes Disibod as sustaining himself and his companions on the roots of plants when they were without other food. He behaved as a good herbalist, one "who plants in his garden spices and aromatic plants, and always endeavors that his garden be green and not dry. . . . People passing through would see him digging roots, or collecting other necessities," and "many sick and weak people were brought to him, whom the Holy Spirit, through his merits, quickly healed."

The present work, which Hildegard called "Subleties of the Diverse Qualities of Created Things," was named *Physica* in a 1533 edition published in Strassburg by Johannes Schott. For a long time Schott's was the only known text, as it was unknown what manuscript Schott had used for the Strassburg edition. The subsequent discovery of several different manuscripts invited confusion in that Schott's arrangement of the "books" differs from that of the manuscripts, including the omission of the book "Stones." Material unattested in the manuscripts is present, and much is left out.

For a later edition published in 1882 as volume 197 of the *Patrologia Latina,* C. Daremberg and F. A. Reuss used the text of a fifteenth-century manuscript now in the National Library in Paris (Cod. 6952).*† Daremberg and Reuss incorporated material from Schott's edition that does not appear in the Paris manuscript, putting these sections in brack-

---

*Of the entire *Patrologia Latina,* or "The writings of our fathers in Latin," a multi-volume work compiled by French cleric and editor Jacques-Paul Migne, only a few volumes out of over three hundred include writings by women. Volume 197 is a collection of writings by Hildegard von Bingen.

†We know of four other manuscripts [two written in the thirteenth century—one in the Herzog-August Library in Wolfenbüttel (Cod. 56, 2 Aug. 4°) and the other in the Biblioteca Medicea Laurenziana, Florence (Ms. laur. Ashb. 1323); one, besides the Paris manuscript, from the fifteenth century—in the Royal Library in Brussels (Cod. 1494); and one from the late fourteenth or early fifteenth century—in the Biblioteca Apostolica Vaticana, Rome (Cod. Ferraioli 921),] and three fragments [Bern, Burger-Bibliothek (Cod. 525, f. 18ʳ–23ʳ); the Freiburg fragment, c. 1496–1505, at Universitätsbibliothek (Cod. 178a); and Universitäts-bibliothek, Augsberg (Cod. III 1, 2°, fol. 43)].

Professor Irmgard Müller of Marburg is preparing a critical edition incorporating all the texts and noting variations, for the *Corpus Christianorum.* Until its appearance, it is futile to make any conjecture about the relationship of the manuscripts.

ets. For this translation, I have followed the *Patrologia Latina,* including its use of brackets for Schott's additions. I have not noted the sections Schott omits nor, for the most part, incorporated material relegated to the footnotes in the *Patrologia.*

The Complete *Physica* consists of nine books: "Plants," which includes a few idiosyncratic items (e.g. butter, salt, and vinegar), which Hildegard used in concocting her remedies, "Elements," "Trees," "Stones," "Fish," "Birds," "Animals," "Reptiles," and "Metals." Some of Hildegard's entries are difficult to identify, as she uses Middle High German colloquial terms not listed in available dictionaries. Names of herbs, as well as other natural beings, change from place to place, and a plant or animal with an identical name may not be the same as the creature bearing its name today.

For each item discussed there is no description of its physical appearance. After a short introduction to each section, Hildegard names the items and tells their basic qualities—whether they are hot or cold, dry or moist. Hildegard then elaborates on their medicinal value, or lack thereof, and explains how to prepare and apply medication. The word "subtleties," used in her title, refers to secret powers hidden in natural creatures for the use of human beings and revealed by God.

Diseases and cures are linked to the four qualities—hot, cold, dry, moist—of which two are often dominant in varying degrees. Medical practice aims to balance these qualities, with some of the applications following the "like cures like" theory, and others using opposite qualities to bring the patient back to health.

"Humors" and their balance are central to Hildegard's theories, but her discussion of the humors has greater affinity with Eastern medicine than with the traditional Greek humoral pathology. To the Greeks, hot is choler, or yellow bile; dry is blood; moist is phlegm; and cold is black bile. Hildegard distinguishes between the dry, damp, foamy, and cool humors. Any humor exceeding its measure endangers a person.

The terms *flegmata* and *livores,* as used in this work (the explanation Hildegard provides in *Causes and Cures* is more involved), can include any of the humors, depending on their prevalence or balance. They are pathological by-products of the metabolic process. *Flegma* is Greek for flame or inflammation. It is also the morbid humor equivalent to the Latin *pituita.* It has been explained as residue left from a burning process within the body, which has turned cold. While *livor,* or "slime," is classically a lead-colored spot or a bruise on the body, in this work the term refers to lymph, pus, or other watery or poisonous secretions. In this translation I have used "phlegm" for the former and "mucus" for the latter.

The word *gicht,* which I have left untranslated, covers a variety of ailments including gout, arthritis, rheumatism, lumbago, and sciatica. Hildegard sometimes explains gicht as involving a commotion in the humors, or one who has it as being troubled by "paralysis," an abolition of function or falling apart. One who is suffering from these ailments is said to be *virgichtiget.*

Vicht is another term I have left as is. It denotes a problem with metabolism, and includes tiredness, weakness, and loss of vitality, with recurrent pains or cramps. *Freislich* denotes a pustule which is terrible, bringing danger and destruction.

"Scrofula" is an ailment of great concern to Hildegard, but one with which we are no longer afflicted. It was caused by a tubercular infection of the lymph glands in the neck, which would sometimes grow very large and rupture. "Scabies" does not refer to what goes by that name today: rather, mange, eczema, scurvy, and scabby head are embraced by that term. Also, "leprosy" designates any scaly disease of the skin, not specifically Hansen's disease; "ulcer" can denote any sore or wound; "crabs" may be crab lice; "worms" can be any kind of vermin; and "pestilence" among animals can cover a range of afflictions.

Recipes for Hildegard's remedies are not as specific as the reader might like. She advises using a certain herb, but how much and whether it is the root, stem, leaf, or flower that is used is sometimes left unsaid. Amounts to be used are frequently expressed proportionally, though she does use two specific weights, the *nummus* (pennyweight) and *obolus* (halfpennyweight). Occasionally, measurements given are in terms of writing implements, as for belladona juice, "a single drop from a pen."

Moderation is Hildegard's key to good health. In a letter to Elisabeth of Schönau, another Benedictine visionary, she advises the use of discretion, "Do not lay on more strain than the body can endure. Immoderate straining and abstinence bring nothing useful to the soul." Hildegard von Bingen advocated a balanced diet, sufficient rest, alleviation of stress, and a wholesome moral life.

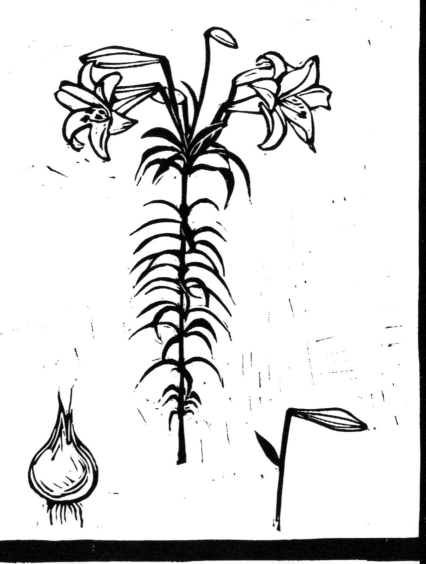

PLANTS

BOOK ONE
Plants

W<small>ITH EARTH WAS THE HUMAN BEING CREATED.</small> All the elements served mankind and, sensing that man was alive, they busied themselves in aiding his life in every way. And man in turn occupied himself with them. The earth gave its vital energy, according to each person's race, nature, habits, and environment. Through the beneficial herbs, the earth brings forth the range of mankind's spiritual powers and distinguishes between them; through the the harmful herbs, it manifests harmful and diabolic behaviors.

Certain herbs, when cooked with particular foods, make a person eager to eat. They are easy to digest and are assimilated into his flesh without making him heavy. When uncooked, the sap of fruit-bearing trees is harmful, but when cooked it can be ingested and is comparable to human blood. Trees which do not bear fruit are not beneficial. They are only wood, not trees. Their leaves are useless to eat. Even if they do no great harm, they are likewise of no benefit and are like decayed matter in a person. The material in trees and wood, which is made into rope, is comparable to human veins. The earth's stones can be compared to human bones, and their wetness is like bone marrow, since a moist stone also has heat. When stones serve to protect roofs, their role is similar to that of human finger- and toenails.

Certain plants grow from air. These plants are gentle on the digestion and possess a happy nature, producing happiness in anyone who eats them. They are like a person's hair in that they are always light and airy. Certain other herbs are windy, since they grow from the wind. These herbs are dry, and heavy on one's digestion. They are of a sad nature, making the person who eats them sad. They are comparable to human perspiration. Moreover, there are herbs which are fatal as human food. They cannot be eaten, their juice is poisonous, and they are comparable to human excrement.

Earth has sweat and moisture and juice: the earth's sweat brings forth harmful plants; its moisture brings forth plants which are edible or otherwise serve useful purposes; its juice produces grapevines and fruit-bearing trees. Plants which are sown by human labor, and spring up and grow gradually, are like domestic animals which are nourished with care in the home. By the labor with which they are planted and cultivated, they throw off the acidity and bitterness of their moisture. Their juices border on the quality of that of a human, and become good and beneficial for his food and drink. There are plants which grow from the falling of their own seed, without human labor, and which, like wild beasts, spring up quickly and suddenly. These are harmful as human food, as a person is reared by sucking milk, eating, and growing in a moderate time, which doesn't happen with these plants. Nevertheless some of these, used in medicine, suppress harmful or feeble humors in people.

Every plant is either hot or cold, and grows thus, since the heat of the herbs signifies the spirit, and the cold, the body. They flourish, according to their nature, when they abound in either heat or cold. If all herbs were hot and none cold, they would cause difficulty to the user. If all were cold, and none hot, they would provide an imbalance in people, since hot things oppose cold, and cold things resist hot. Certain herbs have within them either the power of the strongest aromas or the harshness of the most bitter aromas. Whence, they suppress and hold in contempt many ills which evil spirits make. There are also herbs which have in them the foam, as it were, of the elements. With them, deceived people try to seek their fortunes. The devil loves these and mingles himself with them.

I. WHEAT

Wheat *(triticum)* is hot and full of profit. Nothing is lacking in it. When proper flour is made from it, and bread made from that flour, it is good for both the healthy and the sick. It furnishes a person with proper flesh and correct blood. But, if anyone sifts out the bran from the flour (which is semolina), and then makes bread from that flour, the bread is weaker and more feeble than if it had been made from the proper flour. Without its bran, the flour loses its strength somewhat, and produces more mucus in a person than that made from the whole wheat flour.

Whosoever cooks wheat without the entire grain, or wheat not ground in the mill, it is as if he eats another food, for this wheat furnishes neither correct blood nor healthy flesh, but more mucus. It is scarcely digested. It is not at all good for a sick person, even if a healthy person is able to survive on this food.

Nevertheless, if someone has an empty brain—and because of this is vexed by insanity, and is delerious—take the whole grains of wheat and cook them in water. Remove these cooked grains from the water, and place them around his whole head, tying a cloth over them. His brain will be reinvigorated by their vital fluid, and he may recover his health and strength. Do this until he returns to his right mind.

If someone is ailing in his back or loins, cook grains of wheat in water, and place them, warm, over the place where he is ailing. The heat of the wheat will chase away the powers of that disease.

[If a dog bites a person, a paste of this flour, prepared with the white of an egg, should be placed over the bite for three days and three nights, so it may draw out the poison: because of its breath, the bite of a dog is more poisonous than that of other animals. Afterward, that paste should be removed, and a compound of yarrow and egg white should be placed on the same wound for two or three days. When that is removed, it should be treated with unguents, as any other wound.]

II. RYE

Rye *(siligo)* is hot, but colder than wheat. It has many powers. Bread made from rye is good for healthy people, and makes them strong. Rye is good for fat people, since it diminishes their flesh, and makes them strong. But it is the opposite for those who have a cold stomach, and they are much weakened by it. Their debility cannot weather digesting it, and so, for them, it induces great disturbance.

[Anyone who has a protuberance of any sort on his body should cover the lump with a piece of rye bread, either warmed on the fire or broken from a piece taken from the oven. He should repeat this until the lump disappears. The warmth will destroy the lump and make it vanish.

If one has scabies on his head, he should pulverize a crust of rye bread and apply the powder, which removes this malady. After three days, rub the area with olive oil. It is warm and will heal it. He should continue this until he is cured. If crabs, that is very tiny larvae, eat the flesh of a person, a warm crumb of this bread should be applied. One should do this frequently, and the larvae will die from the heat.]

III. Oats

Oats *(avena)* are hot, with a sharp taste and strong vapor. Oats are a happy and healthy food for people who are well, furnishing them with a cheerful mind and a pure, clear intellect. It also provides good color and healthy flesh. It is good for those who are somewhat, or moderately ill. It does not harm them, whether eaten in bread or as cereal. It is not suitable as food for those who are very ill and cold, since oats always require heat. If people in this condition eat either bread or cereal made of oats, it will coagulate in the belly and produce mucus. It will not furnish them with strength, since they are cold. One who is *virgichtiget*, and from it has been made a bit mad, with a divided mind and crazy thoughts, should take a sauna bath. He should pour the water in which oats have been cooked over the hot rocks. If he does this often, he will become himself and regain his health.

IV. Barley

Barley *(hordeum)* is cold. Because it is colder than the grains just mentioned, it is also weaker. If it is eaten, either in bread or as cereal, it vexes both healthy and sick people. Its powers are not as great as those of other kinds of grain. For an ill person, whose whole body is failing, one should cook barley in rapidly boiling water. Then he should put that water in a large tub, and have the person take a bath in it. Do this often, until he is well, regaining his bodily flesh and attaining health.

And one who is so sick that he cannot even eat bread should take equal weights of barley and oats and add a bit of fennel. He should cook these together in water, then strain the liquid through a cloth. Instead of eating bread, he should drink this broth until he regains his health and strength.

But one whose face has hard and rough skin, made harsh from the wind, should cook barley in water and, having strained that water through a cloth, should bathe his face gently with the moderately warm water. The skin will become soft and smooth, and will have a beautiful color. If a person's head has an ailment, it should be washed frequently in this water, and it will be healed.

V. SPELT

The best grain is spelt *(spelta)*. It is hot, rich, and powerful. It is milder than other grains. Eating it rectifies the flesh and provides proper blood. It also creates a happy mind and puts joy in the human disposition. In whatever way it is eaten, whether in bread or in other foods, it is good and easy to digest. For anyone who is so sick that he is unable to eat, take whole grains of spelt and cook them in water. Add lard or egg yolk, so he might more willingly eat it, on account of the better flavor. Give this to the sick person to eat, and it will heal him inwardly, like a good, sound unguent.

VI. PEAS

Peas *(pisa)* are cold and a bit phlegmatic. They oppress the lungs a bit. Nevertheless, they are good for a warm-natured person to eat. They make him bold. They are not good for the sicknesses of cold-natured people. Eating peas produces much mucus in them.

[Indeed, peas are injurious in all illnesses, and have no power to expel them. Nevertheless, one who is sick with excessive phlegm in his forehead should crush white peas by chewing them, and blend this matter in very pure honey. He should then apply it to his temples, tying a bandage over it. He should repeat this until he is better. If anyone has an ailment in his intestines, he should often swallow warm broth of peas, and he will get better.]

VII. BROAD BEANS

Broad beans *(faba)* are hot. They are good for strong, healthy people to eat—better than peas. There is not much harm if sick people eat beans, since they do not produce as much mucus as peas. Flour from this bean is good, and is useful for the infirm person as well as the healthy. It is gentle and easily digested. One whose entrails are in pain should cook beans in water, with a bit of lard or olive oil. After the beans are taken out, he should drink the warm broth. He should do this frequently, and it will cure him internally.

[Whoever has bubbling pain of any sort on his flesh, whether from scabies or ulcers, should take the flour of the broad bean, and add a bit of powdered fennel seed. He should blend this in water, with a minimal amount of wheat flour, so that it will stick together. He should prepare little cakes, dried by the fire or the sun. He should frequently place them over the area, to draw out the pain, and he will be cured.]

VIII. LENTILS

Lentils *(lens)* are cold. When used as food, they augment neither the marrow nor blood nor flesh of a person. Neither do they contribute to his strength, but only satisfy his stomach, filling its emptiness. They stir a person's weak humors to make a commotion.

[But if spots of scabies, or dirty hair with ulcers at the root, appear on a person's head, he should gently reduce lentils to a powder, over a glowing stone. He should also pulverize a snail shell, with whatever slime there is in it, and add it to an equal weight of lentil powder. Placed over the spots, it will strip off the discharge of this disease, and it will be cured.]

IX. MILLET

Millet *(hirs)* is cold, but a little hot. It does not augment a person's blood or flesh, nor does it provide strength. It only fills his stomach and diminishes hunger, since it does not contain nourishment. It makes a person's brain watery. It makes his stomach lukewarm and slow. It brings about an upset in a person's humors, acts almost as a weed, and is not healthy for a person to eat.

X. PANIC GRASS

Panic grass *(venich)* is cold, but has a little heat. It has very little value, since it has little nourishment, and gives no remarkable powers to one who eats it. It is not as harmful as millet is, nor does it vigorously rouse evil humors and diseases, as millet does. [However, one who has burning fevers should cook panic grass in wine and frequently drink that wine warm, and he will be cured.]

XI. HEMP

Hemp *(hanff)* is hot, and it grows when the air is neither very hot nor very cold, and its nature is similar. Its seed is salubrious, and good as food for healthy people. It is gentle and profitable to the stomach, taking away a bit of its mucus. It is easy to digest, diminishes bad humors, and fortifies good humors. Nevertheless, if one who is weak in the head, and has a vacant brain, eats hemp, it easily afflicts his head. It does not harm one who has a healthy head and full brain. If one is very ill, it even afflicts his stomach a bit. Eating it does not hurt one who is moderately ill.

[Let one who has a cold stomach cook hemp in water and, when the water has been squeezed out, wrap it in a small cloth, and frequently place it, warm, on his stomach. This strengthens and renews that area. Also, a cloth made from hemp is good for binding ulcers and wounds, since the heat in it has been tempered.]

XII. NIGELLA

Nigella *(ratde)* is hot and dry, and it is good as food for no man, since it would make him sick. It is not beneficial to animals, though it is not very injurious. If someone has ulcers on his head, which are not scabies, he should pound nigella and mix it with roasted lard. He should often and thoroughly anoint the ulcers with this, and it will reduce them, and he will be healed.

Also, pound the nigella, and mix honey with it. Where there are many flies, you may streak it on the wall, and the flies on tasting it will sicken and fall dead.

XIII. GALINGALE

Galingale *(galgan)* is totally hot. It contains no coldness and is powerful. A person with a burning fever should drink pulverized galingale in spring water, and it will extinguish the fever. One who is ailing from bad humors in his back or side should boil galingale in wine and frequently drink it warm, and the pain will cease. One with pain in his heart, or with a weak heart, will soon be better if he eats enough galingale.

[Also, a person who suffers from stinking breath—which passes to the lungs, so that he sometimes even has a hoarse voice—should take galingale and fennel in equal weights, with twice the amount of both nutmeg and feverfew. He should pulverize these, and mix them together. He should eat two pennyweights of this powder with a small mouthful of bread every day on an empty stomach. He should soon drink a bit of warm wine, and frequently eat other high-quality herbs, which have good odor, both with food and on an empty stomach. Their good odor checks the stinking breath.

One whose lungs ail in any way should avoid fat foods and abstain from uncooked food as well as food infused with much blood. These create putrefaction around the lungs. Let him also avoid peas, lentils, raw fruits and vegetables, nuts, and oil. These bring mucus to the lungs. If one wishes to eat meat, it should be lean meat. If he wants to eat cheese, it should be neither cooked nor fresh, but dried, since bad mucuses are situated in it. If he wishes to eat oil, he should do it in moderation, lest it attract mucus to the lungs. Indeed, he should not drink water, since it produces mucus around the lungs. He should also not drink new wine. This has not yet thrown off scum by fermenting and thus been purified. Beer does not harm him much, because it has been boiled. He should drink aged wine, since it delights the lungs with its good heat. He should also guard himself against damp and misty air, which harms the lungs with its humidity.

If bad humors have very much overflowed in a person's intestines and spleen, and have brought great sufferings to the heart through melancholy, one should take galingale and feverfew in equal amounts, and a quarter of that amount of white pepper (if he does not have white pepper, he should use four times as much savory as white pepper), and reduce this to a powder. Then, he should take flour of the broad bean, add this to the powder, and mix this with fenugreek juice, without water, wine, or any other liquid. From this, he should prepare little cakes and dry them in the heat of the sun. This should be done in the summer, when the sun is powerful, so he may have them in the winter. Then he should eat these cakes, whether he has eaten or been fasting. Afterward, he should take licorice, five times as much fennel, sugar (of the same weight as the licorice), and a bit of honey. He should make a drink from these things, and drink it for heart pain, with or without food.

If phlegm has made a person's head foggy and his hearing confused he should take galingale, a third part of aloe, twice as much oregano as galingale, and peach leaves of the same weight as the oregano. He should make a powder of these and use it daily, whether he has eaten or been fasting.

One who ails in his chest, heart, or spleen, and one who has a stomach cooled from phlegm, should take galingale, and twice as much oregano, and celery seed of the same weight as the oregano, and a little white pepper. He should reduce this to a powder, and add a little cooked honey to make an electuary. Let him cook it gently, away from sudden boiling, and let him eat this electuary often. Also, he should frequently use good, pure, mild wine.

One who is tormented by palsy should take galingale, with half as much nutmeg, and half as much spike lavender as nutmeg, and equal weights of *githerut* and lovage—but of each one, more than the spike lavender. To these he should add equal weights of female fern and saxifrage. (These two together should be equal to the five previous ingredients.) Pulverize this. If one is well, he should eat this powder on bread; if ill, he should eat an electuary made from it.]

XIV. ZEDOARY

Zedoary *(zituar)* is moderately hot and contains great power. A person whose limbs quiver convulsively and who lacks strength should put zedoary, cut up, in wine. He should add a little less galingale, and cook it with a little honey. He should drink this warm. The tremor will go away, and he will recover his strength.

One who has too much saliva or spume should pulverize the zedoary and tie the powder in a small cloth. He should place this in a metallic jar, with water, so that the water receives the flavor it releases during the night. He should drink it often in the morning, before breakfast, and the saliva and foaming will stop. One whose head aches greatly will be better if he wets his forehead and temples with the same powder, wrapped in a cloth and steeped in water. One whose stomach is very heavy, having been filled with bad food, should pulverize zedoary and make a little cake with that powder, a moderate amount of flour of the finest whole wheat, and water. He should cook it in the sun or in a nearly cold oven and then reduce it back to a powder. He should frequently lick this powder from his hand, before breakfast and when he goes to bed at night. It will take away the distress of his stomach.

XV. GINGER

Ginger *(ingeber)* is very hot and easily diffuses itself. It is injurious as food for a healthy or fat person. It makes him ignorant, languid, and lewd. But, one whose body is dry and almost failing should pulverize ginger and consume the powder in broth, on an empty stomach. He may even eat a moderate amount of it with bread. He will get better. As soon as he is better, he should not eat it, lest he be injured by it. One who has oozing, irritated eyes should tie pulverized ginger in a cloth and place it in wine, so that the wine becomes dark colored. At night, when he goes to bed, he should smear this wine around his eyes and eyelids. If a little gets into his eyes, it will not harm him. It will take away the pus, and the irritation, from his eyes.

[As long as a person has eyesight, this is able to help his eyes; after he has lost his sight, it will not benefit him. One whose eyes are misty should take equal measures of rue and hyssop sap and add three times as much of the above-mentioned wine. He should pour this into a bronze vessel, so that it may retain its power. At night, when he goes to bed, let him smear it around the outside of the eyes and eyelids. If a bit touches the eyes, it will not harm them. Let him do this often, and the mistiness of his eyes will vanish.

One who suffers constipation in his stomach or intestines should pulverize ginger and mix it with a little sap of bugloss. He should make little cakes with this powder and flour of the broad bean, and cook them in an oven in which the heat of the fire has abated a bit. Eating these cakes, on an empty stomach or with food, will diminish the foulness of the stomach and strengthen the person.

A person who suffers from any stomach ailment should pulverize ginger with twice as much galingale and a half portion of zedoary. He should place this powder in wine and drink it frequently, after a meal and at night, when going to bed. His stomach will be better.]

And, one who has pimply eruptions on his body should place the above-mentioned powder, tied in a cloth, in vinegar and add a bit of wine (if he has it) so it doesn't become too dark. He should smear his skin where the eruptions are, and he will be cured.

[However, a person whom *vicht* torments should pulverize a bit of ginger with more cinnamon. He should take less sage than ginger, and more fennel than sage, and a little more tansy than sage, and crush them to a juice in a mortar, and strain it through a cloth. Then he should cook a bit of honey in wine, and add a little white pepper or, if he doesn't have that, a little moneywort, and put it in the powder and juice. Afterward, he should take duckweed, and twice as much tormentil, and mustard which grows in the field—as much as the tormentil, but less than the duckweed (sic). He should rub this to a juice in a mortar, and place it in a little bag, and pour the honeyed wine mixture over it, and make a clear drink. One who suffers the above-mentioned pain should, on an empty stomach, drink as much of this potion as he can in one breath. He should do the same thing at night when he goes to bed, and continue until he is well.

A person who wants to make and consume purgatives should pulverize and strain ginger with half as much licorice, and a third as much zedoary as ginger. Then he should weigh this powder all together, and take as much sugar as the weight of this powder. All this should be equal to the weight of thirty pennies. Then he should take—from the purest, finely ground whole wheat flour—as much flour as is held in a half nut shell, and as much of the milky juice of the soapwort as the slit feather of a scribe is capable of holding in its incision. And so, from the foresaid powder, flour, and soapwort milk, he should make the very thinnest lump of dough or little cake. He should divide this lump into four parts, and dry it in the March or April sun. In those months the rays of the sun are so tempered that they are neither too hot nor too cold, and are especially healthful. If one does not have soapwort milk in those months, he must delay until May, and dry this little cake in the May sun, carefully watching for the proper amout of time. One who then wants to consume a purgative should eat a quarter of the cake, on an empty stomach. If his stomach is so strong and hard that it doesn't feel the effect of the purgative, let him again take half of another quarter of this cake, and smear it completely with soapwort milk. He should eat this, after drying it again in the sun, on an empty stomach. Before anyone takes a purgative, he should warm himself if he is cold, and then eat it. After he eats it, he should rest in bed, calmly keeping watch; when he rises, he should walk here and there in moderation, so that he does not suffer cold. After the loosening, he should eat wheat bread, not dry but dipped in a liquid. He may eat young chickens, and pork, and other agreeable meats. He should avoid coarse bread, beef, fish, and other crude and roasted foods, except roasted pears. He should also abstain from cheese and raw vegetables and fruits. He may drink wine in moderation, but should avoid water. He should also flee the brightness of the sun, and continue this regimen for three days.]

XVI. PEPPER

Pepper *(piper)* is very hot and dry. It contains a certain precipitousness, and harms a person if he eats too much. It causes pleurisy, destroys the humors in a person, and creates bad humors. [A person who is sick from eating an apple or pear should eat pepper, and he will be better.] If someone is splenetic and disdains food to the point of being unwilling to eat, he should eat a moderate amount of pepper in any food, with bread. His spleen will be better, and he will lay aside his loathing of eating.

XVII. CUMIN

Cumin *(kumel)* is dry and of moderate heat. No matter how it is eaten, it is good, useful, and healthful for a person who is congested. But it is harmful for a person who has pain in his heart [because it does not completely warm the heart, which should always be warm]. It is good for a healthy person to eat, since it furnishes a good disposition and moderates the temperature of one who is too hot. Except for one with a lung ailment, it is harmful for an ill person to eat, since it stirs up diseases.

[One who wishes to eat cooked or dry cheese without ill consequences should place cumin on it. One who suffers nausea should pulverize cumin with a third as much pepper and a quarter as much pimpernel. He should mix this powder with pure wheat flour, and make cookies, with egg yolk and a little water, either in a hot oven or under hot ashes. He should eat these cookies, as well as the cumin powder on bread, and it will suppress the hot and cold humors in his intestines, which cause his nausea.]

XVIII. Feverfew or Pellitory

Feverfew *(bertram)* is of moderate heat and somewhat dry. It is absolutely balanced and has good vital energy. It is good food for a healthy person, since it diminishes putrid matter in him, augments his good blood, and creates clear understanding. It restores strength to an ill person whose body is almost completely failing. Providing good digestion, it lets nothing pass through the body without being digested. A person who has a lot of phlegm in his head will find it diminished if he eats feverfew frequently. Eaten often, it expels pleurisy and provides a person with pure humors. It gives him clear eyesight. In whatever way it is eaten, whether dried or in food, it is beneficial for both sick and healthy people. If a person eats it frequently, it will chase illness from him and keep him from getting sick. When it is eaten, it draws moisture and saliva from the mouth. Because it draws out evil humors, it restores health.

XIX. Licorice

Licorice *(liquiricium)* is of moderate heat. No matter how it is eaten, it gives a person a clear voice. It makes one's mind agreeable, and his eyes clear. It soothes his stomach for digestion. It is of great benefit to an insane person. If eaten frequently, it extinquishes the furor in his head.

XX. Cinnamon

Cinnamon *(cynamomum)* is very hot and its power is great. It holds a bit of moisture, but its heat is so strong that it suppresses that dampness. It diminishes bad humors in one who eats it often, and provides him with good humors. [The tree whose bark is cinnamon is very hot. Whence, a person who is paralyzed by gout, or who has quotidian, tertian, or quartan fevers should pour good wine into a steel vessel. He should put into it wood and leaves of this tree, while they still have sap in them. After boiling it on a fire, he should drink it frequently, hot. He will be healed. One whose head is heavy and dulled, and who has difficulty breathing through his nose, should pulverize cinnamon and eat it often with a morsel of bread, or licked from his hand. It dissolves the noxious humors which had dulled his head.]

XXI. NUTMEG

Nutmeg *(nux muscata)* has great heat and good moderation in its powers. If a person eats nutmeg, it will open up his heart, make his judgment free from obstruction, and give him a good disposition. Take some nutmeg and an equal weight of cinnamon and a bit of cloves, and pulverize them. Then make small cakes with this and fine whole wheat flour and water. Eat them often. It will calm all bitterness of the heart and mind, open your heart and impaired senses, and make your mind cheerful. It purifies your senses and diminishes all harmful humors in you. It gives good liquid to your blood, and makes you strong. [The tree on which nutmeg grows is hot. Its wood and leaves are not very useful for medicine. But, one who is troubled by palsy in the brain should pulverize nutmeg and twice as much galingale. He should pound equal weights of the root of gladiolus and plantain, and add salt. He should make a drink from all these, and sip it. He should do this once or twice a day, until he is healed.]

XXII. ROSE

Rose *(rosa)* is cold, and this coldness contains moderation which is useful. In the morning, or at daybreak, pluck a rose petal and place it on your eyes. It draws out the humor and makes them clear. One with small ulcers on his body should place rose petals over them. This pulls the mucus from them. [One who is inclined to wrath should take rose and less sage and pulverize them. When wrath is rising in him, he should hold this powder to his nostrils. The sage lessens the wrath, and the rose makes him happy. Rose, and half as much sage, may be cooked with fresh, melted lard, in water, and an ointment made from this. The place where a person is troubled by a cramp or paralysis should be rubbed with it, and he will be better.] Rose is also good to add to potions, unguents, and all medications. If even a little rose is added, they are so much better, because of the good virtues of the rose.

XXIII. LILY

Lily *(lilium)* is more cold than hot. Take the end of a lily root and vigorously pound it together with old lard. Melt it in a small dish, and put it into a metallic jar. Then frequently anoint one who has white leprosy, having first warmed the unguent, and he will be cured. Red leprosy can be cured in the same way. One who has a rash should drink goat's milk and the rash will completely leave him. One should take the stem and leaves of lilies and pound them, expressing the juice from them. He should knead this juice together with some flour, and keep anointing the part of the body which suffers from rash. Before he anoints himself with this ointment, he should always drink goat's milk. The odor of the first buds of lilies, and indeed the odor of the flowers, makes a person's heart joyful and furnishes him with virtuous ideas.

XXIV. PSYLLIUM

Psyllium *(psillium)* is of a cold nature, and that coldness has a pleasant moderation. A person who cooks it in wine, and drinks that wine warm, will keep strong fevers in check. It makes a person's overwhelmed mind happy by its sweet temperateness. It strengthens the brain by its coldness, as well as by its moderation, and helps restore it to health. One who has fevers in his stomach should cook psyllium in wine. Then he should pour off the wine, and place the psyllium in a cloth. He should tie it over his stomach while it is still warm. It will chase away the fevers from his stomach.

XXV. SPIKE LAVENDER

Spike lavender *(spica)* is hot and dry, and its heat is healthy. Whoever cooks this lavender in wine or, if he has no wine, honey and water, and frequently drinks it when it is warm, will lessen the pain in his liver and lungs, and the stuffiness in his chest. It also makes his thinking and disposition pure.

XXVI. JAVA PEPPER OR CUBEB

Java pepper *(cubebus)* is hot, but the heat has moderation in it. It is also dry. If anyone eats java pepper, it tempers the shameful ardor which is in him. It also brings joy to his mind and makes pure his thinking and disposition [as its beneficial, moderate heat extinguishes the unworthy passions of lust, in which fetid, slimy mucuses lie hidden, and clarifies a person's mind and his disposition by illuminating them].

XXVII. CLOVES

Cloves *(gariofiles)* are very hot, but have some dampness by which they sweetly diffuse, just as the sweet moisture of honey. If one suffers in his head, so that his head is stuffy, and it is as if he were deaf, he should eat cloves often, and the stuffiness in his head will diminish. When sick intestines begin to swell in a person, it frequently happens that dropsy develops. When this happens, he should eat cloves often. They will check the putrefaction of the disease, because their power passes into the intestines. Cloves lessen the swelling, and so get rid of the dropsy, not permitting it to develop further.

The heat of a person's marrow oftentimes comes out in sweat and gives him gout. When this begins to increase, the sick person should eat cloves frequently. Their power goes into his marrow and keeps the gout from increasing and going any further.

[One who has the hiccoughs should chew cloves often. He should also eat zedoary frequently, after eating. He should do this for one month.]

XXVIII. BLACK HELLEBORE

Black hellebore *(cristiana)* possesses both fiery heat and coldness. A person in whom the worst, death-bearing humors are stirred up, so that they bubble up on some limb, with what they call *freislich,* should eat black hellebore constantly, and he will get better. One who has quartan fevers should eat black hellebore at their approach, and he will be better. One who is greatly tormented by *gicht,* and eats hellebore during that torment, will be better. One who has burning fevers in his stomach should cut some up in wine and heat this wine. He should drink it warm, and he will be better.

XXIX. LUNGWORT

Lungwort *(lunckwurcz)* is cold and a bit dry and not much use to anyone. Nevertheless, one whose lung is swollen so that he coughs and can hardly draw a breath should cook lungwort in wine, and drink it frequently, on an empty stomach. He will become well.

If sheep eat lungwort often, they will become healthy and fat, and it does no harm to their milk. But if, as we said, one who has a swollen lung frequently drinks lungwort cooked in wine, his lung will return to health, since the lung has the nature of a sheep.

XXX. HART'S-TONGUE FERN

Hart's-tongue fern *(hirtzunge)* is hot, and it is very effective for the liver, lungs, and painful intestines. Therefore, take hart's-tongue fern and boil it in wine. Add pure honey and bring it to a boil once again. Then pulverize pepper and twice as much cinnamon, and bring it, with the above-mentioned wine, to a boil once again. Strain it through a cloth, so as to make a clear drink. Drink it often, before and after meals. It benefits the liver, purges the lungs, heals aching intestines, and carries away internal decay and mucus. Also, dry the hart's-tongue fern in the hot sun, or gently on a hot tile, and pulverize it. Lick the powder in your hand with your tongue often, having either eaten or not. It checks the pain of your head and chest, and other aches which settle in your body. A person who is intensely and suddenly weak from any pain should immediately drink some of this powder in warm wine, and he will be better.

XXXI. YELLOW GENTIAN

Yellow gentian *(gentiana)* is fairly hot. One who suffers heart pain, as if his heart is just barely alive, should pulverize yellow gentian and eat that powder in broth, and it will strengthen his heart. One who has fever in the stomach should frequently drink this same powder in warm wine, which has been heated by a burning-hot piece of steel. His stomach will be purged of its fever.

XXXII. WILD THYME

Wild thyme *(quenula)* is hot and balanced. A person whose body has unhealthy flesh, as if scabies are thriving, should eat wild thyme often, either with meat or cooked in purees. His flesh will be made well, from the inside, and purified. But one who has a small area of rough skin should pound this thyme with fresh lard and make an unguent from it. When he anoints himself with it, he will have good health. When the brain is ill, as if it is empty, he should pulverize the thyme and mix it with fine whole wheat flour in water. He should make little cakes and eat them often and his brain will be better.

XXXIII. HOREHOUND

Horehound *(andron)* is hot, has much moisture, and is effective against various infirmities. Let one who has deaf ears cook horehound in water. He should take it from the water and permit its vapor to flow—warm—into his ears. He should place warm horehound around his ears and his entire head and he will receive better hearing. One who has a sore throat should cook horehound in water and strain the water through a cloth. Then he should add twice as much wine, and make it boil again in a small dish, with enough lard added. He should drink this frequently and his throat will be made well. One who has a cough should take equal amounts of fennel and dill, add a third part of horehound, and boil it in wine. He should strain it through a cloth and drink it. The coughing will stop. One who has weak and feeble intestines should cook horehound in wine with some honey and put it in a pot. When it has cooled, he should drink it frequently and his viscera will be made well.

XXXIV. GOATSBEARD

Goatsbeard *(hirtzswam)* is cold and harsh. It is noxious if a person or animal without infirmity eats it; its powers are such that it wounds a healthy person or animal internally when it discovers no illness. However, when perilous humors erupt in a person, so that he is tormented by gicht in his limbs, so that his limbs seem to be broken in pieces, if he then eats goatsbeard, it will put to flight the peril of those humors, drawing it off. Goatsbeard's nature is such that it is always accustomed to break whatever exists in the same place it resides. So it dashes to pieces whatever is fetid, where it finds it. Also, if a pregnant woman eats it, it causes her to abort, with great danger to her body.

XXXV. LAVENDER

Lavender *(lavendula)* is hot and dry, having very little moisture. It is not effective for a person to eat, but it does have a strong odor. If a person with many lice frequently smells lavender, the lice will die. Its odor clears the eyes [since it possesses the power of the strongest aromas and the usefulness of the most bitter ones. It curbs very many evil things and, because of it, malign spirits are terrified].

XXXVI. FENUGREEK

Fenugreek *(fenugraecum)* is more cold than hot, and a person who has quotidian fevers, which bring forth frequent sweats, and whom food bothers should take the fenugreek plant in the summer and warm up its seed in wine. If he frequently drinks this liquid, warm, on an empty stomach, he will find himself better. One who has quartan fevers should cook fenugreek in water. After squeezing out the water, he should frequently place the fenugreek around both feet, on the shin bones. He should do this at night, and tie a cloth over it. He should also often drink fenugreek, warmed in wine, as mentioned above, and he will become well.

XXXVII. SYSEMERA

Sysemera is hot. If someone drinks a poison, he should take equal weights of sysemera, rue, and betony and, having pounded them in a mortar, express the liquid. Then he should take twice as much juice of garden spurge and add it to the above-mentioned liquid. When these are well mixed, he should strain it through a cloth and drink it on an empty stomach. When he drinks, he should be seated in a warm place, so he does not get chilled. It would be very dangerous for him to be cold right then. After drinking this, he should drink hydromel, and the poison will foam out, through nausea, or it will travel to the lower regions, and so be released.

One who has many lice should pound sysemera with lard. When it is mixed together, he should rub it around his neck and under his armpits. The lice will die and he will not be harmed by it. But a person upon whom leprosy is seen developing should cook sysemera in water and add lard, preparing a puree. He should frequently eat this, and the leprosy will leave him.

XXXVIII. SAVORY

Savory (pefferkrut) is hot and moist, and that moisture has moderation in it. It is good and beneficial for healthy and ill people to eat. There is something bitter in it which does not bite a person's insides but makes him well. A person who has a frail heart and weak stomach should eat it raw, and it will strengthen him. If one with a sad mind eats it, it will make him happy. Indeed, when it is eaten, it brightens and heals a person's eyes.

XXXIX. HEMLOCK

Hemlock (scherling) is hot and has danger in it so that, if a person eats it, it destroys everything that had been well and correctly established in his blood and humors. It causes bad inundations in him, in the same way that storms make disturbances in the water. After the storm ceases, it leaves the worst mucuses and illnesses in a person. But, one who has been badly stricken by spears and cudgels, or who has fallen from a high altitude so that his flesh and limbs are crushed, should cook hemlock in water and place the expressed water over the limbs which are injured. He should tie a cloth over the area, and so dissipate the humors which have collected there. A person who swells up between the skin and the flesh from an impact or blow, or something thrown, should heat hemlock in water and tie it over the swelling. The swelling will go away. If a limb swells from some infirmity of its own, the swelling will not be expelled by the hemlock. If hemlock is placed on it, the humors which ought to go to the wound, and drive it from the flesh, are compelled to go dangerously back inside the person.

XL. CAMPHOR

Camphor *(ganphora)*, namely its gum, has pure coldness in it, but the tree, which exudes camphor, has a sharp, clean coldness. If a person eats camphor straight, not tempered by herbs, the fire in the person is impeded by its coldness. Even the cold in a person rushes out by its power, so that the person is like wood, because there is neither heat nor cold in his body. Therefore, no one should eat it straight. Take equal amounts of myrrh and aloe, and a little less camphor than either of these. Melt them together in a small dish and add a little wild lettuce. Make little cakes with this mixture and fine whole wheat flour. Dry the cakes either on a stone heated in the fire or in the sun. After they have dried, rub them into a powder and often eat a bit of this powder, in warm hydromel, on an empty stomach. If you are strong and healthy, you will be remarkably stronger and more healthy, and your powers will become well constituted. If you are sick, it lifts you up and strengthens you in a wonderful way, as the sun lights up a stormy day.

XLI. SORREL

Sorrel *(amphora)* is neither hot nor cold in correct measure, whence it is not useful for a person—who is concerned about his disposition—to eat. If a person should eat it, it would make him sad and diffuse that quality in excessive measure throughout his internal organs. It is a beneficial food for herd animals and cattle [since the property in it which harms a person's strengths is useful for animals].

XLII. HOUSELEEK

Houseleek *(huszwurtz)* is cold and not beneficial for a person to eat because of the richness of its nature. If a man who is healthy in his genital nature should eat it, he would be totally on fire with lust and he would become as if crazy. And if any male is dried up in his semen because his semen is deficient from old age, let him place houseleek in goat's milk long enough for it to be drenched by all the milk. Then he should cook it in the same milk, with a few eggs added, so that it can be food. Then he should eat it for three or five days. His semen will receive the powers of begetting, and will flourish for the purposes of offspring. But food prepared in this way is not useful against female sterility. If a female eats it, it provokes her desire, but does not remove her sterility. And one who is so deaf that he doesn't hear should take the milk of a woman, who has given birth to a male child, ten to twelve weeks after her son's birth. He should add to it the juice of the houseleek, and gently instill three or four drops of this into his ears. If he does this frequently, he will receive his hearing.

XLIII. BRYONY

Bryony *(stichwurtz)* is hot and useless for a human, just as a weed is useless. Its heat is dangerous, except in the place where poison is present. If burned in a fire, so that its heat and odor touch that poison, its strength diminishes, just as wine left in a cup all night loses its potency. If it is put in the fire and roasted like turnip, then taken hot from the fire and cut into bits, it gives off an odor. That odor, if it touches a snake or toad, so injures them that the snake foams and the toad is in so much pain that it flees its hiding place. If its odor touches a human it causes him to be in pain, unless he will have eaten rue beforehand. It has such worthless and troublesome humors in it that it kills a person as well as it kills bad vermin. If a person's feet are broken out with ulcers he should cook bryony in water. Pouring off the water, he should place the warmed bryony on his feet, where they are broken out, and moisten them with it. It will take away the puss, and he will be better.

XLIV. WOUNDWORT

Woundwort *(wuntwurtz)* is more cold than hot, and its sap is more dangerous than that of other herbs, just as one kind of worm may be worse or more violent than others. However, when a person has outstandingly large ulcers on him, he should cook woundwort in water and place it, warm, on the ulcers, and frequently moisten them in this way. He will become well. If, however, a person is wounded by a sword, and woundwort is placed on the wound, it will be dangerous for him. Woundwort rapidly heals the skin's exterior surface, but drives the corrupt matter inward [since it suddenly contracts the wounds on the surface, harming the interior parts unless they are first cared for by good aromatic herbs or unguents]. But if there are blemishes and blisters between a person's skin and flesh, that is if smallpox has erupted, then woundwort should be cooked in water and placed warm over it, and it will be healed. Do the same with animals, if they have these types of sores.

XLV. SANICLE

Sanicle *(sanicula)* is hot, and there is much purity in it, and its juice is sweet and healthful, that is wholesome. It is very good for a sick stomach or intestines. Pull it up with the roots in summer, when it is green, and cook it in water. Then strain this water through a cloth, and add honey and a little bit of licorice, and so make hydromel, and drink this often, having eaten. It removes the mucus from your stomach, and makes ailing intestines well. Also, dry sanicle gradually in the sun, lest its powers be diminished. (The sun, unlike fire, does not take away the potency of herbs which are dried in it.) Pulverize it a bit, so it is not totally broken up, and save this powder until winter. In winter, boil wine with a little honey and licorice, and put this powder in the liquid. Drink it often, after eating, and it will purge the mucus from the stomach and return ailing intestines to health. One who is wounded by a sword should squeeze out the juice of sanicle, pour it into water, and drink it after a meal. If it is winter, he should put the powdered sanicle in water, and drink it often, after eating. It purges the inside of the wound and gradually makes it well.

XLVI. COLCHICUM

Colchicum *(heylheubt)* is cold and dry, and in it there is no health or sanity. It is good for no person to eat, for if one eats it, it causes dryness and a failure of his good functions. If a person eats a little bit for only a short time, his flesh [increases on the outside. But his internal strength, which raises up the flesh as if it were growing, is failing], and he often dies, since there is more poison than health. But if an animal eats colchicum, he will not die, but will be slow and depraved.

XLVII. FERN

Fern *(farn)* is very hot and dry and has a little bit of juice in it. It holds within itself great power, namely such a power that the devil flees from it [and it even has certain energy which is like the power of the sun. As the sun lights up dark places, so the fern chases away apparitions, and evil spirits disdain it.] In the place where it grows, the devil rarely practices his deceptions. The fern avoids and shrinks back from any home or place where the devil resides. Thunder, lightning, and hail rarely fall near a home where there is fern. Hail also rarely falls in the field where it is growing. Magic and incantations of demons—as well as diabolic words and other phantasms—avoid a person who carries a fern with him. If any image is prepared for carrying out injury or death, it is not able to harm one who has a fern with him. For a person is sometimes reviled through an image in such a way that he is harmed by it and becomes mad.

In paradise, when the devil drew the human being to himself, a certain sign was made on the devil to remain on him, as a reminder, until the last day. When a person invokes the devil by some words, through which his deceptions are accomplished, the sign is touched. He is often invoked to injure a person, or to fulfill the will of the person over whom the words are spoken. Sometimes a person is blessed by the image which was made, and it furnishes him with prosperity and health. However, hatred and envy make evil, and evil is joined to evil. The wickedness of the devil always lies in wait for a person—looking at what evil has accumulated in him—and adds to it.

A human being has both good and evil knowledge, and good and bad herbs were created for him. Fern sap has been placed for knowledge, and in its honest nature, goodness and holiness are signified. All evil and magic things flee and avoid it. In whatever house it is, poison and phantoms are not able to complete their work. Whence, when a woman gives birth to a child, fern is placed around her, even around the infant in his cradle. The devil beseiges the infant less since, when he first looks at the infant's face, he hates him intensely.

Fern is also effective as the following medicines. One who is virgichtiget should take fern, when it is green, and cook it in water. He should frequently bathe in that water, and the gicht will cease. In summer, when it is green, put the leaves over your eyes often while you sleep. It will purify your eyes and take away their fogginess. One who is deaf, so that he does not hear, should tie fern seed in a little cloth and place it often on the ear. He should be careful that it does not enter the head through the ear, and he will again receive his hearing. And, one who is virgichtiget in his tongue, so that he cannot speak, should place fern seed on his tongue and the gicht in his tongue will cease, and he will again speak. Indeed, if a person who is forgetful and ignorant holds fern seed in his hand, his memory will return, and he will receive understanding; thus he who was incomprehensible will become intelligible.

XLVIII. HAZELWORT

Hazelwort *(haselwurtz)* is very hot and has dangerous power in it, so it should be feared. It is very malignant and of an unstable nature, similar to a storm. Its heat and riskiness run toward danger. More than it profits a person's health it destroys his nature. A person already having had a disease or fever, or gicht, and given it to eat, would be brought greater pain. A pregnant woman who eats it would die or abort the infant, with danger to her body. If a woman who has not yet had a menstrual period eats it, it will afflict her more.

XLIX. ARUM

Arum *(herba Aaron)* is not tepid, nor is it very strong. It has a level and moderate heat, as the sun after dawn has an agreeable heat, and is gentle as the dew in summer before daybreak. Arum can be used many ways, just as a calm person can suffer danger and rightly hold prosperity. When putrid matter in a person turns into a black pustule, in that human death which is called *seltega,* the leaves or root of this herb should be given to him to eat. It mitigates the excessive heat or cold in those pustules, causing them to disappear. And if a person is so virgichtiget that all his limbs are failing and diminished, and his tongue cannot talk, he should right away be given arum leaves to eat, with a bit of salt, and the gicht will cease. If it does not cease, then arum root should be dipped in cooked honey and immediately given to him to eat, and he will be better. But a person who has mucosy fever in his stomach, from which a variety of ague increases, should cook arum root in pure wine and then permit it to cool. Afterward, he should put a hot piece of steel in that wine, and in this way reheat it. He should drink the warm potion, and it will take away the mucus in his stomach and the fever, just as fire melts snow. And a person in whom melancholy rages, who has a fierce mind, and who is always sad, should also frequently drink wine cooked with the arum root. His melancholy and fever will diminish.

L. HUMELA

Humela has tepid coldness in it, and its heat is inactive. It stirs up riotous living in a person, so as to make a fool of him. It makes the person who either eats it or consumes it in a drink extravagant in the same way wine does when one drinks it. It makes him foolish. It furnishes a person with more corrupt matter than blood, and it has almost no utility [since it has not many powers or healthfulness in it, unless it is added to other little herbs or spices].

LI. SPURGE

Spurge *(wulfesmilch)* is said to be a poison. It has sudden heat, which burns a person's flesh. Even its moisture is unsuitable, for it destroys a person's flesh. It has no other utility except that, as doctors of medicine have found, it occasionally is added to certain potions for a hardened stomach. Useful medications are tempered by it, so that the evil in the person's body is chased away by this evil.

LII. BELLADONNA

Belladonna *(dolo)* has coldness in it, and this coldness contains weariness and listlessness. On the earth, at the place where it grows, diabolic influence has some share and participation in its craft. It is dangerous for a person to eat or drink, since it will disorder his spirit, as if he were dead. But, if a person's skin and flesh is bored through with large and very penetrating ulcers, he should take a little bit of goose fat and as much deer and goat tallow as he can get. He should add to this a little bit, as a single drop from a pen, of belladonna juice. He should mix this together and make an unguent. He should infrequently and in moderation—lest he be harmed by it—smear it on the large ulcers. To this unguent he should add a very little bit of belladonna, because if he adds a lot, and rubs it on frequently, it would eat his flesh and perforate it.

LIII. DAUWURTZ

Dauwurtz is hot and dry. It has strong powers in it and is pure in nature. If anyone eats it often, as with any herb, it will purge his stomach and take away fogginess from his eyes.

LIV. TITHYMAL

Tithymal *(brachwurtz)* is hot and dry and useful for many things. One who has in his body arthritic or gouty humor, which feels as if it is eating the inside of his limbs, and who is failing to endure that condition so that he has many different thoughts in his head, as if his knowledge is vanishing, should cook tithymal with wine and honey. He should strain it through a cloth, and frequently drink it warm, with food, and at night. He should place the same warm tithymal, which was cooked in wine, over his breast and tie a cloth over it. If he does this often, he will be better. Also, pulverize equal weights of licorice and bryony. Then mix in powdered tithymal, equal to the amount of the other two, and a little salt. Then often eat the powder prepared in this way, on an empty stomach or with food. It makes your voice cheerful and heals your chest. It furnishes a clearness, like shining bronze, and suppresses and diminishes the gicht, so that your limbs are not impaired by it and you do not lose your intelligence because of it.

LV. CINQUEFOIL

Cinquefoil *(funffblat)* is very hot, and its vital fluid is a bit moist. It prevails against strong fevers. Therefore, take cinquefoil and pound it well, and mix it with fine whole wheat flour and water, as if you want to make a little cake. Moisten it with a little olive oil or, if you do not have this, poppyseed oil, so it becomes soft. Then spread a hempen cloth with it and tie the warm cloth completely around the belly of a person who has violent fevers. After half a day, or half a night, take away that cloth. Warm it again at the fire, and place it on his belly. Do this often and it will chase away the fevers and cause him to vomit. Further, anyone who suffers fogginess in his eyes should take cinquefoil and place it in pure wine, crushing it. Then he should strain it through a cloth and save it in a bronze vessel. When he goes to bed, he should smear it around his eyes so that a little enters his eyes. If he does this often, it will take the obscurity from his eyes. Whoever has jaundice should make small cakes with cinquefoil and fine whole wheat flour and water. If he then eats these cakes for nine days, on an empty stomach, he will be cured. This herb is a beneficial medication for people, unless God forbids it.

LVI. MANDRAKE

Mandrake *(mandragora)* is hot and a little bit watery. It grew from the same earth which formed Adam, and resembles the human a bit. Because of its similarity to the human, the influence of the devil appears in it and stays with it, more than with other plants. Thus, a person's good or bad desires are accomplished by means of it, just as happened formerly with the idols he made. When mandrake is dug from the earth, it should be placed in a spring immediately, for a day and a night, so that every evil and contrary humor is expelled from it, and it has no more power for magic and phantasms. But, if it is pulled from the earth, and set aside with earth sticking to it, and not cleansed in the spring water, it is harmful for many injurious acts of magic and for delusions, just as many evils were at one time done with idols.

If a man, through magic or the burning heat of his body, suffers from lewdness, he should take a root of female mandrake,* which has

---

*Translator's note: There are two kinds of mandrake according to Isidore of Seville. The feminine has leaves like lettuce and produces fruits similar to plums; the masculine has leaves similar to the beet. Poets call the mandrake root anthropomorphic for its humanlike shape.

been cleansed as mentioned. He should tie it between his chest and belly button for three days and three nights. Later, he should divide it into two parts and should keep one part tied over each side of his groin for three days and three nights. Also, he should pulverize the left hand of this same image, and add a bit of camphor to this powder. Eating it will cure him.

If a woman suffers the same ardor in her body, she should put a piece of male mandrake root between her breast and belly button and follow the same procedure as described above. But she should pulverize the right hand of it and add a bit of camphor. After eating it her ardor will be extinguished.

Whoever suffers some infirmity in the head should eat from the top of this plant, in whatever way he wishes. If he suffers in his neck, he should eat from its neck; if in the back, from its back; if in the arm, from its arm; if in the hand, from its hand; if in the knee, from its knee; if in the foot, he should eat from its foot. In whatever part he is ailing, he should eat from the similar part of this image, and he will be better. The male form of this plant is stronger as medicine than the female, since a man is stronger than a woman.

And if someone is always sad and always in hardship, so that he has pain and weakness constantly in his heart, he should take mandrake. This should have been pulled from the ground and placed in a spring for a day and a night. Having taken it from the spring, he should place it near himself in his bed, so that the plant gets hot from his perspiration. Then he should say, "God, you made the human being from the mud of the earth, without pain; now I place next to me this earth, which has never been stepped on, so even my earth may feel that peace, just as you created it." If you do not have mandrake, take the first root mass which sprouts from the beech tree. Happily, it has the same quality for this undertaking. You should pull it out entirely, without breaking the shoots, and carry the whole thing from the tree. Place it next to you in your bed, so that the roots get hot from you and receive the perspiration from your body. Say the same words again over them. You will receive happiness and in your heart will sense recovery. Likewise, you can do the same thing with cedar or aspen, and it will make you happy.

LVII. BINDWEED

Bindweed *(winda)* is cold, does not have strong powers, and is not of much use. If a person eats it he does not get sick, but neither does he derive any benefit from it. If someone's nails begin to develop scabies he should take bindweed and pound it, add a bit of mercury, and mix these things together. Then he should put it on his nails and tie them with a cloth, and they will be beautiful.

LVIII. WINTER CHERRY

One whose eyes are dim should take a red silk cloth and spread winter cherry *(boberella)* on it. When he goes to bed, he should place the silk cloth over his eyes. He should do this often, and the dimness in his eyes will go away. But, for one whose ears are ringing, so that he is practically deaf, he should take winter cherry and daub it on a piece of felt, place that felt around his entire neck, up to his ears, and tie it. He should do this frequently upon going to bed, and the ringing in his ears will cease. Dry the winter cherry somewhat in smoke, and eat it. It will check stuffiness a little bit. One who suffers intestinal ulcers should heat wheat bran in a small dish with winter cherry. He should place this mixture on a cloth and frequently spread it, warm, over his entire stomach and navel, and he will be cured.

LIX. BLIND NETTLE

Blind nettle *(binsuga)* is hot, and a person who eats it smiles with pleasure, since its heat touches his spleen and thence his heart is made happy. When leucoma develops in one's eye, he should pull this plant from the earth and place it in spring water for a night. Then, having taken it from the water, heat it in a small dish and place it, warm, over the affected eye. If he does this for three nights, the leucoma in his eye will be cured and will disappear.

LX. SUNNEWIRBEL

Sunnewirbel* is hot and moist. In its nature it tends toward comeliness and it springs from the earth. A person who carries it with him [such as one who seeks to be above others] is hated by other people. But one who has a pain in his chest, so that his voice is hoarse from it, should take sunnewirbel and an equal weight of common burdock and cook these in pure wine. Then he should strain this through a cloth and, at night, having eaten, he should drink it frequently. His chest and voice will feel better. One who does not digest properly should take equal

---

*Translator's note: The word *sunnewirbel* could mean chicory, heliotrope, wild succory, or dandelion.

amounts of sunnewirbel and common burdock and dry it in the sun or on a hot tile. Then he should reduce it to a powder. To this powder he should add salt, a third as much as either of the other ingredients. Then, with honey, he should make hydromel from it. He should drink this frequently at night, when he has eaten. He will have digestion at the proper time. In this way, the herb is useful for medicine, unless God forbids it.

LXI. HOPS

Hops (hoppho) is a hot and dry herb, with a bit of moisture. It is not much use for a human being, since it causes his melancholy to increase, gives him a sad mind, and makes his intestines heavy. Nevertheless, its bitterness inhibits some spoilage in beverages to which it is added, making them last longer.

LXII. LILIM

Lilim is very hot. A person who has congestion in his spleen or stomach, weak intestines, or difficulty letting his breath in or out, as if he has been bruised in his chest, though he has no pain in his lungs, should take lilim and cook it with a little bit of beer and some honey. He should strain it through a cloth and drink it frequently, whether fasting or having eaten, and when he goes to bed. It brings forth lightness and beneficial belching, so that the foresaid infirmities are better. But one whose humors are weak, so that phlegm rises in him, should cook lilim in pure wine. Then he should pound pennyroyal in a little vinegar and bring it to a boil in the lilim and wine. He should strain it through a cloth, put it in a metal vessel, and cover it while it cools. He should drink this frequently at night and when he eats. It will clear away the chief dampness in him, purge the humors, and diminish the phlegm, as if it were cleansing a wound.

LXIII. SAGE

Sage (selba) is of a hot and dry nature, and grows more from the heat of the sun than from the moisture of the earth. It is useful against ill humors, since it is dry. It is good to eat, raw or cooked, for one whom noxious humors are troubling, since it checks them. Take sage and pulverize it. Eat this powder with bread and it will diminish the superfluity of harmful humors in you. [Also, one who is suffering the stench from some sordid thing should put sage in his nostrils, and it will benefit him.] Anyone who abounds in an excess of phlegm, or who has stinking breath, should cook sage in wine, strain it through a cloth, and drink it often. The evil humors and phlegm will be diminished. If one who has these infirmities is a bit *virgichtiget*, he should cook sage in water and drink it, and the humors and phlegm in him will decrease. [Its heat is moderated by the water, and checks the palsy in the person. If sage is given to someone with wine, the wine makes the paralytic humors in him go beyond their limit.

Someone who disdains eating should take sage, and a little less chervil, and a bit of garlic, and pound these together with vinegar, and so make a condiment. He should dip foods which he wishes to eat in it, and he will have an appetite for eating.

When food containing a wet juice makes a person's head ache, he should take equal weights of sage, oregano, and fennel, and more horehound than there is of all the rest. He should pound this into a juice and add a sufficient amount of butter, or lard if he has no butter. He should make an ointment from these things, and rub it on his head. He will be better. If bad vapors go from a person's stomach to his intestines, making a pain there, he should take sage, and five times as much *seuwurtz* as sage, and ten times as much rue as sage. Let him cook these herbs in a new pot with water, until it comes to the first full boil. Then, with the water squeezed out, he should place the herbs, cooked in this way and still warm, over the place where it hurts, and tie a cloth over this.

If anyone is unable to hold his urine because of the coldness of his stomach, he should cook sage in water, and strain it through a cloth. He should often drink it warm, and he will be cured.

But if evil, solid, and poisonous humors abound in a person, and have made him cough up and expel blood for some time, that person should use no medicine for a time, lest the blood, frightened by the medicine, irritate him internally, and gush out more than usual. After the bleeding ceases a bit, he should cook sage in mild, sweet wine, mixed with a little water. He should also add a bit of olive oil or butter and, when it is cooked, strain it through a cloth. He should drink it, in moderation, when he has eaten, but not when fasting, and it will strengthen him and heal him internally.]

LXIV. RUE

Rue *(rutha)* grows more from the strong, full liveliness of the earth than from heat. It has in it temperate heat, a little more hot than cold. The powers in its moisture are strong, and it is good against the dry bitterness which develops in a person whose correct humors are deficient. It is better and more useful raw than pulverized in food. When eaten it checks the excessive passion in a person's blood. The heat of rue attenuates the harsh heat of melancholy and tempers its excessive cold. A person who is melancholic will be better when he eats rue after a meal. If someone eats a food which brings pain, he should eat rue afterward, and his pain will be lessened.

[Also, a person whose eyes water should take rue, and twice as much sage, and twice as much chervil as sage. He should pound these herbs, a moderate amount, in a mortar, so they give out a little bit of juice. Then he should dip these crushed herbs in egg white. At night, when he goes to bed, he should place this mixture over his forehead, all the way to both temples. This will draw out the bad humors, as if someone is sucking juice from an apple.

A person who has black, turbulent eyes, so that at times there is a cloud which fogs them in some way, should take the sap of rue, and twice as much pure liquid honey, and mix them with good clear wine. He should put a crumb of whole wheat bread in it, and tie it over his eyes, at night, with a cloth.

If someone occasionally has pain in his kidneys and loins, this very often comes from infirmity of the stomach. Then the person should take equal amounts of rue and wormwood, and add a greater amount of bear fat, and pound these together. He should vigorously rub himself with it, around his kidneys and loins, while near the fire.

If a man is sometimes stirred up in delight, so that his sperm arrives at the point of emission but has in some way been retained within his body and he has begun to be ill from it, he should take rue and a bit less wormwood and press out their moisture. To this he should add sugar and honey and as much wine as there is of these juices. He should heat it up five times, with a piece of hot steel in a new pot or a small dish. After having eaten a bit of food he should drink this warm. If it is winter and he does not have these herbs, he should pulverize the berries of the bay tree and twice as much dittany and, after taking a bit of nourishment, should drink this in wine, heated by a hot piece of steel. The noxious mucus which had remained in him is then discharged with the urine and digested matter. If someone eats something which soon brings him pain, he should immediately eat rue and twice as much sage, tempered with salt, and he will be better.]

LXV. HYSSOP

Hyssop *(hyssopus)* is of a dry nature and is moderately hot. It is of such great strength that even a stone is not able to withstand it, and it grows wherever it is sown. Eaten often, it purges the weak and stinking foam of humors, just as heat, boiling in a pot [throws off foam]. It is useful in all foods. It is more beneficial pulverized and cooked than raw. When it is eaten the liver becomes lively, and it cleanses the lungs somewhat. One who coughs and has a pain in the liver, or who suffers from congestion in the lungs, or who suffers from both conditions, should eat hyssop with meats or with lard, and he will be better. Anyone who eats hyssop with only water or wine is harmed more than helped by it. One who ails in his liver or lungs should take licorice, and more cinnamon than licorice, and more hyssop than the other two, and more fennel than the other three. He should cook this in a new pot, with sufficient honey to overcome the bitterness of the herbs. He should cook this vigorously. He should keep the herbs in the pot for nine days and as many nights, then strain it through a cloth and drink it. If he has great pain in his liver or lungs, he should drink this every day for nine days. Before drinking it in the morning, he should eat a little something and then drink. He may eat a sufficient amount at night, and when he goes to bed he may drink some of it. If, however, he is in moderate pain in his liver or lungs, he may do the same thing for three days. Let him do this often, and he will be cured, unless God does not wish it.

[But if the liver is sick because of a person's sadness, before the infirmity abounds in him, he should cook young chicks with hyssop, and frequently eat the hyssop as well as the chicken. Also he should often chew raw hyssop which has been placed in wine, and drink that same wine. The hyssop is more useful to him for that illness than to one who has pain in the lungs.]

LXVI. FENNEL

Fennel *(feniculum)* has a mild heat and is of neither a dry nor cold nature. Eaten raw, it does not harm a person. In whatever way it is eaten, it makes a person happy, and brings to him a gentle heat and good perspiration, and makes his digestion good. Its seed is also of a warm nature and is beneficial to a person's health, if it is added to other herbs in medications. Eating fennel or its seed every day diminishes bad phlegm and decaying matter, keeps bad breath in check, and make one's eyes see clearly [by its good heat and beneficial powers.

One who is unable to sleep for being occupied by some difficulty should, if it is summer, cook fennel and twice as much yarrow. When the water has been squeezed out, he should place the warm herbs around his temples, forehead, and head, with a cloth over them. He should also take fresh sage and sprinkle it with a bit of wine, and place this over his heart and around his neck, and he will be soothed for sleeping. If it is winter, he should cook fennel seed and yarrow root in water, and place it around his head, as described, and put pulverized sage, dampened with a bit of wine, over his heart and neck, and he will be better.

When someone with blue-gray eyes has a dimness of some sort in them, and pain, he should, at the onset of pain, crush fennel or its seed, and take its juice. With dew found on grass which is growing straight, and a bit of fine whole wheat flour, he should make a little cake. At night, he should tie it around his eyes with a cloth, and he will be better. But if someone has eyes similar to stormy clouds, which are neither fully fiery nor fully turbulent but a little bit greenish blue, and if he suffers a fogginess and pain in them, he should crush fennel, if it is summer or, if it is winter, he should put its crushed seed in well-beaten egg white. When he lies down to sleep, he should place this over his eyes, and it will lessen the fogginess of his eyes.

If a person's pain has grown too much from a great outflowing from his nostrils, he should take fennel and four times as much dill and place it on a roofing tile or a thin brick warmed by the fire. He should turn the fennel and dill this way and that, so that it smokes. He should draw this smoke and its odor into himself through his mouth and nostrils, and then eat those herbs, so heated, with bread. He should do this for four or five days, so that the flowing humors might be gently separated from him.

A person who has bad mucus in his sick stomach should take fennel and a greater amount of nettle, and twice as much lovage as there is of the other two. He should eat it frequently with a bit of flour or bread. It will take away the mucus from his sick stomach.

A person whom melancholy is harming should pound fennel to a liquid and rub it often on his forehead, temples, chest, and stomach. His melancholy will stop. But also, one who has eaten roasted meat, fish, or anything else roasted, and has pain from it, should soon eat fennel or its seed, and he will have less pain.

If bad humors cause a very bad tumor to swell up and give a man pain on his virile parts, he should take fennel and three times as much fenugreek, and a bit of cow's butter. He should pound these together and place it on the tumor and it will draw out the bad humors. Then, the same man should take the little cakes from which beer is made, heat them moderately in warm water, and place them over the tumor.

Also, if a pregnant woman labors much in childbirth, one should cautiously cook sweet herbs, such as fennel and asarum, in water. With the water squeezed out, they should be placed, so warmed, around her thighs and back, and be held there gently tied on by a cloth. This should ease the pain, and cause her closed womb to more gently and easily loosen.

A person should also take fennel seed, and half as much galingale, the same half measure of dittany, and half as much mouse-ear as dittany. He should pulverize this and strain it through a cloth. A little while after lunch, he should place this powder in warm—not boiling—wine and drink it. A person who is healthy retains his health, but this powder strengthens the sick person, furnishes him with good digestion, gives him powers, and supplies his face with a good and beautiful color. It is beneficial for anybody, whether healthy or ill, when it is eaten after some food.

If sheep begin to be ill, one should take fennel, and a bit more dill, and place them in water, so that the water takes their flavor. He should give it to the sick sheep to drink].

LXVII. DILL

Dill *(dille)* is of a dry, hot, and temperate nature. In whatever way it is eaten, it makes a person sad. It is not good to eat raw, since it has more of earth's moisture in it than fennel has, and it attracts to itself a little bit of the richness from the earth. Thus it is bad for a person to eat raw, but as a cooked food, it checks gicht, and so is useful in food.

[If much blood is flowing from one's nostrils, he should take dill, and twice as much yarrow, and place these fresh herbs around his forehead, temples, and chest. These herbs must be fresh, since their strength is especially vigorous in the greenness. If it is winter, one should pulverize those herbs and place the powder, sprinkled with a bit of wine, in a little pouch, and place it over the forehead, temples, and chest, as just mentioned.

In order for a man to extinguish the pleasure and lust of the flesh which is in him, he should, in summer, take dill, and twice as much water mint, and a little more tithymal, and the root of Illyrian iris. He should put all these in vinegar, and make a condiment from them, and frequently eat it with all his foods. In winter, he should pulverize these, and chew the powder with his foods, since at that time he cannot obtain the fresh herbs with their vital energy.

In damp and mild wind, when cows easily begin to be ill, mix dill and a little less of Illyrian iris root in their fodder. It consumes any improper humors in them.]

LXVIII. PARSLEY

Parsley *(petroselinum)* is of a robust nature and has in it more heat than cold. It grows from wind and humidity. It is better and more useful for a person when it is raw, rather than cooked in a food. When it is eaten it attenuates the fevers which lightly touch a person when they strike him. Nevertheless, it generates seriousness in a person's mind. But one who ails in his heart, spleen, or sides should cook parsley in wine with a little vinegar and honey. If he strains this through a cloth and often drinks it, it makes him well. [But one whose stomach is ill should take parsley and twice as much fennel and as much soapwort as parsley and make a relish from them. To this he should add butter or beef fat and roasted salt, and eat it often, cooked. But one who is in pain from eating garlic should soon eat parsley, and he will have less pain.]

One who is in pain from a stone should take parsley and add a third part saxifrage. He should cook this in wine, strain it through a cloth, and drink it in a sauna. Also, he should cook parsley and a third part saxifrage in water, and pour it, with the water, over the hot stones in the same sauna bath. If he does this often, he will be better.

[Also, one who is tortured by paralysis should take equal weights of parsley and fennel, with a little less sage. He should grind these herbs together in moderate amounts in a mortar, and add rose-tinged olive oil to it. He should place it over the place where he is suffering, and tie it with a cloth.

And one who has both soft flesh and a limb troubled by gout, from excessive drinking, should take parsley and four times as much rue, and fry this in a small dish with olive oil; or, if he has no olive oil, he should fry them with goat tallow. He should tie these warm herbs on the place where it hurts, and it will be better.]

LXIX. CELERY

Celery *(apium)* is hot and more of a green nature than a dry one. It has much juice in it and is not good for a person to eat raw, because it gives him bad humors. When it is cooked it is not harmful for a person to eat, but makes healthy humors for him. In whatever way it is eaten it induces an unsettled mind in a person [since its vital energy sometimes harms him, and sometimes makes him sad in his instability. A person who has watery eyes, which overflow with dripping tears from superabundant humors, should take celery, and a little more fennel, and pound these to a juice. He should dip this in egg white, without its yolk. When he goes to sleep at night, he should tie it over his watering eyes. If he does this often, he will be cured].

One who is so tortured by gicht that his face is twisted by contraction and his limbs tremble, and he is even contracted in other parts of his body, should pulverize celery seed. He should add to it a third part rue, and nutmeg (less than there is of rue powder), cloves (less than nutmeg), and saxifrage (less than cloves) and reduce all this to a powder. He should eat this powder with or without food and the gicht will cease, since this is the best remedy against it. If anyone tortured by gicht eats this powder frequently, the gicht will flee from him, without doing any damage.

LXX. Chervil

Chervil *(kirbele)* is of a dry nature and grows from neither strong air nor the strong moisture of the earth, but arises in weak breezes, before the fertile heat of summer. It is more hot than cold, and that heat is healthful. It is a bit like weeds since, if it is eaten raw, it brings much vapor to a person's head. It is not useful for the human body, whether eaten cooked or raw, but it is beneficial as a medicine, and heals broken wounds of the bowels. Pound chervil, and pour the expressed juice in wine, and give it to a person who has broken wounds of the bowels. Do this often, and he will be cured.

[When a person eats raw food, and the evil humors of those foods, untempered by any condiment, rise to the spleen, causing pain there, a person should take chervil, and a little less dill, and make a condiment. He should eat this frequently with little lumps of whole wheat bread in vinegar. Afterward, he should take the seed of flax, and cook it in a frying pan. With the water squeezed out, it should be poured into a pouch and placed on the area where the spleen is, as hot as the person can endure.

Also, a person who suffers from various ulcers or scabies should take chervil, and three times as much female fern, and five times as much elecampane as chervil, and cook these in water. After, when the water is squeezed out and filtered through a cloth, pour the herbs into a frying pan and add a bit of fresh frankincense and sulphur, and add fresh pork fat, more than there is of the already mentioned things, so that it might be thickened a bit, as an unguent, over the fire in the frying pan. Then the one in pain should anoint himself around his wounds. He should do this for five days. It should be liberally applied to his skin and flesh, and afterward the patient should wash himself in a bath to remove the humors and the stench.]

LXXI. BROOKLIME

Brooklime *(pungo)* is of a hot nature. If someone eats it cooked as a puree, with lard or oil added, it will loosen his stomach as if it were a purgative. When eaten, it even checks gicht.

LXXII. CRESS

Cress *(crasso)* is more hot than cold, is indeed moist, and grows more from the life force of the earth than from the sun. When eaten, it increases bad humors in a person and injures the spleen [since it is a tender, easily injured organ].

LXXIII. WATERCRESS

Watercress *(burncrasse)* is of a hot nature and, when eaten, is not much use to a person, nor is it very harmful. If anyone has jaundice or fever, he should heat watercress in a small dish and frequently eat it warm, and it will cure him. One who can scarcely digest the food he has eaten should likewise heat the watercress in a small dish, and eat it. Because its powers come from water, it will help him.

LXXIV. PURSLANE

Purslane *(burtel)* is cold and, when eaten, produces mucus in a person. It is not profitable for a person to eat.

LXXV. WATER MINT

Water mint *(bachmyntza)* is hot, but a little bit cold. It can be eaten in moderation, but it is not much use to a person when eaten, though it is not detrimental. When one's stomach is heavy from many foods and drinks, and thence is stuffed, he should frequently eat water mint, either raw or cooked with meats, or in a broth, or cooked as a puree. The stuffiness will cease, since this cools his fatty, hot intestines, diminishing the stuffiness. For anyone who is congested from a sick lung, produces phlegm, and coughs with the slightest movement, or who is stuffed with many rich foods and drinks, and only with difficulty draws a breath, though he does not produce phlegm—it should be determined that he use water mint, as just described.

LXXVI. HORSEMINT

Another mint, horsemint *(myntza maior)*, which is large, is more hot than cold. This may be pounded, and tied over the place where vermin or parasites harm a person by eating, and they will die.

LXXVII. FIELD MINT

The mint, field mint *(myntza minor)*, which is called "lesser" is more hot than cold. This should be pounded, and placed on the eyes where there is discharge, tied with a cloth. It draws out the discharge. But one who has a cold stomach and is unable to digest food should eat field mint raw, or cooked with meats or fish. It will warm his stomach, and provide good digestion.

LXXVIII. SPEARMINT

Spearmint *(rossemyntza)* is of moderate and sharp heat, although it is a little bit temperate. One whom gicht is harming should pound this mint, and strain the juice through a cloth, and add a bit of wine. In the morning, evening, and at bedtime he should drink it, and the gicht will recede. Just as salt tempers all food, if too much or too little is added to foods it is bad, so too spearmint, added moderately to meat, fish, purees or other nourishment, offers a good flavor to that food, and is a good condiment. Indeed, eaten so, it warms the stomach and furnishes good digestion.

LXXIX. GARLIC

Garlic *(allium)* has proper heat and grows and has its liveliness from the vigor of the dew, from the first sleep of night until daybreak nearly arrives, in the morning. For sick as well as healthy people, garlic is more healthful to eat than leeks. It ought to be eaten raw. If cooked, it becomes insipid like ruined wine. Its juice is balanced and it has the proper heat. It does not harm the eyes, although, because of its heat, the blood around a person's eyes becomes very excited, afterward becoming clear. It should be eaten in moderation, lest a person's blood become too hot. When garlic is old, its healthy and proper advantage vanishes; but if it is then tempered by other foods, its power returns.

LXXX. SHALLOT

Shallot *(alslauch)* is cold and poisonous. It is valuable for neither a healthy nor a sick person to eat. Nevertheless, one who wishes to eat it should first put it in wine, and temper it. Then both healthy and sick people may eat it. For a sick person it is better consumed raw (in moderation) than cooked; if cooked it would eat at his stomach. If someone wishes to eat it raw, he should first temper it in wine, as already mentioned.

LXXXI. LEEK

Leek *(lauch)* has in it quick and injurious heat, as cheap brushwood, which is quickly kindled and quickly dies. It produces disquietude in one's sexual passion. Eaten raw, it is as bad and injurious for a person as a poisonous, injurious herb. It acts contrarily on a person's blood, decayed matter, and humors, so that his blood does not increase properly, his corrupt matter is not diminished, and the bad humors in him are not made clean. But one who wishes to eat a leek raw should first temper it in wine, with salt added, or in vinegar. It should lie in the wine or salt long enough for it to be so tempered that the evil powers in it are destroyed: from morning till midday, or from noon till evening. So tempered, it is good for healthy people to eat. It is better for healthy people to eat it raw in this way than cooked. For sick people it is not beneficial to eat, whether raw or cooked, because their blood does not have the correct heat, their decayed matter is stirred up, and their humors are foamy. If a sick person eats it, it disturbs all these things. If, however, sick people have great desire to eat a leek, they should eat it raw, in moderation, tempered as mentioned above. It is better raw than cooked. [And, leeks are not very suitable for medicines, because they grow in unstable breezes, that is, when the heat of the breeze has moisture in it, and when the moisture has heat.]

LXXXII. WELSH ONION

Every leek *(lauch)* that is hollow, such as *surige* and *prieslauch,* and *planza* and the like, is not very hot, but temperate, and has some almost winelike liquid. Welsh onions grow from the wind and the humidity of the earth. They are remarkably less noxious than other leeks. They do not create storms in a person's humors, and can be digested easily. Eaten raw, they do not harm healthy people. They should be cooked for sick people, lest their moisture be joined to the noxious fluids which are in ill people.

LXXXIII. ONION

Onion *(unlauch)* does not have proper heat. It has sharp moisture and liveliness from the dew which is present at daybreak, when the powers of dew dissipate. Raw, they are as harmful and poisonous to eat as the juice of injurious herbs; cooked, they are healthful to eat [since fire diminishes their noxious properties]. It is good for those who have ague, fever, or gicht when it is cooked. Raw or cooked, it creates pain for those who are sick and have a weak stomach, because it is moist.

LXXXIV. CABBAGE

Cabbage, kale, and red cabbage *(koles)* are of a moist nature, and cauliflower is a little more cold than hot, and a bit dry. They grow from the mucus of dew and air. From that they have something like powers and internal organs, and their juice is a bit injurious. They generate maladies in humans and injure weak intestines. Healthy people who have strong veins and are not very fat can eat them and overcome their powers. They are harmful to fat people, whose flesh abounds in moisture. Eating them is nearly as harmful for them as for sick people. They are even harmful in a relish or cooked with meats. They increase rather than diminish bad humors.

LXXXV. MEADOW GRASSES

Meadow grasses *(wiszgras)* are of a temperate nature, are moderately dry, and are like medicine or lettuces for both sick and well people to eat. They do not generate harmful humors and are easily digested, with soundness.

LXXXVI. STUTGRAS

Stutgras, which are smaller, furnish ill people with weak and sick humors and augment their melancholy. They are heavy to digest, and injurious for a person to eat, just as weeds [since their vital energy is evil].

LXXXVII. SQUASHES

Squashes *(kurbesa)* are dry and cold, grow from the air, and are good for both sick and healthy people to eat. [But melons are moist and cold and] grow from the wetness of the earth, and stir up bitter humors in people, and are not healthful for sick people to eat.

LXXXVIII. TURNIP

Turnip *(ruba)* is more hot than cold. Although it is heavy in a person's stomach, it is easily digested. One who wishes to eat it raw should take off the whole exterior rind. It is thick, and its natural vigor is harmful to a person. When the rind is removed, one can eat what is inside. It is better cooked than raw and does not supply bad humors. If at some time a humor rises up into ulcers, one should eat turnip and the ulcer will be checked. But if someone who is congested in the lungs eats turnip, cooked or raw, it will torment his lungs a bit [since it does not have powers to resist serious illnesses].

LXXXIX. RADISH

Radish *(retich)* is more hot than cold. After it is dug up, it should be placed underground in a damp place for two or three days. This tempers its energy, so that it is much better for eating. When it is eaten it cleanses the brain and diminishes noxious humors in the intestines. If a strong and fat man eats radish, it cures him and cleanses him internally, but it will harm a sick, lean body. If a sick person wishes to eat it, he should first dry it over a hot tile and reduce it to a powder. He should add salt and fennel seed, and eat it thus with bread. It purges the foulness inside him and strengthens him. One who has much phlegm should pulverize radish in the same way. Then he should cook honey and wine and put the powder into it. When it has cooled a bit, he should drink this, with or without food. The powder purges the phlegm and the honey keeps him from becoming lean. It is thought that eating it expels a person's evil humors and stenches. One who eats radish should eat galingale afterward. This checks the stench of his breath and does not harm him.

XC. LETTUCE

Domestic lettuces *(latich),* which can be eaten, are very cold. Eaten without condiment, their injurious juice makes a person's brain empty, and they fill his stomach with illness. Whence, one who wishes to eat it should first temper it with dill, vinegar, or garlic, so that these suffuse in it a short time before it is eaten. Tempered in this way, lettuce strengthens the brain and furnishes good digestion. [If someone suffers pain or a swelling in his gums, he should take lettuce or, if he has none, oak leaves that are just budding. He should add a slightly greater quantity of chervil. He should crush these a moderate amount, then add wine. He should place this in his mouth, and hold it there for some time. This drives off the harsh humors from the gums.]

XCI. PRICKLY LETTUCE

Prickly lettuce *(lactuca agrestis)* has nearly the same quality (as common lettuce). This lettuce is injurious, and is called a weed. Whoever eats it, either raw or cooked, becomes mindless, and empty in his marrow. These lettuces are neither hot nor cold, but are just like an injurious wind which dries up the fruit of the earth, and brings forth no fruit. These lettuces grow from the foam of the sweat of the earth, and are therefore injurious. [But if an ass has pain in its stomach, break prickly lettuce into its bran which has been heated slightly in water. Do this often, and the ass will be cured. If someone has scrofula that has not yet ruptured, he should take a fairly big lettuce leaf, one that is white on the outside and green on the inside. He should break pieces of it off according to the width of the scrofula, and throw the rest away. He should smear honey on these pieces of lettuce, and for three days and three nights place them over the scrofula. When they have dried up, he should cover them again in the same way, and they will become smaller.

XCII. WILD LETTUCE

Wild lettuce *(wilde latich)* is cold, and it extinguishes lust in a human. A man who has an overabundance in his loins should cook wild lettuce in water and pour that water over himself in a sauna bath. He should also place the warm, cooked lettuce around his loins, while still in the sauna. If he does this often, it will extinguish his lust while not harming the health of his body. If a woman's womb is swelling with uncontrollable lust, she should make a sauna bath with the wild lettuce. Sitting in the sauna, she should pour the water in which wild lettuce was cooked over the hot stones. She should place the warm, cooked lettuce over her belly. She should do this often. It will chase the lust from her without diminishing the health of her body. Indeed, anyone with uncontrollable lust should dry wild lettuce in the sun and reduce it to a powder in his hand. They should often drink this powder in warm wine. It will extinguish the lust, with no damage to the body.

XCIII. CHARLOCK

Charlock *(herba senff)* grows in fields and vineyards and can be eaten. It is hot, but its heat is unstable. It is humid, but in its moistness it has an improper torpor, since it grows from changing breezes and whirling winds. It is not useful to eat [although poor people eat the herb, even if it is injurious]. It is poisonous and furnishes a person with ill humors and weighs down his stomach. Nevertheless, it can be digested easily. It does not harm healthy and lean people, but it harms those who are infirm and fat; it weighs down the stomach of sick people, and makes it difficult for fat people to draw their breath.

XCIV. MUSTARD

Mustard *(sinapis)* is of a very hot, and somewhat dry, nature. It grows in temperate heat and cold, that is, in temperate breezes. It has the powers of trees and herbs, since it grows from the same wind which brings forth fruits. Because it grows from the vital energy of the earth, it has a bit of juice. The herb itself is harmful to eat, since its power is weak and unstable. It destroys the insides of a person who eats it.

Its seed flavors other foods. It is not good for a sick person with a weak, cold stomach because it weighs it down and does not cleanse it. A strong stomach overcomes it. When eaten, it makes the eyes clear but puts a vapor in the brain, and a certain harshness in the head, so that it draws forth some moisture from the head. It introduces headache and is very harmful for the head. It does not furnish good, correct digestion, but rather makes it painful and produces something like smoke in a person. Whoever wishes to eat it should do so in moderation, since it harms sick people, who do not have the power to resist it. It does little harm to healthy people, since their strength restores them.

However, one who likes to eat mustard should pour over it wine which he has heated. Consumed in this way, it does not harm sick people. Its injuriousness is removed by the heat of the wine. If one does not have wine, he may pour cold vinegar on it. Eaten in this way it is not harmful. If it is not tempered by wine or vinegar, it is not good for human consumption. If it harms even healthy people, it is not beneficial to the sick.

XCV. ELECAMPANE

Elecampane *(alant)* is of both a hot and dry nature, and has beneficial powers in it. Dry or green, it may be put in pure wine all year long. After it has shriveled in the wine its powers have faded, and it should be thrown out and replaced by new. One who has pain in his lungs should drink this in moderation, every day, before and after eating. It carries away the poison from the lungs, suppresses migraine, and clears the eyes. But if someone drinks this frequently, it would injure him by its strength. If you do not have wine, make pure hydromel with water and honey, put the elecampane in it, and drink as described. Also, take fig, and twice as much elecampane. Add galingale, and from this make a clear drink. Drink it if you have sick lungs, with no other infirmities, for it is good for your lung illness. If you have additional maladies, do not drink it, for it is too strong, and you would be injured by it.

XCVI. POPPY

Poppy *(papaver)* is cold and moderately humid. Its seed, when eaten, brings sleep and prevents prurigo. The seeds check hungry lice and nits. They can be eaten after being steeped in water, but are better and more useful when eaten raw rather than cooked. The oil which is expressed from them does not nourish or refresh a person, nor does it bring him health or sickness. This oil is cold, but the seeds are hot.

XCVII. MALLOW

Mallow *(babela)* has in it a moderate coldness, just as the dew, but it is colder. [If melancholy, brought forth by various fevers, makes a person's brain ail, one should crush mallow and twice as much sage in a mortar, and sprinkle it with olive oil. He should put this on his head, from the forehead, over the top, and to the back of the head, and tie it with a cloth. Repeat for three days, and for these three days refresh it at night with additional oil, or vinegar.

A person wishing to clear his vision should look for dew on the mallow (or on bindweed, pear leaves, or leaves of oak or beech trees, since these are tender). He should smear his eyes and eyelids with this dew, which he will have found in the morning or at night, when the night is clear, pure, and calm. He should then sleep for a while.]

No person should eat raw mallow. Eaten raw, it would be poison, because it is slimy and has thick, poisonous humors, which it imparts to a person. For those who have a weak stomach, it is good eaten cooked fresh, when it is just beginning to grow. It should be prepared as a puree, with lard added. Eaten, it facilitates digestion a bit. One with a sick stomach must eat it in moderation, lest he be harmed. The healthy person should avoid it altogether.

XCVIII. BURDOCK

Burdock *(cletta)* has some injurious heat in it. It grows from the sap and sweat of the earth. It is both useful and harmful. Its root has no utility, and its leaves, whether raw or cooked, are dangerous for a person to eat, except for a person who is born with a stone in his body. This person should cook the leaves of the herb in the finest wine. He should drink the warm wine, before or after a meal, after it has been strained through a cloth. Its strength will wear down the stone. Also, reduce its flowers to a powder and, having thrown away the snail, reduce the snail's shell to powder. Mix them together, so that there is more powdered snail shell. If someone has scabies on his head, cast the powder on the sores for nine or fifteen days. On the fourth and fifth days wash his head with lye made from beech wood, and he will be healed.

XCIX. THISTLE

The thistle *(distel),* whether smooth or prickly, has a quick heat, which quickly dulls since it exudes from the earth. The sweat of the earth, from which the herb is born, is prickly and makes twisted herbs. Just as sweat exudes from a human when he is in difficulty so the sweat of the earth sends out twisted herbs, which lacerate a person. And, indeed, even when the thistle is smooth it is harmful for a person to eat raw. If anyone eats it raw, it would weaken his blood, and put decaying matter in him. It would diffuse his humors, just as pouring water into good wine weakens it. From it a person would become void of sense and lacking in blood and humors. Nevertheless, if thistle is cooked and then eaten, it does no great harm or profit to a healthy person. It does not enrich the blood, nor does it relieve hunger. It is harmful for sick people, whether cooked or raw, since it creates weariness in them.

But, lady's-thistle has coolness in it and is very useful. Anyone who has a stitch in his heart, or pain in any other part of his body, should take lady's-thistle and a little less sage, and reduce them to a juice in a little water. When he is tormented by the stitch, he should immediately drink this, and he will be better.

C. NETTLE

Nettle *(urtica)* is very hot in its own way. It is not at all good eaten raw, because of its harshness. But, when it newly sprouts from the ground, it is good when cooked, as food for a human. It purges his stomach and takes mucus away from it. Any kind of nettle does this. [If worms have grown in a person from noxious and evil humors which are poisonous, he should take equal weights of the juice of stinging nettle and mullein, and the leaves or bark of the walnut tree, as much as there is of the two other ingredients. He should add a bit of vinegar, and a lot of honey, and bring it to a boil in a new pot. He should remove the foam from the top and, after it has boiled, take it from the fire. For fifteen days he should drink a small amount before breakfast, and a greater amount after eating. The worms which are in him will die.

And, a person who is unwillingly forgetful should pound stinging nettle to a juice, and add a bit of olive oil. When he goes to bed, he should thoroughly anoint his chest and temples with it. If he does this often, forgetfulness will diminish.

Also, if a watery discharge foams from the nostrils of a horse, so that he coughs from it, cook stinging nettle and a greater amount of lovage in water and, having put the reins on him, let that warm vapor enter his nostrils and mouth, and he will be better. If the horse has pain in his stomach, frequently mix stinging nettle and a greater amount of lovage with his fodder, so he might eat them at the same time, and he will be better.]

CI. PLANTAIN

Plantain *(plantago)* is hot and dry. Take plantain and express its juice. Give it, strained through a cloth, and mixed with wine or honey, as a drink to a person tormented by gicht, and the gicht will cease. But one who has swollen glands should dry the root of the plantain by fire and place it warm over the swollen glands. He should tie a cloth over it and he will be better. Do not, however, place it over scrofula, which would be harmed by it. One who is bothered by a stitch should cook plantain leaves in water. Having squeezed out the water, he should place them warm over the place where it hurts, and the stitch will cease. And, if a spider or other bug touches or stings a person, the spot should soon be smeared with plantain juice, and it will be better.

If a person, man or woman, eats or drinks a love enchantment, then plantain juice, with or without water, should be given to him to drink. Later, he should take some strong drink, and he will be purged inside and be relieved. [If, however, a bone is broken by a fall, one should cut up plantain root in honey. He should eat it daily, before breakfast. He should also gently cook the green leaves of mallow and five times as much plantain leaves or root in water in a new pot. He should frequently place these, warm, over the injury, and the fractured bone will be healed.]

CII. MENNA

Menna is hot and dry, and its leaf, placed over an open wound, draws out the poison and heals it. Cooked as a puree and eaten, it heals painful, ulcerated intestines.

CIII. VIOLET

Violet *(viola)* is between hot and cold [and is of an especially sober color]. Although it is cold, it grows from the [mild, gentle] air which after winter is beginning to warm up. It is valuable against fogginess of the eyes. Take good oil, and make it boil in a new pot, either in the sun or over a fire. When it boils, put violets in so that it becomes thickened. Put this in a glass vessel and save it. At night put this unguent around the eyelids and eyes. Although it shan't touch the inside of the eyes, it will expel the fogginess. [Someone with inflamed eyes that are foggy and painful should take violet, twice as much rose juice, and fennel juice (a third as much as there is of the rose juice). He should add a bit of wine and, when he goes to bed, rub this salve around his eyes, being careful that it doesn't touch the inside of his eyes.

A person who has a heaviness in his head or kidneys, or for whom any other place is fatigued by palsy, should squeeze juice of violets through a cloth and add to it a sufficient amount of goat tallow and half as much old fat. Melt these together in a small dish and make an unguent. When this is rubbed onto the head or other ailing place, there will be an improvement.

If someone has pain in his head, if crabs are eating his flesh, or if he has any kind of ulcer on his body, he should take juice of the violet and a third as much olive oil and goat tallow (the same amount as the violet juice). He should boil these in a new pot and prepare an unguent. One whose head has pain should rub it across his forehead, and he will be better. Crabs or other vermin which eat a person will die upon tasting this, smeared over the afflicted places.

One suffering tertian fevers should take violet and a third as much plantain and two-thirds as much savory. He should frequently eat these herbs with vinegar or roasted salt.]

Anyone oppressed by melancholy with a discontented mind, which then harms his lungs, should cook violets in pure wine. He should strain this through a cloth, add a bit of galingale, and as much licorice as he wants, and so make spiced wine. When he drinks it, it will check the melancholy, make him happy, and heal his lungs.

CIV. ORACH

Orach *(melda)* is more cold than hot, but it has a good balance, and when it is eaten it provides good digestion. And if glands filled with poison—that is, scrofula—begin to develop on a person, he should often prepare a puree using orach with a little less hollow leek, and even less hyssop. When he eats it, the scrofula will dry up. Also, if one cooks orach in water and places this warm on the scrofula, after squeezing out the water, the person will be better.

CV. GROUND IVY

Ground ivy *(gunderebe)* is more hot than cold, and it is dry. It has somewhat the quality of spices. Its vital energy is profitable, so that if a person who languishes, and whose reason is failing, soaks it in warmed water, cooks it in a puree or a broth, and eats it often, with meat or small tarts, it will help him. And if someone frequently washes his head with it and with lye, it will chase away many illnesses from his head and prevent it from getting ill. If bad humors trouble one's head, so that even his ears ring, boil ground ivy in water. When the water is squeezed out, place the warm ivy around his head. It diminishes the bad humor in his head, and opens up his hearing. Also, if he has pain in and around his chest, as if he has internal ulcers, he should, while he is in a bath, place this warm, cooked ivy around his chest, and he will be better.

CVI. SOUTHERNWOOD

Southernwood *(stagwurtz)* is hot and dry, and when one is rubbed with it the odor it gives off excites melancholy and rage in him, and torments his head. But, where scabies begin to break out on a person's head, the juice of the plant should be poured on the sores, and they will be cured. And, where boils arise on a person's body, or where any one of his limbs is withered, southernwood should be pounded and placed around it. The place should also be thoroughly anointed with this juice, and it will be better. [When the scabies or withered limbs persist, the southernwood should soon be removed, since it then does more harm than good.] One who is troubled by gicht in his limbs should take some southernwood, some old lard, and a bit of olive oil and heat them together in a frying pan. Then place this, warm, over the limb in which the gicht is raging. He should then bind it together with a cloth. If this is done frequently, the gicht in that place will cease.

CVII. MUGWORT

Mugwort *(biboz)* is very hot, and its juice is of very great value. If it is cooked and eaten as a puree, it heals ailing intestines and warms a cold stomach. But, if someone eats or drinks something which has given him pain, then he should cook and eat warmed mugwort with meat or lard, or as a puree, or with any other condiment. It will attract the rotten matter which was in the previously ingested food or drink, and chase it away. [If bad humors gather in some part of the body, flowing out from broken skin where there is no poisoned wound, the person should take mugwort and express the juice. To the juice he should add a smaller amount of honey. He should spread this on the afflicted area, then cover it with egg white, and tie it with a cloth. He should do this until he is better.]

CVIII. CLOVER

Clover *(cle)* is as hot as it is cold. It is also dry and is beneficial nourishment for herd animals. It is of little value as medicine, except against obscured vision. Put its flowers in olive oil, stirring them around in it, without cooking, and then smear this around the eyelids and foggy eyes. The flowers should be thrown out as soon as the eyes have been anointed. They quickly lose their power and do not last long in the oil. If one will do this often, the fogginess in his eyes will disappear.

CIX. WORMWOOD OR ABSINTHE

Wormwood *(wermuda)* is very hot and has much strength. It is the principal remedy for all ailments. Pour a sufficient amount of its juice into warm wine. For one who has a headache, wet the entire head, from the eyes to the ears and neck. Do this at night, upon going to bed. Cover the whole head with a woolen cap, until morning, and it will suppress the pain of the swollen head. It will chase away the pain that pulsates on the head from gicht, as well as the pain inside the head.

[If any kind of vermin has entered a person's ears, he should take wormwood, half as much rue, and half as much hyssop as rue, and cook them in water. He should then tip his head and let the warm vapor rise up from the warm herbs through a reed pipe and enter the healthy ear. The vapor will reach the ear where the vermin are, and they will flee. Earlier this ear will have been smeared with honey with a bit of lard in it. Upon sensing the wormwood, the vermin would turn away from it and toward this sweetness. One may also burn a spike of barley, with or without the grains, so the smoke might enter the ear through the reed, as described. A person should do this many times a day and he will be relieved, unless God does not wish to relieve him. When the vermin have come out of the ear, one should boil olive oil in a new vessel and permit the vapor to go into the ear where the vermin have been, and thus oil the sores. Then he should cool the oil and smear it all around the entrance of the ear. If a little enters the ear, it will do no harm. One may also cook chamomile in water and let the vapor pass into the healthy ear. He should block this ear with his hand so the vapor cannot get out. If he does this frequently, he will be healed.

A person who has a toothache, either from rotten blood or from purging of the brain, should cook equal weights of wormwood and vervain in a new pot of good wine. He should strain it through a cloth and drink it with a little sugar. When he goes to bed, he should tie the warm herbs around his jaw. He should do this until he is well.]

Pour wormwood juice into olive oil, so that there is twice as much oil as wormwood. Heat it in a glass jar in the sun, and keep it for a year. When some person has pain in or around his chest, which is making him cough, smear it on his chest. When the remedy is rubbed in, one whose side aches is cured from the outside. Also, pound wormwood to a juice in a mortar, add deer tallow and deer marrow, and make a salve; there should be twice as much wormwood as tallow, and twice as much tallow as marrow. A person who is greatly tormented by gicht, so that his limbs threaten to break, should be thoroughly massaged with it where it hurts, while he is near the fire, and he will be cured.

When wormwood is fresh, pound it and express its juice through a cloth. Then gently cook wine with honey, and pour the juice into this wine, so the wormwood overcomes the wine and honey flavor. Drink this every other day before breakfast, from May to October. It will check your melancholy and sickness in the loins, and make your eyes clear. It will strengthen your heart, prevent your lungs from becoming sick, warm your stomach, purge your intestines, and furnish you with good digestion.

CX. HENBANE

Henbane *(bilsa)* is cold and soft, and without powers. If anyone eats it, or the oil made from its seed, it would become a deadly poison in him. When a person has parasites, which irritate his flesh, rub that place with henbane juice, and the parasites will die. Oil made from its seed is not much use; but when there is too much heat in one area of a person's limb, that place should be anointed with the oil. It will cool without other medicine. This oil is not useful for other ailments. [When a drunk returns to himself, he should put henbane in cold water and wet his fore-head, temples, and throat with it, and he will be better.]

CXI. TANSY

Tansy *(reynfan)* is hot and a bit moist, and is effective against all over-abundant humors which flow out. Whosoever has catarrh, and coughs because of it, should eat tansy, taken either in broth or small tarts, or with meat, or any other way. It checks the increase of humors, and they vanish. Whosoever has a harsh cough should prepare a tansy draft with whole wheat flour and eat it often. The dryness and internal injuries of the cough will loosen, and the person will get rid of the nasty filth by coughing it out, and he will be better.

One who has heaviness in his stomach from a variety of bad foods should take broth, cooked without vegetables or other herbs, and put tansy in it. He should cook it again, and eat it often. It will soothe his stomach and make it light, and give him smooth digestion. And, when one is unable to urinate, because he is constricted by a stone, he should pound tansy, strain its juice through a cloth, add a bit of wine, and drink it frequently. The constriction will be loosened, and he will urinate freely. [A woman who is in pain from obstructed menses should take tansy and an equal weight of feverfew and a bit more mullein than either of the others. She should cook these in water from a freely flowing stream, which is tempered by the sun and air. Then she should put tiles in a fire, and make a sauna bath with the foresaid water and herbs. When she enters this bath, she should place the warm herbs on the bench and sit on top of them. If they become cold, she should warm them again in the same water. She should do this as long as she sits in the sauna, so her skin and flesh, as well as her womb, may be softened by the humors of these herbs, and the veins which were closed might be opened. Then she should take bearberries and add a third as much yarrow, and rue (a third as much as the yarrow), and as much birthwort as there is bearberries and yarrow, and a bit more dittany. She should pound these in a mortar and cook them in a jar with good, pure wine. Then she should put this mixture in a little sack. Further, she should crush as many cloves as she has, with a smaller amount of white pepper, and add fresh honey, which is free from impurities. She should boil this in a new pot and pour it on the forenamed herbs in the sack, and so prepare claret. She should drink this every day, before or after eating, but not while in the foresaid bath, since a bath constricts a person somewhat. She should do this until she is well. But, while she suffers this constriction of blood, she should avoid beef and other rich, strong foods, eat agreeable foods, and drink wine. When she drinks water, she should drink well water and avoid waters from leaping, flowing springs, since these are a bit harsher than other waters.]

CXII. Oregano or Wild Marjoram

Oregano *(dost)* is hot and dry, but neither property is strong. If anyone were to eat or drink it, or in any way let it into his body, it would give him leprosy and swell up his lungs. It would weaken his liver. But one who has red leprosy, whether recent or long established, should take oregano and a little less horehound juice, and add henbane oil (more than there is of the other two) and a bit of wine, and mix these together. When he is about to leave the sauna, he should pour this liquid over himself. After he has come out of the bath and is perspiring very much, he should completely smear himself with goat tallow, which has been dissolved in a small dish on the fire. He should stay in bed while it dries up. After it has dried, he should again pound oregano, and add bran to its stem pieces, and mix these together in a small warm dish. He should put this, warm, over the leprous sores. He should tie a bandage over this and keep it there for some time, until he becomes warm from it. If he does this frequently, he will, without a doubt, be cured, unless he dies [or unless God does not wish him to be cured. Also, one who suffers quotidian fever should pulverize oregano with a bit of camphor and more tormentil than there is of the other two. At the onset of fever he should put this powder in wine and drink of it and stay in bed, and he will be well.]

CXIII. Yarrow

Yarrow *(garwa)* is a little bit hot and dry. [A person whose vision is darkened from flowing tears should pound yarrow a moderate amount and place it over his eyes at night, not letting it touch the inside of his eyes. He should take it off when it is almost midnight. Then he should rub the best and purest wine around his eye lashes, and his eyes will be healed.] Yarrow also has distinguished and subtle powers for wounds. If a person has been wounded by a blow, the wound should be bathed in wine. Then yarrow, cooked gently in water, and that water squeezed out, should be tied gently, while warm, over the cloth which covers the wound. It will take away the putrid matter and the ulcer from the wound, and the wound will be healed. He should continue to do this as long as it is necessary. But, after the wound begins to be drawn together and healed a bit, discard the cloth and place the yarrow directly on the wound. It then heals completely. One who receives an internal injury, so that there is an internal break or constriction, should pulverize yarrow and drink it in warm water. After he is better, he should take the same powder in warm wine until he is well. [Also, a person whom tertian fever torments should cook yarrow and twice as much female fern in sweet, good wine. He should strain this wine through a cloth, and drink it at the onset of the fever. He should drink these herbs in wine for three days and, if necessary, he should renew it with similar, fresh herbs. It will mitigate his fever and he will be well.]

CXIV. AGRIMONY

Agrimony *(agrimonia)* is hot. A person who has lost his knowledge and understanding should have his hair cut from his head, for that hair creates a shaking tremor. Agrimony should be cooked in water, and that warm water used to wash his head. The same herb, so warmed, should be tied over his heart, when he first senses enervation from madness. Then it should be placed, warm, over his forehead and temples. It will clear up his knowledge and understanding, and take the insanity from him. If someone produces or throws off mucus and much phlegm from his sick intestines, and has a cold stomach, he should frequently drink wine in which agrimony is placed, before and after meals. It diminishes and purges the mucus, and warms the stomach. [Also, in order that a person be purged from saliva, discharge, and runny nose, one should take agrimony juice and twice as much fennel juice and add to these one half pennyweight of herb Robert juice. Then take as much galingale as there is of the other three, and six pennyweight of storax, and two pennyweight of female fern, and pulverize these. Blend this with the forenamed liquid, and make little pills the size of beans. Afterward, take a quarter pennyweight of the juice of celandine, and dip the pills in it, and place them in the sun to dry. If the sun has no heat, place them in a light wind or gentle breeze, so that they might be gently dried. When a person wishes to eat these pills, he should wrap his belly with lamb skins, or skins of some other animal, so that he becomes warm with their healthful heat. He should not get too close to the fire, but use the heat of this covering. He should consume the pills before sunrise, since dawn is a smooth and gentle time. He should take five or nine pills, dipping each one in honey before swallowing them. After eating them, he should walk around a bit in a shady place, not in the direct sun, until he feels a loosening. Around noon, after he has felt the loosening, or if his obdurate stomach has not yet had it, he should sip a porridge of the finest whole wheat flour, so that the gentle porridge may heal his intestines or his hardened stomach might soften.

If a person becomes leprous from lust or intemperance, he should cook agrimony, and a third part hyssop, and twice as much asarum as there is of the other two in a cauldron. He should make a bath from these, and mix in menstrual blood, as much as he can get, and get into the bath. He should also make an unguent from goose fat, twice as much chicken fat, and a bit of chicken dung. When he comes out of the bath, he should smear himself with this ointment and go back to bed. If he does this often, he will be cured.] Also, if someone's eyes are clouded, pound agrimony in a mortar and place the crushed matter over the eyes at night, being careful that it not enter the eyes, and bind with a cloth. It will attack the fogginess of the eyes and make them clear.

CXV. DITTANY OR FRAXINELLA

Dittany *(dictamnus)* is hot and dry, and has the powers of fire and stone. Just as stone is hard and holds heat when it comes out of a fire, so dittany is powerful against illnesses in which these qualities prevail. If a stone is beginning to grow in a person who is fat by nature, he should pulverize dittany, and frequently eat this powder with wheat bread. It will keep the stone from growing. A person in whom a stone has grown should put dittany powder in vinegar mixed with honey and drink it frequently, on an empty stomach. The stone will break up. One who has a pain in his heart should eat powdered dittany and the pain in his heart will cease. [When someone has begun to grow lame in any limb, he should cook dittany vigorously in water, and throw out that part which is, like the heart, in the middle. While it is cooking, he should add twice as much *huszmoszes** and four times as much stinging nettle and mix these together. After it is cooked, and the water gently squeezed out, he should place the warm herbs over the joints and veins of the limb which was beginning to be lame. If he does this often, he will be cured.]

---

*Translator's note: The word *huszmoszes* could mean moss that grows on houses, but this can't be confirmed. It may be a misprint for houseleek, *huszwurtz.* See Moss entry on p. 133 for mention of moss growing on house roofs as a remedy for ague.

CXVI. GERMAN CHAMOMILE

German chamomile *(metra)* is hot, has a pleasant juice, and is like a gentle ointment for painful intestines. If one has pain in the intestines, he should cook German chamomile with water and lard or oil. He should add fine whole wheat flour, and thus make a porridge. He should eat it, and it will heal his intestines. When women menstruate, they should eat or drink that same porridge. It will gently provide a purgation of mucus and internal fetid matter and bring on menses. [However, a person who suffers a stitch should mix the juice of German chamomile with cow butter. He should rub the area which hurts, and he will be cured.]

CXVII. MOUSE-EAR

Mouse-ear *(musore)* is cold. When eaten, it strengthens the heart and diminishes bad humors which have gathered in one spot in a person. A person should not eat it by itself, for it is too harsh. He should add a bit of dittany, galingale, or zedoary, and eat it like that [and it will dissipate cold humors].

CXVIII. GLADIOLUS

Gladiolus *(swertula)* is hot and dry. All its power is in its root, and its natural vigor ascends to its leaves. In May, take the juice from its leaves. Melt fat in a small dish and add to it this juice, preparing an unguent which will be green. If someone has a bit of scabies on his head, he should rub this on frequently, and he will be cured. If the skin on his face is hard like bark, or has boils or a bad color, he should squeeze the juice from gladiolus leaves, pour it into a vessel with water taken from a large river, and warm it gently. Then he should wash his face with this water. If he does this often, it will make his skin smooth and of good color. Also, one may cook the root and leaves of gladiolus in water, squeeze out the water, and place it warm around the head of a madman, tied with a cloth, so that he sleeps like this. Do this often. Then, slice up the root of that same gladiolus. Season the rounds in honey, and frequently give them to the madman to eat, and he will be healed.

Also, pound gladiolus root in a mortar with good wine, and heat this wine, after straining it, and give it as a drink, so warmed, to someone who has a stone and whose urination is painfully constricted. His stone will be softened and his constricted urinary tract will open. Against a recent case of leprosy, pound the root of the gladiolus and place it in ass's milk, making it coagulate. Pour pork lard into a small dish, and add the crushed root and ass's milk. Cook this, stirring vigorously. Strain it through a cloth into a vessel, and you will have an unguent. Then make lye from ashes of alder. One who is starting to become leprous should first wash the place where he feels the incipient leprosy, then rub in the ointment. If he does this often, he will be healed.

CXIX. HORSERADISH

Horseradish *(merrich)* is hot. In March when all herbs grow green, the horseradish gets soft, but only for a short time. When eaten then, it is good for healthy and strong people. It strengthens the vital energy of their humors. After it grows hard, when its rind is tough, it is dangerous to eat. It then has no vital energy and makes a person dry, as if he were eating wood. Therefore a person should not eat it, but may suck the juice, and spit the rest from his mouth. If a lean and dry person wants to eat horseradish, a moderate amount will strengthen him. Eating too much might make him sick, since he has in him only moderate strength. When horseradish is green, it should be dried in the sun. Then an equal amount of galingale powder should be added to its powder. Whoever has pain in his heart should eat this powder, with bread, before or after a meal. He will be better. Whosoever has pain in his lungs should eat this same powder in warm wine or warm water, before or after a meal, and he will be cured.

CXX. DWARF ELDER

Dwarf elder *(hatich)* is cold and moist, and contrary to the nature of a human, so that it would be dangerous to anyone who eats it. If in someone's head there is a ringing, as of rushing water, from bad humors, dwarf elder should be placed, cold, around the person's head, and he will be better. If the nails on someone's fingers or toes are mangy, he should frequently tie dwarf elder berries over his nails so they might be cleansed, or otherwise fall off, letting other, beautiful ones grow back.

CXXI. BLACK NIGHTSHADE

Black nightshade *(nachtschade)* is hot and dry. One who has pain in his heart, or whose heart is not strong, should gently cook nightshade in water. When the water has been squeezed out, he should place the nightshade, warm, over his heart, and he will be better. If one has toothache, he should warm nightshade in water and, when he goes to bed at night, place it warm over his upper and lower jaws, where it hurts, and the pain will cease. When one's feet swell up, he should place nightshade, moderately warmed in water, over his feet. The swelling will disappear. One who has pain in the marrow of his legs should cook nightshade in water and place it, warm, around his legs. He should wrap it with a cloth, and he will be better.

CXXII. CALENDULA

Calendula *(ringula)* is cold and moist. It has strong vital energy, and prevails against poison. Whosoever has eaten poison should cook calendula in water and, after squeezing out the water, place it, warm, over his stomach. It weakens the poison which can be excreted. The same person should quickly warm up good wine, place some calendula in it, and warm it again. Because he has consumed poison, he should drink the wine semiwarm. He will get rid of the poison through his nose, as foam. If cows or sheep have eaten something bad that causes them to swell up rapidly, calendula should be pounded, and its juice expressed. The juice should be poured into their mouths, with a little bit of water, so they swallow it and are cured. If a cow or sheep coughs, pour the calendula juice, without water, into their nostrils. Soon they will expel the noxious humors and become well. A person whose head is crusty should cut the soft part off bacon, and even the rind of that bacon, and throw these parts away. He should take the hard part, which was next to the rind, and pound it with calendula in a mortar. He should then frequently anoint his head with it. The crust will fall off, and his head will be beautiful. And one who has scabies on his head should take the flowers and leaves of calendula, squeeze out their juice, and, with this juice and a little water and fine whole wheat or rye flour, prepare paste. He should put it all over his head, covered by a cloth cap, until it grows warm, and the paste breaks down. He should then remove it, and again prepare paste in a similar way, and place it around his head. He should do this for nine days. Every time the paste is removed from his head, he should wash his head with lye prepared from calendula juice, and he will be better.

CXXIII. MULLEIN

Mullein *(wullena)* is hot and dry and a little bit cold. One whose heart is weak and sad should cook, and frequently eat, mullein with meat, fish, or small tarts, but with no other herbs. It will strengthen his heart and make him happy. Also, one who is hoarse or who has a pain in his chest should cook equal amounts of mullein and fennel in good wine. He should strain this through a cloth, and drink it often. He will recover his voice, and his chest will heal.

CXXIV. GERMANDER

Germander *(gamandrea)* is hot and rich, and is profitable for neither man nor beast to eat or drink. It flees, avoiding mucus and scabies, and ends up in the blood, weakening and diminishing it. It undermines the blood and increases its rotten matter, since it does not remove it. Disease ensues when one takes it as a purgative, because his blood has been weakened, and the gore remains in him, and his flesh is enfeebled. Nevertheless, whosoever suffers a slight case of scabies between his skin and flesh should pound germander with old lard and smear himself with it. His flesh will be healed. Once he has begun to heal a bit he should no longer use it. It will harm his blood if he uses it for very long. It is not useful for scabies that lie very deep in the skin, for it would weaken the blood and send the putrid matter further into the body. [If a person's blood, stirred up by bad humors, begins to flow out from his backside with digested food, he should not impede it, since it purges him. If it is excessive, he should add germander to vegetables and other good herbs, making a food which will revive him.]

CXXV. CORNFLOWER, CENTAURY, OR BACHELOR'S BUTTON

Cornflower *(centaurea)* is hot and dry. If one has a broken bone anywhere in his body, he should often drink cornflower or its root mixed in wine or water, and the broken bone will become firmly united. Also, he should warm cornflower in water and, when the water has been expressed, place the cornflower, so warmed, over the place where the bone is broken, and so massage the place with it, and it will be healed. One who is virgichtiget, to the point that his tongue fails to speak and some limb is failing, should mix the root and leaves of the cornflower with fresh deer tallow. Adding flour, he should make small cakes and eat them frequently. The gicht which bothered him will be suppressed. Also, the same person should often drink cornflower in wine, and the gicht will cease.

CXXVI. PENNYROYAL

Pennyroyal *(poleya)* has a pleasant heat, but is nevertheless moist. [It has in it some of the virtue of these fifteen herbs—zedoary, cloves, galingale, ginger, basil, comfrey, lungwort, birthwort, yarrow, southernwood, female fern, agrimony, storax, geranium, and watermint. All these plants are good against fevers.] One whose brain is afflicted should cook pennyroyal in wine and place it, so warmed, around his entire head. He should tie a cloth over it. This will warm his brain and suppress his madness. If one's eyes are obscured, he should extract pennyroyal juice, and smear it around his eyes and eyelids, but not touch the eyes. It will chase away the cloudiness. [If it does touch the interior of the eyes, their substance will be irritated by its strength.] Also, take bile of chicken and twice as much pennyroyal juice. Add a bit of pure wine to make an eye salve. Place it in a metallic jar. Anoint the eyes and eyelids of an adolescent, or even those of a middle-aged person, whose eyes are clouded because of sickness. Let a little bit enter the eyes. Do this for twelve nights, when he is going to bed, and the fogginess will disappear.

Also, pulverize pennyroyal, and put the powder into a mixture of half honey and half vinegar. Drink it frequently on an empty stomach. It will purge the stomach and clear the eyes. Also, if one frequently eats raw pennyroyal leaves and meat, with salt, but nothing else added, it will warm his cold stomach. It even purges a poison-filled stomach and makes it well.

CXXVII. PEONY

Peony *(beonia)* is fiery, and has good strength. It is effective against tertian and quartan fevers. Crush its root a little, place it in wine, and drink it frequently. It will chase the tertian and quartan fevers from you. One may also pulverize the peony and put the powder in flour. Add lard or poppyseed oil, making a kind of porridge. Eat it often and, again, the tertian and quartan fevers will cease. If a person goes out of his mind, as if he knows nothing and is lying deranged in ecstacy, dip the seed of the peony in honey and put it on his tongue. The powers of the peony will ascend to his brain and stir it up, so that he will quickly return to his own mind and receive his understanding.

If someone has much phlegm in his head and around his chest, and therefore is expelling much filth, and even has bad breath, he should cut the peony root into medium-sized circles. He should add some peony seed, and bring this to a boil in wine. He should drink a little bit, frequently, while it is warm. It will purge his head and chest and give his breath a good odor. After he drinks the wine, he can heat more wine with the same peony seed and pieces of root, up to three times.

Also, take the peony seed and dip it in the blood of a swallow. Roll it, so dampened, in fine whole wheat flour. When anyone falls with epilepsy, place it in his mouth while he lies there, and do this every time he falls with this disease, and he will finally be cured.

And, if gnawing worms destroy a person's hair, he should make a lye with the root and seed of the peony, and wash his head with it often. The worms will die. Also, put peony root and leaves in his clothing. When this is done, the worms flee and do not harm the clothing.

CXXVIII. BETONY

Betony *(bathenia)* is hot and it displays, more than other herbs, signs for people's knowledge, just as clean, domestic animals are more engaged with humans than are wild animals. At times the deceit of the devil extends his shadow over it, and over similar herbs. Because of his dewy nature, he knows all powers in plants. For one who is foolish or silly and lacks knowledge, betony should be crushed to a juice and placed over his entire chest at night. It should be tied on with a cloth until morning. If this is done often, he will return to his senses. If someone is regularly tormented by false dreams, he should have betony leaves with him when he goes to bed, and he will see and feel fewer false dreams. [A woman who suffers inordinately with great menstruation at the wrong time should place betony in wine, so that its flavor passes into the wine. She should drink it often, and she will be cured.]

If a man, by a woman, or a woman, by a man, will have been deceived by some magic art, or touched by some illusion, or conjured by fantastic and diabolic incantations, so that the man is insane with love for the woman or the woman insane with love for the man, they should seek betony which has not previously been used for medicine or magic. Previous entanglement with magic would negate its value as a medical remedy. When found, one leaf should be placed in each nostril, and one under the tongue. One leaf should be held in each hand, and one under each foot. The person should fix his eyes intently on the betony. He should do this until the leaves grow hot on his body. This should be repeated until he is better. This will release him from the madness of his love, if he has eaten or drunk or drawn into his body nothing which would incite love. If anyone, whether a man or a woman, has been ensnared by magic words into love of someone else, he should always have betony with him, and he will be better. If it is winter, and betony leaves are unavailable for the foresaid remedy, he should do the same thing with its root. No one should eat betony, since eating it harms his understanding and intellect, and makes him nearly mad.

CXXIX. BLACK DOCK

The dock *(sichterwurtz nigra)* which is called "black" is hot and cold, and its heat is hard and harsh. If one's head is tormented by any disease or weakness and he has lost his senses and intelligence, so that he is out of his mind, crush together black dock and a little less wild thyme. Heat them in a small dish with old lard and place this, warm, over his entire head and around his neck, tied with a cloth. Do this for five days, once in the morning and once at night, heating it each day. After the fifth day, make lye with ashes of the beech tree. Wash his head, and he will be cured. If he has not yet gotten his mind back, put the same ointment around his head and neck, for five more days, as described. Again, after the fifth day, wash his head with the lye. However strong the mental illness might be, it will be chased from him, and he will recover his senses and intelligence.

CXXX. WHITE DOCK

White dock *(sichterwurtz alba)* has the same nature as the black dock, except that the black is harsher than the white. White dock, mixed with wild thyme and fennel and lard, as described above, chases madness from a person. It is a valuable addition to other medicinal mixtures and ointments. A young girl whose menstrual periods fail to come at the right time should put roses, and one sixth as much white dock, in oil, and vigorously and often rub her groin, navel, and hips with that oil. The menses will be moved and loosened. But if she is entangled by some obstacle, and this does not bring on her menses, the described ointment diminishes the menses, so she will have less pain from it, when it pours out, even if it does not come at the right time. [But if a person has pain in his heart or uvula, pound together white dock, with a third as much southernwood, and less *menua* than southernwood. Add to this cow butter, which had been prepared in May, to make an excellent ointment. Then when he has pain in his heart, anoint him there, and if he has pain in his uvula, rub it around his throat. Do this often, and he will be better.]

CXXXI. PIMPERNEL OR BURNET SAXIFRAGE

Pimpernel *(bibenella)* is more cold than hot and is not very valuable for humans, because its juice is harsh. Nevertheless, you should always have it hung from your neck. This enables you to withstand demonic invocations, magic formulas, and other enchantments which are not caused by something you have eaten or drunk.

CXXXII. COLUMBINE

Columbine *(agleya)* is cold. A person on whom freislich begins to spring up should eat raw columbine, and the freislich will disappear. And one on whom scrofula is developing should eat raw columbine, and it will decrease. But one who ejects much phlegm should soak columbine in honey and eat it often. It will diminish the phlegm, and he will rid himself of it. One with fever should pound columbine, strain its juice through a cloth, and add wine. He should drink this frequently, and he will be well.

CXXXIII. GARDEN SPURGE

Garden spurge *(springwurtz)* is cold. The little sap it has is sharp. By itself it is not good for humans. Eaten pure, mixed with nothing else, it would diffuse through a person's body, and pass through unhealthfully, with great peril. But, one who wishes to take a small, gentle purgative should take equal weights of cinnamon and licorice and pulverize them. He should roll this powder with a bit of wheat flour in spurge sap and form it into bean-sized pieces. He should let these dry in the sun or in the oven. In the morning, he should take as many pieces of it as five, nine, or fifteen pennies weigh. This will gently purge him. Afterward, he should be heedful of practicing moderation with his food and drink.

CXXXIV. FORGET-ME-NOT

Forget-me-not *(frideles)* contains neither correct heat nor correct cold. It holds no powers useful for humans. It is like a weed and is not valuable as medicine. If someone should eat it, it would do more harm than good.

CXXXV. HOG'S-FENNEL

Hog's-fennel *(berwurtz)* is hot and has dry vital energy. A person with strong, burning fevers should pulverize it and eat the powder with bread, before or after a meal, and he will be better. Anyone who has gicht should also frequently eat this powder, and gicht will cease. For jaundice, one should pound the root of hog's-fennel, when it is green, in vinegar, and eat it. If he also prepares broth with that vinegar and eats it frequently, he will be cured.

CXXXVI. SAXIFRAGE

Saxifrage *(stembrecha)* is cold and possesses strong powers. It is not good for a thin person to eat, because it would be too strong for his body. When mucus coagulates, in either a person's stomach or bladder, and becomes hardened, like a stone, he should crush saxifrage seed in water and drink it often after eating, but not on an empty stomach. When drunk in this manner, it breaks anything hard and harmful in a person's body, so that he is healed. For jaundice, one should grind the seed in wine and let it lie in that wine for a moderate time. He should then drink it, after having eaten. This extinguishes the jaundice which arises from an excess of gall, often producing in a person matter as hard as stone.

CXXXVII. UGERA

Ugera is very hot and sharp. Its sharpness is very strong and breaks down large, strong ulcers. Pound the ugera in a mortar, and add some olive oil. Place it, cold, on the ulcer. If you do not have olive oil, add a bit of deer tallow, and heat it in a small dish. Let it cool, and place it on the ulcer. Its power softens the ulcer and draws out the poison, healing it. If a person has large red ulcers, pound the ugera and add olive oil or deer tallow as explained above. Place this over the ulcers to extract the poison. When the ulcers begin to grow red, take away the ugera and make a plaster of hempen cloth with olive oil or deer tallow. Place this over the ulcers, and they will be healed, since the poison is drawn out. Also, soak the ugera root in vinegar and place it, for the night, on a place where warts have recently developed on the body. Tie a cloth over it. Do this often, and the warts will disappear.

CXXXVIII. CELANDINE

Celandine *(grintwurtz)* is very hot, has poisonous juice which is dark and bitter, and can confer no health to a person. Even if it might give a person good health in one area, it would bring a greater illness to another internal spot. If anyone eats or drinks it, it ulcerates and harms him internally, making alimentation and digestion painful and unhealthy. Whosoever eats, drinks, or touches something unclean, from which his body becomes ulcerous, he should take old fat and add some celandine juice to it. He should crush this and liquefy it in a small dish. When he rubs himself thoroughly with this unguent he will be healed.

CXXXIX. LOVAGE

Lovage *(lubestuckel)* is of a temperate heat. If eaten raw, it breaks down a person's nature, making it worse. If one should eat it by itself with no other condiments, even though it is cooked, it would make him heavy and listless in both mind and body. But if it is cooked, and eaten with condiments, it does no great harm. One who suffers pain in the glands in his neck, and whose neck veins are swollen, should cook lovage in water with a slightly greater amount of ground ivy. Having poured off the water, he should place these warm herbs around his neck and over the distended veins, and he will be cured. [And if someone has a chest cough, which is beginning to be painful, he should take lovage and an equal amount of sage, and twice as much fennel as there is of the other two, and place them together in good wine, until the wine takes their flavor. Then he should throw out the herbs and heat the wine. He should drink it warm, after eating, until he is well. If the cough is minor, and the pain mild, the person should drink the foresaid potion, unheated. If the pain is great, he should drink the same wine heated, until the condition is broken down and becomes less harsh.

If rheum flows from a horse's nostrils and causes him to cough, whosoever wishes to relieve him should take lovage and a little less stinging nettle and cook them in water. Take them from the water and, with the reins in place, let the warm vapor go into the mouth and nostrils, and the horse will be cured. If, however, a horse has pain in his belly, as if from bites, the person should take lovage and a little less stinging nettle and frequently mix them with his fodder, so that he eats them both together, and he will be cured.]

CXL. IVY

Ivy *(ebich)* is more cold than hot and, like a weed, useless as human food. But, a person who has jaundice should heat it in a small dish with deer tallow or old fat. He should place it, warm, over his stomach, so that the jaundice passes into the herb, and the yellow appears on the exterior skin of that person. When these herbs have been placed over his stomach, as explained, one should immediately crush watercress in cold water, strain it, and give the water to him to drink cold. The jaundice will be expelled, and he will be cured.

[A woman who suffers inordinately great menses at the wrong time should cook ivy in water and place it, warm, around her thighs and navel. Its coldness halts the contrary flow. If the interior membrane, which encloses the intestines, is cut by some accident, ivy and twice as much comfrey should be cooked in good wine. After these herbs are cooked, they should be taken from the wine. Then a bit of pulverized zedoary, sugar equal to the amount of ivy, and some cooked honey should be added to the wine and brought to a moderate boil. This should be poured through a little sack, making a clear drink. The ill person should drink this frequently, after food, and at night. He should also place the herbs which were cooked in the wine over the place where the interior membrane was ruptured. This draws together the torn places. He should also cut comfrey root into minute bits and place them in wine, so that it takes their flavor. He should drink this wine often, until he is healed.]

CXLI. MARSHMALLOW OR ALTHAEA

Marshmallow *(ybischa)* is hot and dry and prevails against fevers. If a person has fevers of any kind, he should pound marshmallow in vinegar and drink it in the morning, on an empty stomach, and at night. The fever, whatever its nature, will cease. A person who has pain in his head should crush marshmallow with a bit less sage and mix in a little olive oil. He should warm it in his hand, near the fire, and place it on his forehead. He should tie it on with a cloth, and go to bed, and he will be better.

CXLII. VALERIAN

Valerian *(denemarcha)* is hot and moist. One who suffers from pleurisy, or is in pain from gicht, should pulverize valerian and add a bit less catnip powder. He should mix flour and water in a small dish with lard and these herbs, making little cakes. He should eat them often. The pleurisy or gicht in him will cease, and he will be better.

CXLIII. CATNIP

Catnip *(nebetta)* is hot. A person with scrofula, which has not yet ruptured, on his neck should pulverize catnip. He should often eat this powder with bread or in a puree, or in little cakes, and the scrofula will vanish. If the pustules are broken, place fresh, uncooked catnip leaves over them. The scrofula will dry up.

CXLIV. HERB ROBERT OR STORKSBILL

Herb Robert *(cranschnabel)* is very hot and has a bit of moisture. It has nearly the powers of spices. Therefore, take herb Robert and a little less feverfew, and even less nutmeg, and reduce them to a powder and mix them together. One with heart pain should eat this powder with bread or, if eaten without bread, he should lick it from his hand. He will be better since this is the best powder for a healthy heart. And, whosoever has a runny nose should place this powder near his nose and inhale its odor. The runny nose will dissipate gently and mildly, dissapearing quickly without danger to the person. Also, one who has a cough and constriction in his chest should mix flour, this powder, and lard or butter in a small dish and make little cakes. He should eat them often, with or without food. This gently and tenderly weakens the cough and chest wound, and brings them to an end, making the person better. And, one who has a pain in his chest, because his chest is congested, or one who has a pain in his throat, so that he has lost his voice, should drink this powder in warm wine. His chest and throat will be better. But, one who has a pain in his head will be better if he adds salt to this powder and eats it, with bread or licked from his hand.

CXLV. COMFREY

Comfrey *(consolida)* is cold. If a person eats it for no reason, it destroys all the humors that had been correctly established in him. But if some part of a person is deficient, ulcerated, or wounded, and he then eats comfrey, it quickly pursues the mucus which is coming out there, healing it as well as the ulcers on the surface of the skin. It does not heal ulcers within the body. Similar to rocks thrown into a large ditch which keep water from flowing out and cause slime to settle, and worms and other evil things to remain there, comfrey, eaten immoderately and not in the right way, heals surface wounds but sends putrid matter further in.

CXLVI. BIRTHWORT OR ARISTOLOCHIA

Birthwort *(byverwurtz)* is hot, and a bit cold. Therefore, pulverize its root and leaves and add half as much feverfew powder and one-fourth as much cinnamon powder. Mix them together and eat it daily, either with bread or with warm wine, or in broth. You will have no great or lasting infirmity until the time you die. No one should shun powder prepared in this way. If a healthy person eats this powder daily, he will not be lying sick in bed a long time. If he is sick and eats it, he will be well. In order to conserve this powder safely throughout the year, it should be placed in a new, earthenware vessel, enclosed in the earth. It will retain its powers.

CXLVII. SILVERWEED

Silverweed *(grensing)* is a weed and is not useful for a person's health. If someone eats it, it neither benefits nor harms him.

CXLVIII. WATER PARSNIP

Water parsnip *(morkrut)* is a repast of the human being. It is neither beneficial to his health, nor does it harm him. When it is eaten, it fills his stomach.

CXLIX. GOOSE GRASS

Goose grass *(gensekrut)* is cold and is a weed. If a person should eat it, it is not profitable to his health, but it harms him more.

CL. FLAX

Flax *(linsamo)* is hot, etc., as below in CXCIV, about flaxseed, in which there are many things written which are absent here.

CLI. CHICKWEED

Chickweed *(hunsdarm)* is hot and is a weed. If a person has fallen by accident, or has been struck by cudgels, so that his skin is bruised, he should cook chickweed in water, then squeeze out the water. He should frequently place the warm herb over the wounded area and tie a cloth over it. It will dispel the mucus collected there.

CLII. BLACK HELLEBORE

Black hellebore *(nyesewurtz)* is hot and dry. It has a bit of moisture and a certain vital energy which is useful. One who is troubled by gicht or has jaundice should pound black hellebore and strain its juice through a cloth. He should add that juice to wine. If he has gicht, he should frequently drink it this way, on an empty stomach; if he has jaundice, he should drink it often, after a meal, and he will be cured. One can also cook black hellebore in wine with honey, and strain it through a cloth. He should drink this when he has eaten and at night when he goes to bed. If he does this frequently, he will be cured. It will gently soothe his chest, purge his stomach, and diminish whatsoever is filthy or stinking inside his body.

CLIII. GOUTWEED

The herb which is called "gout" *(herba gicht)* is very hot and has some vital energy in it. One who has pain in his stomach should moderately pound it, with its seed, and cook it in wine and a bit of honey. He should strain this through a cloth, and drink it warm. One who wishes to take measures so that his stomach should not become sick should often drink that same potion cold. His stomach will retain its good health. But, one who is often troubled by gicht should pound this herb, with its seed, and add bear fat and a third as much olive oil. He should cook this in water and make an unguent. He should anoint himself where it hurts. It shall immediately penetrate the skin, and the stormy period of his gicht will cease.

CLIV. VERVAIN

Vervain *(ysena)* is more cold than hot. When someone's flesh is rotten from ulcers or worms, he should cook vervain in water. He should then place a linen cloth over the putrid ulcers or places made putrid by worms. Having squeezed out the water slightly, he should lay the vervain, moderately hot, over that linen cloth. When the vervain has dried out, he should put on more, cooked in the same way. He should do this until the putridness is gone. If someone's throat swells up, he should warm vervain in water and place it, so warmed, over his throat. He should tie it with a cloth and continue this treatment until the tumor vanishes.

CLV. SUMMER SAVORY

Summer savory *(satereia)* is more hot than cold. If someone is tormented by gicht, so that his limbs are always moving, he should pulverize summer savory. To this he should add pulverized cumin and sage (less cumin than sage), and mix these powders together in hydromel. He should often drink this, after he has eaten, and he will be better.

CLVI. ARNICA

Arnica *(wolfsgelegena)* is very hot and has a poisonous heat in it. If a person's skin has been touched with fresh arnica, he or she will burn lustily with love for the person who is afterward touched by the same herb. He or she will be so incensed with love, almost infatuated, and will become a fool.

CLVII. INDIAN CHICKWEED

Indian chickweed *(symes)* is cold. If maggots or worms are eating a person, he should pulverize this chickweed on the fire, and place the powder on the wound. The worms or maggots will die.

CLVIII. RUSH

Rush *(juncus)* is not rightly hot, nor rightly cold, but lukewarm, and therefore not effective as medicine.

CLIX. MEYGELANA

Meygelana is cold, and its coolness is like the earth when it brings flowers to fruit. If scrofula or freislich or any kind of poison-filled ulcers develop on a person, he should often eat meygelena on an empty stomach, and they will disappear. One who has epilepsy should also eat meygelana before a meal. When he is lying on the ground, with that illness, place this herb under his tongue. He will stand up much more quickly, with less suffering.

CLX. TORMENTIL

Tormentil *(dornella)* is cold. Its coldness is good and healthy and prevails against fevers which arise from noxious food. Take tormentil and cook it in wine, with a little honey added. Strain it through a cloth, and drink it frequently at night, on an empty stomach, and you will become well.

CLXI. CLARY SAGE

Clary sage *(scharleya)* is hot and is effective against poison. If someone has swallowed poison, cook clary sage with a little honey and rue. After this has cooked, add a bit of thorn apple and strain it through a cloth. This should be drunk three times, after some food. The poison will pass through by either vomiting or evacuation of the bowels, unless the poison is so great that it brings death to the person. One whose stomach is so weak that he is easily made sick by food should take clary sage, and a third as much pennyroyal, and one-twelfth as much fennel. He should cook these together in good wine, with a bit of honey, and strain it through a cloth. He should often drink it after a meal and at night. His stomach will be gently cured, or purged, and he will have an appetite for food. And, one with a pain in his head should cook clary sage in water, express the water, and place the warm herb around his head. He should cover it with a cloth, and go to sleep, and he will be better.

CLXII. GERANIUM OR CRANESBILL

Geranium *(storcksnabel)* is more cold than hot and is effective against stones. One who has a stone in his body should take geranium and a little less saxifrage and cook them in water. He should strain this through a cloth and prepare a sauna. He should also cook oats in water and pour that water over the hot rocks. After he has sweated in this bath, he should drink the warm water in which the geranium and saxifrage were cooked. The stone will be gently broken up. And, one who has pain in his heart and is always sad should take geranium, and less pennyroyal, and even less rue and pulverize it. He should often eat this powder with his bread. His heart will be strengthened, and he will be happy.

CLXIII. BENNET

Bennet *(benedicta)* is hot. If someone consumes it in a drink, it fires him up with lustful desire. But, if anyone is failing in all his corporeal powers, he should cook bennet in water, and often drink that water warm. He will recoup the powers of his body. After his body is better, he should avoid bennet.

CLXIV. MADDER

Madder *(risza)* is cold and effective against fever. One who has a fever and disdains eating should cook madder gently in water. He should remove the herb, and drink the warm water in the morning and at night. He should place the herb, which he took out of the water, over his stomach for a short time. He should do this for three days, and the fevers in him will cease. [Someone who suffers quartan fevers should cook equal weights of madder and the leaves from thorn bushes, with three times as much tithymal as there is of the other two, in wine. Then, he should pour some very fine, clear wine and immerse a hot piece of steel in it ten times. Afterward, he should take the wine which has been cooked with the herbs and pour it into the wine in which he had immersed the steel. He should bring this to a boil. He should drink this at the onset of fever until he is well.]

CLXV. MUSETHA

Musetha is more hot than cold, and any unguent becomes better and more powerful when it is added. By itself, it is not much good as medicine.

CLXVI. BLOODWORT

Bloodwort *(birckwurtz)* is more cold than hot. A person who has superfluous and poisonous humors in him should take bloodwort and pound it together with twice as much tithymal, until it is liquid. He should put this in an earthenware vessel, and pour good, clear wine over it. Taken after meals, and at bedtime, for fifteen days, it will benefit a person for a year. This potion lessens his superfluous and poisonous humors.

CLXVII. MASTERWORT

Masterwort *(astrencia)* is hot and effective against fevers. For any kind of fever, one should pound masterwort. Once it is shredded, he should pour half a glass of wine over it, and leave it over night. In the morning, he should add wine to it, and drink it, before breakfast. If he does this for three to five days, he will be cured. [A person who is unable to digest the food he has eaten should take two pennyweight of aristolochia juice, one pennyweight of pimpernel juice, and a half pennyweight each of soapwort juice and ginger. He should mix fine whole wheat flour with these juices, and make little cakes as wide as pennies, but a bit thick. He should cook them in the sun or in a nearly cool oven. The person who cannot digest because he is internally warm, and food burns up inside him, should take one of these little cakes in the morning, on an empty stomach. If he is cold internally, which makes the food congeal and compress, he should take two or three little cakes in the morning, on an empty stomach. Afterward, his first food should be broth or a draft, then some good, gentle foods. He should do this until he feels his stomach is freed up.]

CLXVIII. SMARTWEED

Smartweed *(ertpeffer)* is cold. It grows from clear air. A person who has fever should take sufficient smartweed and put it in good wine for a night. He should then throw out the smartweed and heat the wine with a hot piece of steel. In the morning, before breakfast, and at night when he goes to bed, he should drink it. He should continue until he feels good health in himself.

CLXIX. BRAMBLE

The bramble *(brema)* on which dewberries or blackberries grow is more hot than cold. [If someone's tongue either swells up or has ulcers, he should use a bramble, or a small lancet, to cut his tongue, so that the mucus breaks through. If he has a toothache, he should do the same thing to his gums, and he will be better.] If worms eat a person or animal, pulverize bramble and place the powder on the flesh where the worms are eating. The worms will die, and the person will be healed. If someone's lungs are ailing and he has a chest cough, he should take feverfew, and a little less bramble, even less hyssop, and a smaller amount of oregano. He should boil this in good wine, with honey, then strain it through a cloth and drink a little after eating moderately. Later he may drink more of it, after a full meal. If he does this regularly, his lungs will recuperate, and the mucus will be carried away from his chest. Moreover, the dewberry fruit which grows on the bramble harms neither a healthy nor a sick person, and is easily digested, although medicine is not found in it.

CLXX. WILD STRAWBERRY

The plant on which wild strawberries *(erpere)* are grown is more hot than cold. It produces mucus in the person eating it and is not valuable as medicine. The wild strawberries themselves make a kind of mucus in the person who eats them. They are beneficial as food for neither a sick nor a healthy person because they grow near the ground and, indeed, in putrid air.

CLXXI. BILBERRY

The plant on which bilberries *(walt bere)* (which are black and sometimes called whortleberries) grow has very great cold. It is the cold which cedes a bit to heat, when the cold humor of the earth and stones does more harm than good. It is not useful as medicine, and the fruit harms the person who eats it, stirring up gicht in him.

CLXXII. MUSHROOMS

Mushrooms *(fungi)* of any kind, which spring up on top of the ground, are like the foam and sweat of the earth, and are a bit harmful to the person who eats them. They create mucus and scum in him. Nevertheless, mushrooms which grow in dry air and on dry land are more cold than hot, and are better than those which grow in damp air and on damp earth. Not much medicine is found in them. Mushrooms which grow in damp air and on damp earth are neither fully hot nor cold, but lukewarm. If a person eats them, they stir up a bad humor in him. There is not much medicine in them. However, the mushrooms which spring from certain trees, whether standing or lying on the ground, are of some value as human food, just as some small garden herbs. They are less harmful to eat, and sometimes are valuable as medicine.

The mushroom that grows on an almond tree is not rightly hot or cold, but has a torpor in it. It is not valuable for eating because it stirs up . . . But if worms are nascent on a person, before they are alive, take the mushroom which grows on the almond tree, when it is fresh and recently taken from the tree. Hold it over boiling water so that it becomes warm and moist. Place it frequently, warm and moist, over the swelling where the worms are developing, and the swelling will vanish. If the worms have grown, so that they are alive, dry the same mushroom in an oven which is warm, but without coals. Reduce it to a powder, and frequently place it over the sore, and the worms will die.

The mushroom which grows on the beech tree is hot. It can be eaten in food by both healthy and sick people. A person who has a cold, or a mucusy stomach, should take a mushroom from the beech tree when it is fresh. He should cook it in water with good herbs and a bit of lard. He should frequently eat a bit of it after a meal. It will warm his stomach and remove mucus. But, if a pregnant woman is fatigued because her body is slow, heavy, and oppressed from the weight of the child, she should take a mushroom from a beech tree. She should boil it in water until it is completely broken down, strain it through a cloth, and make a broth from this juice, adding sufficient lard. She should have some once or twice a day, after having eaten, and she will be gently released from the pain of her offspring.

The mushroom which grows from the elder tree is cold and not good for a person to eat. If someone does eat it, he will become weak. It does not have much medicinal value.

The mushroom which grows from the willow is hot and good to eat. One who has pain in his lungs, and whose chest is oppressed because of it, should cook this mushroom in wine and add a bit of cumin and lard. He may sip this broth and eat the mushroom itself. Eaten this way, the mushroom mitigates pain in the heart and spleen. The heart often has pain because the stomach, lungs, and spleen afflict it with bad humors. If you want to consume a purgative potion, take a fresh mushroom from the willow. Dry it in the sun or warm oven. Pulverize it and then, when you wish to use a purgative, take some thorn apple, and add a pennyweight of this powder to it, and a half pennyweight of milk from garden spurge. Mix them together and take that potion, just as any other, on an empty stomach, and it will purge you. The powdered mushroom tempers the thorn apple and garden spurge, and it searches out evil humors, as if they were good aromas.

And, if he has leucoma in his eye, he should dry the mushroom of the willow tree in the sun. Afterward, whenever he wishes to cure leucoma, he should place the mushroom in water for a short time, then shake out the water which it has soaked up. With a feather, he should streak this water on his eyelids so that it even touches the inside of the eyes a bit. He should do this for three or five nights when he goes to bed, and he will be cured.

The mushroom which grows on the pear tree is cold and moist. It neither harms nor profits the person who eats it. But, the person whose head is scabby should take a fresh mushroom from the pear tree, squeeze its juice into olive oil, and then throw away the mushroom. He should often anoint his head with this oil, and he will be cured. For mangy nails, he should take from the pear tree a mushroom, as wide as the mangy nails, and dip it in ox, not cow, bile. When it has been intincted with the bile and placed over the nail, it will dry up on the inside. He should again dip it in the bile and put it on the nail, which will grow beautiful from it.

The mushroom that grows on the aspen is hot and slimy. It is not good for a human to eat, and no medicine is found in it.

CLXXIII. ASAFOETIDA

Asafoetida *(wichwurtz)* is more cold and moist than hot. A person who has burning fevers should take asafoetida, and twice as much basil, and cook this in pure wine. He should allow it to cool, and drink it daily, while fasting, both in the morning and at night when he goes to bed. He should do this until he gets well.

CLXXIV. ALOE

The juice of this plant *(aloe)* is hot and has great strength. For strong, daily stomach fevers one should make a plaster with aloe on hempen cloth. When placed over the stomach and navel, the fever will cease. Its odor strengthens a person internally; it purges a similar affliction in the head. One who has a cough should put an aloe plaster on his chest, so that he can smell the odor. The cough will cease. But, one who has ague should take horehound juice or, if it is winter, horehound powder and put it with a greater amount of aloe, and licorice. He should cook this in wine, strain it through a cloth, and add hydromel. Any ague, except quartan, will quickly be cured. One who has jaundice should place aloe in cold water and drink it in the morning and when he goes to bed. He should do this three or four times, and he will be cured.

CLXXV. FRANKINCENSE

Frankincense *(thus)* is more hot than cold, and its odor ascends even without fire. It clears the eyes and purges the brain. Pulverize frankincense and add it to a bit of fine whole wheat flour and egg white. Make little cakes, and dry them in the sun or on a hot tile. Afterward place them frequently near your nostrils. Their odor will strengthen you, clear your eyes, and fill your brain. But, one whose head is ailing, who thinks his head is splitting, should place the little cakes, just described, on both his temples. He should tie them on with a cloth when he goes to bed, and the pain will cease. For quotidian fevers, one should pound frankincense and spearmint together, and place this frequently over his navel, in order to warm it up, tying it on with a cloth. He will be cured [because the fevers torment his stomach and liver].

CLXXVI. MYRRH

Myrrh *(myrrha)* is hot and dry. If you wish to carry myrrh with you, first heat it in the sun, or over a tile warmed by the fire, so that it melts slightly. Then hold it near you so that it heats up from your flesh or perspiration. It chases from you phantasms, magic spells, and demonic invocations made with malign words over bad herbs. They will be less likely to hurt you, if you have neither eaten nor drunk magic things. Streaked on the chest or stomach, it chases overflowing desire from someone who is burning with lust. Although myrrh's odor chases lust from a person, it does not make his mind happy. It oppresses it and makes it heavy and sad. Therefore, along with myrrh, he should also carry gold with the impurities burnt out. This makes a person's mind happy. When great fevers invade a person, myrrh drunk in warm wine expels them. One beset by lust can extinguish it by eating myrrh, but it also makes him dry, so it is not helpful. It is not useful for anyone to eat, except in great necessity.

CLXXVII. BALSAM

Balsam *(balsamon)* is of a royal nature and is very hot and moist. It is of such temperament that it is used as medicine with great caution, lest its strength harm a person, in the same way noble people ought to be venerated and feared, lest they be provoked to anger. For great stomach fevers, one should make an unguent with a bit of balsam, some olive oil, and a greater amount of deer marrow. Rubbing it around the stomach expels the fevers. If someone is insane, use this unguent to anoint his temples and neck, so that it touches neither the top of his head nor the brain, which might be harmed by its strength. This restores his right mind and good health. One who is virgichtiget should add a bit of balsam to *paulinum* or another good electuary, and eat it. The gicht in him will cease. Dead bodies may be kept in balsam for a little while, lest they putrify. Balsam juice should be strongly feared by all natural things. They may be correctly tempered by it, but it could easily dissipate them.

CLXXVIII. HONEY

If a person who is fat and has thick flesh eats honey *(mel)* often, it makes decayed matter in him. If honey is cooked, one who is thin and dry is harmed by it. If someone eats the honeycomb wax it stirs up melancholy, and so harms him. It makes a heaviness in him and causes his melancholy to increase.

CLXXIX. SUGAR

When sugar *(zucker)* is still raw, and not yet useful to the human being, dry it in the summer sun or, if it is winter, over a heated stone. Thus dry, it refreshes one who eats or drinks it. One who ails in his brain or chest, and is so blocked that he is unable to purge himself or cough the congestion up, should eat or drink this. It will purge his brain and unloosen his chest.

CLXXX. MILK

Milk *(lac)* of cows, goats, and sheep is more healthful in the winter than in the summer. In winter it does not draw into itself the variety of saps that it does in the summer. If healthy people drink milk in the summer, it harms them only a bit. Weak and sick people should consume very little. If healthy people wish to consume milk in the winter, they should take the root of stinging nettle and dry it and air it. They should place it in milk before they drink it, since bad humors are checked by nettle. If weak or sick people desire milk in the winter, they should boil it and place dried nettle in it. In summer, when the nettle contains humors and saps and greenness, it is not beneficial to place it in milk. The fresh sap harms the milk.

CLXXXI. BUTTER

Cow butter *(butyrum)* is better and more healthful than the butter of sheep or goats. A person who is congested or has a cough, or whose body is dry, should eat butter. It shall heal him internally and refresh him. For a healthy person, or one who has a moderate amount of flesh, eating butter is good and healthful.

If, however, one's body has fatty flesh, he should eat butter in moderation, lest his weak flesh become fatter.

CLXXXII. SALT

Salt *(sal)* is very hot and a bit moist. It is useful to the human being in many ways. If someone eats foods without salt, it makes his insides tepid. If he eats foods seasoned with a moderate amount of salt, he is strengthened and healed. However, one who eats his food with too much salt becomes dry internally, and is harmed. Then [the salt falls over the lungs, like sand, and] dries them out. Since the lungs need moisture, it harms and congests them. If salt falls on the liver, it harms it a bit, even if the liver is strong and able to withstand it. Thus, all food ought to be salted, so that it has more flavor, which the salt brings out. But, salt is more healthful roasted over a fire than raw. Its moisture is then dried out. If a person eats it, in moderation, on bread or with any other food, it is good and healthful for him. [Salt is like blood and, like flowing waters, gives strength in moderate use. In immoderate use it is as a flood or storm.] Crystallized salt has greater heat than other salt and has some moisture. It is fit for human use, and for all medicines; adding a tiny bit makes them very much better. It excels other kinds of salt, just as spices are more valuable than herbs. Eating a little of this salt with bread or other food, even with some other condiment, strengthens and heals and is good for the lungs. Eating it extravagantly, without moderation, is debilitating and harms the lungs. [It exudes from the strongest moisture of waters and earth. In moderate use its good heat and powers are strengthening. Used immoderately it destroys the user, like a sudden flood.] A person suffers great thirst when he ingests much salt. The salt desiccates his lungs and dries his good humors. The lungs and humors seek moisture, so the person is thirsty. If someone drinks a great quantity of wine in order to quench his thirst, he induces senseless behavior [as happened with Lot*]. Thus it is more healthful and sane for a thirsty person to drink water, rather than wine, to quench his thirst.

---

*Translator's note: According to the Old Testament (Gen. 19:30–38), Lot's daughters bore him sons, begotten when he had drunk too much wine.

CLXXXIII. VINEGAR

Wine vinegar *(acetum)* is useful for all foods when it is added in a manner which does not destroy the flavor of the foods, but allows a bit of vinegar to be perceived. Vinegar consumed with a bit of food purges the foulness in a person and diminishes his humors, causing the food to journey through him as it should. If so much vinegar is added to food that it overpowers the flavor of the food, making the food taste more like vinegar than itself, it is harmful. Its heat in some way cooks the food inside the person, making it hard and scarcely digestible. If a person has broken scrofula on his body, he should take the mother of vinegar, which lies atop the vinegar. He should squeeze out the vinegar, just as one presses cheese. He should allow it to dry, and reduce it to a powder. It should be placed on the scrofula, which will dry out and heal. Scrofula that has not ruptured will diminish when mother of vinegar, with its juice, is tied over it with a cloth. Vinegar made from beer is not as good as that made from wine. It is weak and lukewarm, and it easily gives fever to a person. It will easily harden his stomach, and it is of little value to the person who consumes it.

CLXXXIV. MERANDA

One who wishes to make *meranda* should put little pieces of bread into wine, beer, or water. When the liquid has soaked into the bread, he should eat it. Softened in this way, the bread is much more tender and easy to digest. If someone merely intincts the bread and eats it right away, before it is saturated, it constricts him, and makes him heavy inside, and is not easily digested. Meranda of wine is strong, and makes a person's insides a bit dry. It is not very beneficial, even if it does no great harm. Meranda of beer is more healthful than that of wine because the juice of the bread is joined with its near relative, the juice of the beer. Though it does not dry out a person internally, it does not profit him much. The meranda of water is more healthful than that of beer. It is light and gentle in the stomach and easily digested. Just as soft food, it passes through a person easily and without injury. Taking meranda frequently is not good for a person with a hot, strong stomach; it cools the stomach and dries it out. A person with a cold stomach is also not much helped by meranda; it cools his stomach all the more, and hardens it a little. Meranda is not very helpful for a person with a weak and tender stomach; it weighs it down. Nevertheless, it diminishes mucus and carries it away.

CLXXXV. EGGS

Eggs *(ova)* of any kind are more cold than hot. They are able to do great outrage. They are harmful to eat, since they are sticky and slimy, and almost like poison. A person should not eat them, for if he does, scrofula and the bad worm that eats on humans develop on him very quickly. It is possible to eat eggs from domesticated hens. They should be eaten in moderation because, like excessive, uncooked flour, they are harmful to weakened intestines; they stick to them like insipid matter, and produce mucus and putrid matter in the stomach. A person whose intestines are healthy will be able to overcome this, if he eats them. But, since one is easily sickened by them, he should eat them in moderation. For a healthy person, soft eggs are better than hard, which make pain in a person's stomach. Neither soft nor hard eggs are fit for a sick person to eat. If an ill person wishes to eat eggs, he should pour a bit of wine into water, and bring it to a boil in a small dish. He should then break the eggs into the water, and throw away the shells. If cooked that way and eaten, they do not harm him. The poison and rot which is in them is cooked out by the fire. However, an egg roasted in its shell on the fire is better and more healthful to eat than an egg cooked in water in its shell. The fire draws out the rot through the shell; the water does not remove the putridness, since some of the shell floats above it. Also, the yolk of the egg is more healthful to eat than the white. A moderately hard yolk is better as food than one entirely soft. If anyone should eat a raw egg it harms him very much, since it generates putridness.

Goose eggs are harmful to eat unless they are cooked in some food. Duck eggs are bad to eat and harm the human being. But, they are better to eat than duck flesh, since all the fetid matter in a duck remains in its flesh, and does not fully pass into the eggs.

CLXXXVI. SPRUCE PITCH

Spruce pitch *(pix)* is very hot. It is healthful in drinking vessels. If maggots eat a person, place spruce pitch over the wound. It will draw the worms to itself, so that it is possible to pull them out and scrape them off. When they have been removed, place spruce pitch on the wound a second time, until the worms are completely gone. After the flesh has been purged of them, anoint the place with olive oil and other good ointments, and it will be healed.

CLXXXVII. PINE RESIN

Pine resin *(hartz)* is tepid. A vessel in which it is placed is not healthful. It torments the head and creates stuffiness.

CLXXXVIII. SULPHUR

Sulphur *(sulphur)* is hot and, when burned or used in concoctions, it draws bad humors to itself. It is not useful as medicine, unless a person has had some poison or enchantment prepared for him, or if he has delusions. If sulphur is burned, its odor is so strong that all things are weakened by it, and they are less able to do damage, just as where there are two evil companions, one exceeds the other in wickedness.

CLXXXIX. LUPINE

Lupine *(vigbona)* is cold. One who has a pain in his intestines, as if he is swelling up, should reduce lupine to a powder and add to it a bit of bread, which has been reduced to a powder, and a bit of fennel seed, or some lovage juice. He should cook this with water, as a food, and eat a little. If done often, it will heal his ailing intestines.

CXC. GARBANZO BEANS OR CHICK-PEAS

Garbanzo *(kicher)* are hot and gentle. They are light and easy to eat and do not increase bad humors in the person who eats them. One who has fevers should roast garbanzo beans over live coals. He should eat them, and he will be better.

CXCI. BITTER VETCH

Bitter vetch *(wisela)* is cold and dry. When eaten, it excites fevers and makes the stomach cold. It is not very suitable for medicine.

CXCII. VETCH

Vetch *(wichim)* is cold. It does not harm animals much, but it is not good for a human to eat. However, if a person's flesh bubbles up between the skin and the flesh, as if a wart is springing up, he should take vetch and cook it in water, and place it, warm, over the place. The wart, which had begun to grow from perverse humors, will vanish.

CXCIII. MILLET

Millet *(milium)* is cold and not useful for eating. It augments neither the blood nor the flesh. It does not give strength. It fills a person's swelling stomach and diminishes hunger. It does not have a refreshing taste. It also makes a person's brain watery and his stomach lukewarm and slow. It incites a storm in a person's humors and is nearly like a useless field herb, not healthy for a person to eat. But if someone ails in his lungs he should pulverize millet over a hot stone and add twice as much powdered hart's-tongue fern. He will get better if he eats it with a mouthful of bread, on an empty stomach or after a meal.

CXCIV. FLAXSEED

Flaxseed *(semen lini)* is hot and not good to eat. For pain in the side, one should cook flaxseed in water and dip a linen cloth in that warm water. He should frequently place that cloth, without the seed, over his side. The pain is attenuated and relieved a bit, even though it was somewhat serious. Also, for pain in the side take flaxseed, and a bit less gum arabic, so that the flaxseed exceeds the gum arabic by a fourth part. Cook them, like glue, in a frying pan. Then pound mistletoe from a pear tree to a juice in a mortar. There should be more of this juice than there is gum arabic. Put deer marrow, of a greater weight than the gum or juice, in the pan with the flaxseed and gum, and bring it to a boil. Tallow of a young bull can be substituted for the deer marrow. This should be strained through a cloth sieve, completely perforated, and put in a new earthenware vessel, coated with wax. Use this frequently, while near the fire, to anoint the painful side.

Whosoever has been burned anywhere on his body should boil flaxseed in water, dip a linen cloth in the water, and place the cloth over the area of the burn. This draws out the burn.

CXCV. COSTMARY

Costmary *(balsamita)* is more hot than cold. If anyone's knowledge and understanding are lost from many diverse thoughts, so that he has become a madman, take costmary and three times as much fennel and cook them together in water. Having thrown out the herbs, have the person frequently drink this water, cold. The afflicted person should avoid dry foods, and eat good, delicate things which furnish him with good blood. He should also eat semolina porridge made with butter or lard, not oil, since oil fills the brain and attracts phlegm. He should not drink wine, since it scatters his already dissipated humors. Neither should he drink straight water, since it would bring his senses to greater inanity. For three days he should drink the foresaid potion, and beer, and cover his head with a cap or piece of felt made of pure wool. This slowly and gently heats up his head.

Also, a person who has eaten or drunk poison should soon pound equal weights of costmary, rue, and betony in a mortar and squeeze out the juice. Then he should add twice as much purgative juice, mix this, strain it through a cloth, and drink it on an empty stomach. He should be seated in a warm place, lest he get cold. It is dangerous for him to be cold at this time. After drinking it, he should imbibe a drink made from honey. He will either vomit the poison he has consumed or it will pass through his backside, and he will be freed from its effects.

One who has many lice should pound costmary with fat and mix them together. He should rub it around his neck and armpits, and the lice will die. Just as the costmary resists poison, so it counteracts lice.

But, a person who is developing leprosy should cook costmary in water with some lard and prepare it as a food. He should eat it often, and the leprosy will go away. For tertian fevers one should take equal weights of costmary and butterbur and three times as much radish as there is of the other two. He should cook this in wine and strain it through a cloth. He should pulverize twice as much cloves, and a third as much ginger as there is of the first two plants, and make a pure drink from this and the wine he filtered. He should use this at the onset of the fevers, and for the next nine days, so it may be fully useful to him.

CXCVI. STUTGRAS*

The smaller variety of stutgras is cold and weak in nature. It furnishes weak humors and augments melancholy. It is heavy on digestion and harmful for humans to eat, since its vital energy is bad.

CXCVII. STORAX

Storax *(stur)* is more cold than hot. Eating it is neither very profitable nor very injurious. By itself it has no powers and is useless. Added to certain other herbs it helps expel some harmful humors.

CXCVIII. PRICKLY LETTUCE†

CXCIX. SKIRRET

Skirret *(gerla)* is hot and dry. Eaten in moderation, it is not very helpful or harmful. If someone should eat a lot of it, its heat and dryness would stir up fevers in him and harm his intestines. A person whose face has weak skin, which easily splits, should pound skirret in a mortar and add oil. When he goes to bed at night, he should rub it on his face, continuing until he is healed.

---

*See also Stutgras entry on p. 47.
†See Prickly Lettuce entry on p. 49.

CC. PARSNIP

Parsnip *(pastinaca)* is cold, and is a food for the human being. It doesn't particularly lead to good health, nor is it harmful, but only fills the stomach.

CCI. BORAGE

Borage *(borith)* is hot and moist. A person whose vision is obscured should break borage into pieces and smear it on a red silk cloth. He should put it over his eyes at night. If he does this often, the dimness will go away from his eyes. It is not harmful to touch the inside of the eyes with this ointment. If the silk is white or green, he should put borage juice on it, then smear it on felt, and wrap that around his entire neck, over the back of his head, and up to his ears, but not covering them. If he does this often, it will stop his ears from ringing. Anyone whose chest is congested should put a very little bit of borage in wine. The evil humors which harm the lungs will go away. But, if someone ails internally from intestinal ulcers, he should take wheat bran and heat it in a small dish with borage. He should place it, so warmed, over his whole belly and navel, and he will be cured.

CCII. SPIKE LAVENDER*

CCIII. COMMON HOUSELEEK†

Common houseleek *(semperviva)* is cold and not useful for a person to eat, since it is of a rich nature. If anyone is so deaf that he lacks hearing, he should take the milk of a woman who has just given birth to a male child, ten or twelve weeks after the birth of the child, and add a bit of houseleek juice to it. He should let three or four drops be put into his ear. Whenever he allows this to be done, he will receive his hearing.

CCIV. BRYONY‡

CCV. FEMALE FERN

Female fern *(polypodium)* is hot and dry. If a lean person, who is not very sick, ails in his intestines, he should pulverize female fern and a third as

---

*See Spike Lavender entry on p. 22.
†See also Houseleek entry on p. 27.
‡See Bryony entry on p. 28.

much sage. Eating this powder diminishes bad humors. For a very ill person, cook wine over a fire, with added honey. After straining it and allowing it to cool, put this powder in and have the patient drink it. A person whose intestines are well, but whose flesh is fat, should not eat this powder nor drink the potion, lest it debilitate his healthy humors.

CCVI. LADY'S-THISTLE*

Lady's-thistle *(vehedistel)* contains coldness, which is from the dew, and is very useful. One who is ill from a stitch in his heart, or other part of his body, should reduce lady's-thistle and a little less sage to juice in a little water. At the very time the stitch torments him, he should drink it, and he will be better.

CCVII. FICARIA OR LESSER CELANDINE

Ficaria *(ficaria)* is cold and moist. For a person who suffers from burning fevers, cook Ficaria and twice as much basil in pure wine, and let it cool. Let him drink some of this wine each day, on an empty stomach, and at night when he goes to bed. He should do this until he is well.

CCVIII. WOAD

Woad *(weyt)* is cold, and that coldness is very sharp. A person who is tormented by some sort of palsy, no matter how strong, should cook it in water. He should strain it through a cloth, and throw out the herbs. Then he should place vulture fat and half as much deer tallow in that water and cook them together. He should make an ointment from this and anoint himself with it very frequently, and the palsy will cease.

CCIX. PRIMROSE

Primrose *(hymelsloszel)* is hot. All its vital energy is from the sharpness of the sun. Now, certain plants are strengthened by the sun, others by the moon, and certain others from the sun and moon together. But this plant takes its strength especially from the power of the sun, whence it checks melancholy. When melancholy rises in a person, it makes him sad and agitated in his moods. It makes him pour forth words against God. Airy spirits notice this, and rush to him, and by their persuasion turn him toward insanity. This person should place primrose on his

---

* See also Thistle entry on p. 52.

flesh, near his heart, until it warms him up. The airy spirits dread the primrose's sun-given power and will cease their torment.

A person whose head is so oppressed by bad humors that he has lost his senses should shave his hair and place primrose on top of his head. He should bind it on and should do the same thing to his chest. If he leaves these bindings on for three days, he will return to his senses. One whose whole body is tormented by palsy should put primrose in his drink, which will then get its flavor. He should drink it frequently, and he will be cured.

CCX. BUTTERBUR

Butterbur *(hufflatta major)* is cold and moist. Because of this, it grows vigorously. When placed over ulcers, it draws bad humors into its sharp coldness. If someone has scrofula on his body which has not yet rup-tured, he should break off, close to the stalk, a piece of this herb, as wide as the scrofula. He should throw the rest away, and smear honey over the part he retained. For three days and three nights he should place this over the scrofula. When the herb has dried up, he should repeat this treatment with a fresh piece of herb. The scrofula will begin to get smaller. On the fourth day he should moisten wheat flour with honey and mix them together. He should first place columbine over the area where the scrofula was, and over that the honeyed lump of flour. He should do this for nine days, or more, until the scrofula vanishes.

CCXI. COLTSFOOT

Coltsfoot *(hufflatta minor)* is hot. If a person has eaten many foods with-out moderation, and his liver is injured and made hard, he should make incisions in coltsfoot, and twice as much plantain root, and insert the mush from mistletoe from a pear tree (the same amount as the coltsfoot). [He should bore through the cuttings with an awl or other small instru-ment, thrust the mush into the openings, and place the cuttings in pure wine. A pea- or beanlike swelling, about the weight of a penny, which has grown on a walnut leaf or twig, should also be put into the wine. He should drink it just as it is, uncooked, with or without food, and he will be cured.]

CCXII. ASARUM

Asarum *(asarum)* is hot and dry and has the power of spices, since its vital energy is gentle and useful. A person who languishes a long time, and whose flesh is weak, should drink this in heated water. He should frequently eat it, cooked, either in a relish, or with meats, or with small cakes. It is very beneficial, since its good sap heals a person internally. If someone makes lye with it, and frequently uses it to wash his head, its good qualities keep infirmities away from the head and prevent illness. If one's head is troubled by bad humors, like vapor, so that he hears ringing in his ears like the sound of water, he should boil Asarum in hot water. After squeezing out the water, he should place the warm herb around his head. Its good powers will diminish the vapor in his head, and his hearing will clear up.

A person who ails in or around his chest, or who has internal ulcers, should, while in a bath, place warm, cooked Asarum around his chest. Its gentle strength, tempered by the gentleness of the water, will make him better. At the onset of any lung pain which afflicts the whole throat and causes hoarseness, one should cook Asarum and a little more basil, and even more humela, with the water exceeding the herbs by a third. When this is cooked, he should strain it through a cloth. Then he should take as much nutmeg as he can hold, and a third as much galingale, and twice as much mistletoe from a pear tree, pulverize it, and cook it with the best wine in a new pot. The wine should exceed the powder by a third. After adding honey, he should boil it again. Then he should add the water in which the Asarum and herbs were cooked, so there is twice as much wine as water. He should drink a little bit of this before a meal. After a meal, he may drink as much of this as he can in one draft, warming it first with a hot piece of steel. The heat of the Asarum will take the rotten matter from the lungs, and the coldness of the basil will enrich the lungs, and make him sad. The coldness of the humela will also purge the lungs. These will have been tempered in the warm water, as described above. The heat of the nutmeg and the heat of the galingale will have been tempered by the coldness of the mistletoe, strengthened by the heat of the wine and water, and altered by the hot steel. This will preserve the lungs so that there is neither depletion nor overrichness. When all these things are blended together, as described, moderation is retained in the lungs.

CCXIII. Mountain Parsley

Mountain parsley (*hirceswurtz*) has a sharp heat and is moist. By its sharpness, coldness, and moistness it checks evils that spring up into palsy from unregulated heat and cold and from humidity.

CCXIV. SCAMMONY

Scammony *(scampina)* has in it a sharp, harsh, harmful cold, and it works destruction. It has the nature of useless herbs. When doctors wish to make their customary potions quick, and to speed them up, they add scammony to them. It expels healthy as well as ill humors from a person by its harmful cold and its nature. If given to a person to eat or drink, straight and not mixed, it cuts him internally, in his intestines. It leads out vital as well as deadly humors, and it destroys his body.

CCXV. WATER LILY

Water lily *(nimphia)* is cold and uncultivated. Just as a useless herb, it is neither very beneficial nor particularly harmful.

CCXVI. MARE'S-TAIL

Mare's-tail *(catzenzagel)* has in it neither perfect heat nor perfect cold, but is tepid. It springs from the bad humors of the earth. It does not confer any strength to the person eating it. Nevertheless, if someone prepares it in a way that results in flies tasting it, it kills the flies by its torpor and bad humors.

CCXVII. ZUGELNICH

Zugelnich is hot and excites lust in a person. Its powers could be useful against leprosy and palsy, except that the heat of this herb, which brings lust to a person, keeps back its powers, so that it is not much good against these illnesses.

CCXVIII. PSAFFO

Psaffo has a temperate cold and is useful. It grows in weak heat. If its juice is added to unguents or potions, it renders them more useful.

CCXIX. THE PLANT ON WHICH BEARBERRIES GROW

The plant on which bearberries *(rifelbere)* grow has neither a strong heat nor a strong cold, and it is not very useful to the body. Its fruit, while cold, has a certain affinity to blood, since it grows from the air, which nourishes blood, whence it provokes menstruation. The fruit does not greatly benefit or harm the person who eats it.

CCXX. Duckweed

Duckweed *(merlinsen)* is cold. In itself it has no great powers, unless it is added to other profitable things. If it is added to them, it diminishes a person's harmful humors.

CCXXI. Cattail

The herb on which the cattail grows *(dudelkolbe)* is more cold than hot. It is not useful for human medicine because its juice is thick and slimy.

CCXXII. St. John's Wort

St. John's wort *(hartenauwe)* is cold and is good in the fodder of herd animals. It is not used much as medicine because it is a small, unculti-vated, and neglected herb.

CCXXIII. Thyme

Thyme *(thymus)* is hot and dry. If someone adds thyme to good herbs and condiments, it carries off the putrid matter of his ailment by its heat and strength. If it were not seasoned with other herbs or condiments, its strength would perforate ulcers, but would not heal them if placed over them. If someone has leprosy, season thyme with other herbs and spices. Rub this on the leprosy. Its heat and strength will diminish the rotten matter in any kind of leprosy. One should take the thyme and some of the earth around its root and make it boil in a fire. He should prepare a steam bath for himself. He should also cook the thyme, with the earth sticking to it, in a caldron with water. He should use it often in the sauna. The heat and dryness of this herb, heated with the dry earth, diminishes bad humors, unless it is not pleasing to God. If someone is tormented by palsy or a stitch, or by that disease which vexes one's limbs, as if he is being eaten and nibbled away, he should take sage and twice as much tithymal, and six times as much thyme. He should cook these in water and then add goat tallow and twice as much old fat and make an unguent. One should rub it on the afflicted parts, while near the fire. The heat of the sage, as well as that of the tithymal and thyme, tempered with the added gentleness of the warmed water, along with the heat of the goat tallow and old fat, diminish the unjustly hot and cold pains of the humors. The same ointment kills lice on a human, if he rubs himself with it. If old age or some other infirmity is causing blood and water in someone's eye, weakening him beyond measure, he should stare at green thyme until his eyes are damp, as if by crying. This makes them pure and clear, since the greenness of that herb carries away the eye disorder.

CCXXIV. ALOE*

CCXXV. PLIONIA

Plionia is cold. A person who is frequently vexed by palsy from gout, or is agitated, should crush plionia root and place it in wine, so that it takes on its flavor. At night when he goes to bed, he should drink it, and he will be better.

CCXXVI. COCKSCOMB OR YELLOW RATTLE

Cockscomb *(rasela)* has a sudden heat. If worms are eating the flesh of a human or a beast, one should put salt into the sap of cockscomb and put it on the place where worms are injuring the flesh. It will kill the worms completely.

CCXXVII. DORTH

Dorth is hot. If someone has bad, thick scabies on his head, he should reduce dorth to a powder and mix it with old fat. Rubbing the scabies diminishes the putrid matter.

CCXXVIII. THISTLE

Thistle[†] *(cardo)* is hot. A person who has eaten or drunk poison should pulverize the top, root, and leaves of thistle. He should consume this powder either in food or drink, and it will expel the poison. If someone has a rash on his body, he should mix this powder with fresh fat and anoint himself with it, and he will be healed.

CCXXIX. DANEWORT

Danewort *(ebulus)* is cold and moist. It has a nature opposite to that of the human, making it dangerous for a person to eat. But if there is a sound, like rushing water, in someone's head, Danewort should be placed, cold, around his head. And, if someone's fingernails or toenails are mangy, he should frequently bind the fruit which grows on Danewort over them. The nails will either be cleansed or destroyed, and new ones will grow.

---

*See Aloe entry on p. 81.
†See also Thistle entry on p. 52.

CCXXX. BASIL

Basil *(basilica)* is cold. A person who has palsy in his tongue, so that he is unable to speak, should place basil under his tongue, and he will receive speech. Also, one who has strong fevers, whether tertian or quartan, should cook basil in wine, with honey added. He should strain it and drink it frequently, with or without food, and at bedtime. His fevers will cease.

ELEMENTS

BOOK TWO

Elements

I. AIR

Air *(aer)* is the breath that, with the dew of its moisture, perspires on all budding things, that they all grow green. With its blowing, it brings forth flowers, and by its heat it gives all things the strength to mature.

The air situated near the moon and stars wets the heavenly bodies, just as terrestrial air enlivens and sets in motion the earth, as well as both irrational and sensible animals, according to their nature. The air compresses within them. But, when these animals die, the air reverts to its original state. It does not increase, but remains as it had been.

Terrestrial air, which dampens the earth and makes trees and plants grow green and move, does not diminish when it is in these things. Nor does the air increase when it leaves plants which are being cut down or pulled up, but remains in the same state as it was before.

II. WATER

Water *(aqua)* is from a living source. Waters springing forth from their source wash away all filth. If there is blood and water in a person's eye, from either old age or an infirmity, one should go to a river or pour fresh water into a vessel. Leaning over, he should take the moisture of this water into his eyes. That moisture will stir up the water drying up in his eyes and render them clear. He should also take a linen cloth and dip it in pure, cold water. He should tie it around his temples and eyes, being careful that it not touch the eyes, lest they be aggravated by the water.

The cold water on the soft linen cloth will dampen the eyes until the water of the eyes is restored to sight by this water. Because the eyes are fiery, their membrane thickens. When that membrane is touched by the water, as mentioned, the coldness and dampness of the water thin it.

One who wishes to have hard, healthy teeth should take pure, cold water into his mouth in the morning, when he gets out of bed. He should hold it for a little while in his mouth so that the mucus around his teeth becomes soft, and so this water might wash his teeth. If he does this often, the mucus around his teeth will not increase, and his teeth will remain healthy. Since the mucus adheres to the teeth during sleep, when the person rises from sleep he should clean them with cold water, which cleans teeth better than warm water. Warm water makes them more fragile.

A woman who suffers inordinately great menses for an excessive amount of time should dip a linen cloth in water and place it frequently around her thighs so that she grows cold internally, since the unreasonable flux of blood is restrained by the coldness of the linen cloth and the frigid water. She should then massage the veins in her legs, belly, chest, and arms by gently squeezing them with her hands. This keeps them within bounds, so the wrong route is not created for the blood. She should also be careful not to work too much, and not to be worn out by too much traveling, lest that blood be agitated. She should also be careful not to eat hard and bitter foods, lest they give her indigestion. During this time she should eat soft and sweet rations insofar as they heal her internally. She should drink wine and beer, since she is strengthened by them, and is thus able to retain her blood.

III. THE SEA

The sea *(mare)* sends forth rivers, by which the earth is irrigated, just as the body of a human is inundated by the blood of its veins. Some rivers go out from the sea with a rapid motion, some with a gentle motion, and others by storms. The earth along the course of each river has some sort of grassy vegetation, unless it is too rich, or too dry, or too rough, so that from it vegetation is unable to grow. But, from land which is moderate in these things, vegetation grows.

IV. THE SAAR

The Saar *(Seh)* starts from an impetus of the sea. Its bottom and sands are soiled, like a swamp, since it rises and falls with storms. Its water is healthful neither for drinking fresh nor for being taken cooked in food. It is not good for ingestion or any other healthful purpose, since it comes from the froth of the sea. Because it is salty, one who uses it to bathe in, or to wash his face, makes his skin white and healthy on the outside, but it harms him internally. In the Saar dwell various fish from the sea. They become fat and healthy from the saltiness of its sandy bottom.

V. THE RHINE

The Rhine *(Rhenus)* is sent forth from a thrust of the sea. Therefore, it is clear, and it runs through sandy land, the sand of which is light and properly mingled. In it is found vegetation. Because it sets out from an impetus of the sea, it is somewhat harsh—as lye—and, taken uncooked, it consumes mucusy humors in humans. But if it does not find harmful and mucusy humors in a person, its water, taken uncooked, rather aggravates a healthy person, since it finds nothing to purge. Therefore, when it is cooked with foods it consumes the mucus of that food, and so renders that food somewhat wholesome. Nevertheless, if the same water is consumed in foods or drinks, or if it is poured over a person's flesh in a bath or in face-washing, it puffs up the flesh, making it swollen, making it dark and distorted. It even darkens and swells up meats cooked in it. Because of its harshness it quickly passes into the flesh of a human. When fish from this river are freshly caught they are healthful to eat, but when they stand long they quickly rot, because they are bruised by the harshness of the water.

VI. THE MAIN

The Main *(Mogus)* is thrust forward a bit languidly from its sea origin. Because it is slow, it is easily blocked and is inactive. Therefore, the water of this river is rich, and its sand muddy. Its water, consumed in food or drink, poured over a person's flesh in the bath, or used to wash the face, makes the skin and flesh clear and smooth. It does not change a person or make him sick. It swells and whitens meats which are cooked in it, since it is gentle and not harsh in its course. Freshly caught fish are healthful and can last a long time since, because of the mildness of this water, they are not worn out. They do not have to suffer, and so their flesh endures.

VII. THE DANUBE

The Danube *(Donauwia)* arises from an impetus of the sea. Its water is clear and harsh, and its sand is healthful and beautiful. But its water is not healthy for food or drink since its harshness injures a person's internal organs. This harshness makes a person's skin very dark, but does not make the skin weak, because the water is clear as well as harsh. The fish of the Danube are healthful and, since the water is harsh, can last a long time.

VIII. THE MOSELLE

The Moselle *(Mosella)* arises from waters that flow from the sea, and so it is gentle and clear. Its turbulence falls to the bottom, whence its sand is muddy. Its fish are not healthful, nor do they last a long time, because they feed on filth.

IX. THE NAHE

The Nahe *(Na)* arises from filthy waters that pour from the sea. From it, clear brooks sometimes flow. Completely irregular in its course, it sometimes flows with great impetus, and other times languidly. Because it occasionally runs speedily, it is quickly blocked and becomes inactive. It does not produce a very deep sand-bed, nor high banks. It makes a person's skin white and thick, yet wrinkled. It does not injure his internal organs since the impetus and listlessness of its course are, though variable, not harmful. Its fish are fat and healthy and do not rot quickly. The water with its unstable movement—quick one moment, languid the next—does not dig into the sand. Because of the many kinds of nourishment found in the river, the fish in the Nahe are durable.

X. THE GLAN

The Glan *(Glan)* has its beginning in other rivers, so its water is a bit harsh. It is healthful and useful for food, drink, baths, and face-washing. Its fish are also healthful, but are not long-lived because of the harshness of the water. The sand of the Glan is beautiful and healthful.

XI. EARTH

Earth *(terra)* is naturally cold, and has many powers in it. In summer the lower part is cold, and the upper part is warmed with heat generated by the sun's powerful rays. In winter the interior part of the earth is warm, lest it be split by cold dryness, and the upper part is cold, since the sun at that time draws its powers back from the earth. The earth shows its greenness in heat, its dryness in cold. In winter the sun over the earth is sterile and drives its heat into the earth, so the earth can preserve its various grasses. Through heat and coldness, it brings forth all grasses.

There is white, that is to say pallid, earth, as well as black, red, and slightly green. White earth, which is pallid and sandy, is somewhat dry and holds great moisture and large drops of rain. From this great moisture it brings forth wine, fruit-bearing trees, and a moderate amount of grain. Earth which holds in itself a bit of moisture, in minute drops, produces from that small amount of moisture grain, a bit of wine, and few fruit-bearing trees.

Black earth with a correct balance has a cold moisture, neither too great nor too little, but moderate. From this moisture it engenders not all fruits, but it brings forth plentifully the fruit it does engender. When its moisture is disturbed at times by storms, there is a failure in the fruit.

Red earth has a correct balance in its moisture and dryness. It brings forth many fruits that, because of their abundance, are unable to come to completion. Having correct balance, it is not easily harmed by storms.

XII. CALAMINE

That earth which is called calamine *(calaminum)* is neither hot nor cold in due proprtion, but tepid. Because of this tepidness, it does not grow fruit to completion, but brings forth certain fruits that do not come to perfection. If added to other spices, it diminishes mucus in some decaying matter.

XIII. CHALK

That earth which is called chalk *(crida)* is cold and dry. Because of these qualities it does not engender much fruit. When put on pelts it keeps spoilage from them so they do not rot, but it is not useful as medicine.

XIV. GREENISH EARTH

That earth *(terra subviridus)* which has neither a white, nor black, nor red color, but is greenish and stony, is cold and dry. It engenders neither wine nor grain nor other fruitful produce, since it does not have the correct balance in its dryness. If it produces some, they quickly fail.

If someone is overwhelmed by numbness, another person should take a bit of the earth from the right and left side of the bed where the sick person's head is, and in the same way take earth from near the person's right and left foot. While he is digging it he should say, "You, earth, are sleeping in this person, N." And he should place the earth which had been taken from both sides of the patient's head under his head, until it grows warm there. In a similar manner, he should place the other earth under his feet, so that it might receive heat from them. When the earth is placed under his head and feet, this should be said, "You, earth, grow and be useful in this person, N., so that he may receive your vital greenness, in the name of the Father, and the Son, and the Holy Spirit, who is the all-powerful, living God." This should be done for three days.

TREES

BOOK THREE
Trees

ALL TREES HAVE EITHER HEAT OR COLD IN THEM, in the same way that plants do. Certain trees are hotter than others and some colder, since some trees have more heat in them than other hot trees, and some more cold than other cold trees. Trees are productive, and those which bear proper fruits, as those in forests, are more cold than hot. The forest trees which are larger and produce more fruits than others do are hotter than other forest trees. Those which produce small and few fruits are colder than other forest trees.

I. APPLE TREE

The apple tree *(affaldra)* is hot and moist and is of such great moisture that it would even flow forth, if not constrained by the heat. A person, whether old or young, who suffers a fogginess in his eyes for any reason should take the leaves of this tree in springtime, before it produces its fruit for the year. When these first come out at the beginning of spring, they are tender and healthy, as young girls before they produce children. He should pound these leaves and express their sap, and to this add an equal measure of the drops that flow from the grapevine. He should place this in a metallic jar and, at night when he goes to bed, he should moisten his eyelids and eyes with a feather dipped in a bit of it. It should be like dew falling on grass, and care should be taken that it not enter the eyes. Then he should sprinkle the crushed leaves with a bit of the drops that flow from the grapevine, and place them over his eyes. He should hold this on with a cloth, and sleep with it on. If he does this often, the fogginess will be driven from his eyes, and he will see clearly.

When in springtime the first shoots of the apple tree burst forth, tear off one little branch, without cutting it with iron, and draw a strap of deer hide back and forth over the break in the tree and the branch, so that it becomes damp with sap. When you sense that there is no more moisture, then hack, with very tiny blows, this broken spot with a small knife, so that more of the moisture flows out. By drawing the deer-hide strap over the same place and on the same branch, drench it with as much sap as you can. Then put it in a damp place, so that it may absorb even more sap. Anyone who has pain in his kidneys or has trouble urinating should gird himself with this strap, over his naked flesh, so that the sap which it drew in from the apple tree might pass into his flesh, and he will be better.

Anyone who has pain from an illness of the liver or spleen, from bad humors of the belly or stomach, or from a migraine in his head should take the first shoots of the apple tree and place them in olive oil. He should warm them in a little jar in the sun. If he drinks this often when he goes to bed, his head will be better.

Also in springtime, when the blossoms come out, take earth which is around the root of this tree, and heat it on the fire. Anyone who has pain in his shoulders, loins, or stomach should place it, thus warmed, over the painful place, and he will be better. After the fruits of this tree have increased, so that they begin to enlarge, this earth is no longer powerful against these infirmities. The humor of this earth and sap of the tree will have ascended to the fruits, leaving that in the earth and branches much weaker.

The fruit of this tree is gentle and easily digested and, eaten raw, does not harm healthy people. Apples grow from dew when it is strong, namely from the first sleep of the night until day is nearly breaking. They are good for healthy people to eat raw, since they are ripened by the strong dew. Raw apples are a bit harmful for sick people, because of their weakness. But cooked or dried apples are good for both sick and healthy people. After apples have gotten old, and the skin has contracted as happens in winter, then they are good for both sick and healthy people to eat raw.

II. PEAR TREE

The pear tree *(birbaum)* is more cold than hot and is powerful and strong. It is to the apple tree as the liver is to the lungs. For, just as the liver, it is stronger and more useful, and indeed more harmful, than the apple. Because of its hardness, its roots, leaves, and sap are not useful for medicines, but its mistletoe is somewhat useful for medicine. If someone has pain in his chest or lungs, he should take its mistletoe and pulverize it. He should add some pulverized licorice to it and eat it often, whether fasting or with meals. His chest and lungs will be better. One who suffers gicht should place this same sweet-tasting mistletoe, cut in bits, in olive oil for three days and nights. Afterward, he should melt twice as much deer tallow as olive oil on a fire, and place well-crushed and ground spikenard in that tallow for two days and nights. Then he should pound well the oil with the mistletoe which was placed in it, and express the juice through a cloth, and gently heat it with the deer tallow and spikenard. [Then the man should be anointed where the gicht is raging, and it will be chased off, unless the foundation of death is there.]

The fruit of the pear tree is powerful, heavy and harsh. If someone eats too much when it is raw, it gives his head a migraine and makes vapor in his chest. The lungs draw in the pear sap, which hardens like lead slag and tartar around the liver and lungs, creating great infirmities in those organs. Just as a person is sometimes filled with the odor of wine, so also his breath mixes with the sap of the pear, and takes its sharpness. Whence, after eating raw pear, he will have difficulty drawing breath. Many infirmities come into the chest from this, since pears grow from the dew at close of day when dew's power is weak. Unless they are cooked, pears create noxious humors in people, since they grow when the dew is flagging.

Anyone who wishes to eat pears should place them in water or roast them on fire. Boiled pears are better than those roasted, since the warm water gradually cooks out the harmful sap which is in them. Fire is too quick and in roasting not all the moisture is expressed from them. Cooked pears sometimes oppress one who eats them, since they seek out any rotten matter in him and diminish it, breaking it up. Nevertheless, they give him good digestion since they remove rotten matter. The fruits are easily digested and do not bring in rotten matter with them. Take pears, cut them, and throw out their cores. Cook them vigorously in water. Then take hog's-fennel and a little less galingale, licorice (less than the galingale) and savory (less than the licorice). If you do not have hog's-fennel, take the fennel root and reduce it to a powder. Mix it with the other powders, and put them in a bit of warm honey. Add the prepared pears, mix this well, and place it in a small container. Every day eat one small spoonful before breakfast; eat two spoonfuls with a meal; and three spoonfuls at night, in bed. This electuary is very good, and more precious than gold, since it carries away migraine and diminishes the vapor which the raw pear creates in a person's chest. It consumes all bad humors in a person, and so cleanses the person, just as a vessel is washed of its impurities.

III. WALNUT TREE

The walnut tree *(nuszbaum)* is hot and holds bitterness. Before it produces fruit, its bitterness and heat are in the lower trunk and leaves. This bitterness sends forth the heat and brings forth the walnuts. When the kernel begins to grow, the bitterness is lost, and sweetness springs up. But, when the sweetness has increased in the kernel, it has a sharpness. The sweetness and sharpness mingle, producing the nut. The bitterness and heat remain in the lower trunk and make the outside of the nut grow. After the fruits of all fruit-bearing trees enlarge and ripen, their leaves are no longer useful for medicine, since their sap has passed into the fruit.

Whence, when the walnut tree's leaves first appear until the fruits grow, when the nuts are still immature and not to be eaten, take the leaves of this tree, while they are still fresh. Squeeze the juice from them onto the place where worms are eating a person, or where maggots or other worms are growing on him. Do this frequently, and they will die. But, if worms are originating in his stomach, he should take leaves of the walnut tree, with an equal amount of peach tree leaves, before their fruits are ripe, and pulverize them over a fiery hot stone. He should eat this powder often, either with an egg, or in a broth, or cooked in a bit of cereal. The worms in his stomach will die.

If leprosy has begun to grow on someone, squeeze the juice from these leaves and add old fat to it, making an ointment. When the leprosy is still new on him, he should anoint himself with this near the fire. Without a doubt he will be healed, unless God does not wish it.

One who is virgichtiget should take the earth which is around the roots of this tree, before its fruit matures, and heat it, like rocks, in the fire. He should make a sauna bath and, seated in that bath, he should pour water over that fiery earth, receiving its heat and sweat. So bathing himself, the gicht which had wanted to contract and weaken his limbs will be chased away. If he does this frequently when he first begins to be ill with gicht, his weak limbs will be cured.

One who has much phlegm in him should take that which exudes from the walnut tree when its branches or rootstock are cut. He should cook it gently in wine with fennel and a little savory, strain it through a cloth, and often drink it warm. It will throw off the phlegm, and he will be cleared out.

One who has bad scabies on his head should take the outer skin of the walnut, that is its shell, and squeeze its juice over the wounds, that is over the scabies on his head. When they have swollen up from the bitterness of the juice, he should anoint them with olive oil, which will check the bitterness. If he does this often, the scabies will be cured.

Fever is easily stirred up in a person who has eaten many walnuts, fresh or old. Although healthy people are able to overcome this, sick people are harmed. The oil expressed from walnuts is hot and makes the flesh of those eating them fat. It makes their minds happy. But phlegm increases from it, so that it fills a person's chest with mucus. Sick people as well as healthy are able to tolerate it as food, but it does congest a weak chest a bit.

IV. QUINCE TREE

The quince tree *(quittenbaum)* is very cold and of a subtlety which is assimilated, sometimes usefully, other times not. Its wood and leaves are not of much use for human beings. Its fruit is hot and dry and has a good balance in it. When it is ripe and eaten raw, it harms neither a sick nor healthy person. It is very useful, cooked or roasted, for a sick or healthy person to eat. One who is virgichtiget should frequently eat this fruit, either cooked or roasted, and it will check the gicht in him, so that it does not blunt his senses, nor break his limbs nor leave the person helpless. One who produces much saliva should eat this fruit frequently, cooked or roasted. It will dry him up internally and diminish his saliva. Where there are ulcers or foulness on a person, one should cook or roast this fruit and place it, with other spices, over the wounds, and he will be cured.

V. PEACH TREE

The peach tree *(persichbaum)* is more hot than cold, but has something else in it. It has something like envy in it, and its sap is more useful for medicine than its fruit. One who, in various illnesses, has any kind of spots on his body should take the inner bark of this tree before its fruit matures. He should pound this bark, express its sap, and add a little vinegar to it, and as much cooked honey as there is of the other two things. He should place this in a new clay jar, and frequently anoint his body where these bad spots are, until they are diminished.

When one's breath stinks badly, he should take the fruits of the peach tree before they are ripe. He should pound them, then take a handful of licorice, a bit of pepper, and some honey and cook these things in pure wine, and so prepare a spiced wine. He should drink this often, with a meal and at night. It will make his breath fragrant and take rottenness away from his body and chest.

For one with worms in his stomach or belly, the root and leaves of betony should be pulverized. Add to this twice as much pulverized leaves of the peach tree, taken when it has just sent out its flowers. Cook this in a new pot with good, pure wine. Drink it often, before breakfast and at night, and the worms will die.

The fruit of this tree is good for neither a sick nor a healthy person to eat. It weakens the good humors in a person and produces mucus in his stomach. Anyone who wants to eat this fruit should throw away the outer skin and the pit and place the rest in wine with salt and a bit of pepper. Prepared in this way, it does not harm him much, though it does not have a good flavor.

Take also the raw, inmost kernels of the fruit and, having thrown away the shell, pound them to a milk and squeeze five spoonfuls through a cloth. Then pulverize three pennyweight of galingale, two of licorice, and a half pennyweight of spurge, and add this to the peach-kernel milk. Prepare a small cake of fine whole wheat flour and garden spurge, and dry it gently and gradually in the sun or a warm oven. Then mix this cake with a half pennyweight of the forenamed milk. Before sunrise, take spoonfuls of this—equal to the weight of two and a half pennies—after heating it on a fire. Then put yourself to bed for a short while. This checks gicht and carries congestion away from your chest, and mucus away from your stomach. As a pleasant potion, it gently purges you. If you need to, take it twice in a month, and on the day you take it, refrain from strong food, rye bread, peas, and lentils. Eat soft foods and drink wine.

One who has pain in his chest, so that his throat is a bit constricted, either because some bad thing is growing on it or there is some bad vapor in it, with no ulcer or tumor, should take a paste of wheat flour and dissolve it in gum from the peach tree. He should often place this, warm, over his throat for a little while, and he will be better. If, however, there is pain in his throat from an ulcer or tumor, he should not place this on it, because it would be painful. If a person has glands on his neck that are contracted or more distinct than usual, and if there is no ulcer or tumor, he should place the same prepared paste on them. If the neck were ulcerated or tumescent, this paste would make it worse.

One who has pain in his head should take the wheat paste, dissolve it in the gum of the peach tree, and place it, warm, on the top of his head for some time, and he will be better.

For one whose eyes water, press gum from the peach tree, or from the shell of a walnut, and warm it a bit on a hot tile. Then place it around the eyes, until they grow warm. Do this once a day, every four days, lest in doing it too often the eyes are harmed. The gum of the peach tree has in it the first strength of its wood and draws to itself natural moisture.

VI. CHERRY TREE

The cherry tree *(cerasus)* is more hot than cold, and it is much like a joke, since it shows forth happiness but is harmful. Its sap and leaves are not much use as medicine, since there is a weakness in it. Its fruit is moderately warm and is neither very useful nor very harmful. Eating it does not harm a healthy person, but it creates pain if a sick person, or one with bad humors in him, eats much of it. Take the inmost kernels of this fruit, when raw, and pound them well. Dissolve bear fat in a small dish, and mix this with it, making an unguent. Use it often to anoint one whose body has bad ulcers, which are very like leprosy, but are not, and he will be cured.

One who has wrenching pains in his belly, although not from worms, should often eat the kernels raw, and he will be better. One who has worms in his belly should place the kernels in vinegar and often eat them on an empty stomach, and the worms will die.

One who has pain in his eyes, so that they are red from the pain and ulcerous, should take warm crumbs of rye bread and put the gum of the cherry tree on them. He should tie them with a band, so the gum is placed on the skin of the eyes. If he does this often, it will draw the drips from his eyes, and he will be cured.

If some disease or bad humors fall upon one's ears, so that he becomes as if deaf and his ears ring, he should take the forenamed gum and dissolve it in a small dish over the fire. He should pour it, thus warmed, over crumbs of rye bread and place this in the openings of his ears at night. He should also cover his ears and temples with these crumbs smeared with the gum and tie a linen cloth over them. If he does this often, the disease, bad humors, and ringing will be chased away, and he will be cured.

VII. Plum Tree

The plum tree *(prunibaum)* is more hot than cold and is even dry, and prickly like a thorn, and indicates anger. If some worms are eating the flesh of a person, take the upper bark of that tree, down to the sap, and its leaves and pulverize them. Dry them in the sun, or in a pot by the fire, or in a pot which had been warmed by fire. Put this powder on the place where the worms are eating the person. When the worms begin to move from there, so that the person feels it, take vinegar mixed with a bit of honey and pour it where the worms are, and they will die. When they have fallen from the wounds, dead, dip a linen cloth in wine and place it over the wounds. It will draw out the rotten matter, and the person will become well.

Also make ashes from the bark and leaves of this tree. From these ashes make lye, and if your head is either pockmarked or withered, wash it often with this lye. Your head will be cured, and will be beautiful, will produce much beautiful hair.

If someone through magic or by evil words is rendered insane, take the earth which is around the roots of this tree and warm it vigorously in the fire, until it burns a little bit. When it has burned a bit in the fire, place rue and a little less pennyroyal on it. Let it absorb their sap and odor. If you do not have pennyroyal, place fresh fenugreek on it. If it is winter, place on it the seeds of these herbs, moderately warmed. After the person has eaten, place this, with the herbs, on his head, naked stomach, and naked sides, and tie it with a cloth. Put him in bed and cover him with clothing, so that he might sweat a bit with that earth. Do this for three or five days, and he will be better. For when the ancient serpent hears magic and evil words, he takes them up and sets traps for the one for whom they were said, unless God stops him.

Take the gum of this tree and, if someone's lips swell up, or if he reports gicht springing up in them, heat this gum moderately and at night when he goes to bed tie it, with a cloth, on his lips where it hurts. Do this often and the pain will cease. One whose fingers and hands are always moving from the tremor of gicht should tie this same gum, warmed, over his whole hand, and the tremor will cease.

The fruit of this tree is harmful and dangerous for healthy and sick people to eat. It stirs up melancholy in a person, augments bitter humors in him, and makes all diseases bubble up in him. It is as dangerous as a weed for a person to eat. Whence, when someone wishes to eat it, he should eat moderately. A healthy person is able to survive eating it, but it harms a sick person.

Whoever has a dry cough should take the inmost kernels of this fruit and, throwing away the covering, place them in wine. They should soak in the wine until they have swelled a bit. Then he should eat them often and prepare a drink with good wine. He should consume this by sipping, and he will be quickly cured. Every kind of plum tree has these powers in their bark and leaves, and the same nature in their fruit, except the trees which are larger bring forth larger fruits with greater strength.

VIII. ROWAN

The rowan tree *(spirbaum)* is hot and dry, but its heat is not very useful. By its splendor it signifies pretense. Its bark, leaves, and sap are not much use as medicine. Nevertheless, throw the earth from around the root of this tree into gardens, strewing it where caterpillars and butterflies eat and devastate the vegetables. When they are troubled by this, they withdraw and can no longer flourish there.

The fruit of this tree aggravates a person, puffing him up. It stirs up his humors but does not make mucus in a person. Eating it does not profit or harm a healthy person, but it is not good for sick people.

IX. BLACK MULBERRY

The black mulberry *(mulbaum)* is cold in its property. One who has scabies should cook the leaves of this tree in water and bathe in that water; or, in a sauna, wash himself vigorously with that water. If he does this often, his skin will be healed. One who has consumed poison by eating or drinking should pound these leaves, expressing their juice. To this juice he should add a bit less absinthe, and mix it with twice as much good, pure wine. He should cook this until it boils. After it has cooled, he should drink it moderately, with a meal. Either he will spit up that poison through nausea or it will pass through him as he evacuates his bowels. There is a richness in its fruit, and the fruit harms neither a sick nor a well person. It helps a person less than it harms him.

X. ALMOND TREE

The almond tree *(amygdalus)* is very hot and has a bit of moisture in it. Its bark, leaves, and sap are not much use as medicine, because all its power is in the fruit. One whose brain is empty, and whose face has a bad color from a pain in the head, should frequently eat the inmost kernels of this fruit. They fill his brain and give him the correct color. Also, one who ails in his lungs, or whose liver is weak, should often eat these kernels, either raw or cooked. They give strength to the lungs, since they in no way burden a person. Neither do they make a person dry, but render him strong.

XI. HAZEL TREE

The hazel tree *(haselbaum)* is more cold than hot and is not much good for medicine. It symbolizes lasciviousness. Take the shoots, that is, the parts where the flowers first bud. Dry them in the sun and reduce them to a powder. Put this powder where there is scrofula on a person, and he will be healed.

[A male whose semen has a diffuse quality, so that it does not engender offspring, should take large hazelnuts, a third as much smartweed, and a quarter as much bindweed as smartweed. He should cook this with some pepper and the liver of a young he-goat which is old enough to procreate. Then he should add it to a little raw, fatty pork meat. Having thrown out the herbs, the man should eat this meat. He should also dip bread in the water in which this meat was cooked, and eat it. If he does this often, he will flourish with progeny, if the righteous judgement of God does not prohibit it.]

Its fruit, that is its nuts, are not very harmful for a healthy person to eat, nor do they benefit him much. They harm a sick person, because they congest his chest.

XII. CHESTNUT TREE

The chestnut tree *(kestenbaum)* is very hot but has great power mixed with that heat. It symbolizes discretion. The virtue in it, and its fruit, is useful against all infirmity in a human. A person who is virgichtiget, and is thence irascible, since gicht always is accompanied by anger, should cook the leaves, bark, and fruit in water. He should make a sauna bath with this, and take it often. His gicht will cease, and he will have a calm mind.

Should some disease kill herd animals, pound the bark of this tree and put it in water, so that it takes its flavor. Put this often in the drink for asses, horses, cattle, and sheep. The disease will go away, and they will be cured. But, if a horse or cow or ass, or any kind of herd animal, has given himself pain, because of avidity for food or drink, give the animal leaves of this tree to eat with its fodder, if possible. If the animal is unable to eat, pulverize the leaves, put them in water, and give it to him often in his drink, and he will be cured.

A person who makes a staff from the wood of the chestnut, and carries this staff in his hand, so that his hand becomes hot from it, is strengthened by that heat in his veins and all the powers of his body. Also, frequently taking in the odor of this wood brings health to your head.

A person whose brain is empty from dryness, and who because of that is weak in the head, should cook the inmost kernel of the fruit of this tree in water. He should add nothing else. Having poured off the water, he should eat it often, on an empty stomach or with a meal. His brain will improve and be filled, his nerves will be strong, and the pain in his head will cease. One who has a pain in his heart, so that his heart does not prosper in health and he becomes sad, should frequently eat these same kernels, raw. The juice will infuse his heart, which will benefit from its strength, and he will receive happiness. One who ails in the liver should pound those same kernels, place them in honey, and often eat them with the honey, and his liver will be cured. One who suffers a pain in his spleen should dry those kernels gently on a fire and then frequently eat them, somewhat warm. His spleen will be warmed and tend toward full health. For one who ails in the stomach, boil these kernels in water. When they are cooked, mash them in the water. Then blend water and bread crumbs in a small dish. Add powdered licorice, and a little less powder from the root of the female fern to the mixture, and cook them again with the chestnuts, to prepare a mush. When the person eats this, it will purge his stomach and make it warm and strong.

XIII. MEDLAR TREE

The medlar *(nespelbaum)* is very hot. It signifies sweetness. Its bark and leaves are not much good as medicine, because all its strength is in its fruit. Nevertheless, a person who suffers from ague should, at the onset of this infirmity, pulverize its root and drink this powder in warm wine, before breakfast, with meals, and at night. He should do this frequently, and he will be cured. The fruit of this tree is good and useful for healthy and sick people, however much they eat. It increases their flesh and cleanses their blood.

XIV. FIG TREE

The fig tree *(fickbaum)* is more hot than cold. It will always have heat, and its cold is not strong. It signifies fear. Take its leaves and bark, and pound them moderately. Cook this well in water, and then make an unguent with bear fat and a little less butter. If you have a pain in your head, anoint your head with it. If your eyes hurt, rub it on your temples and around your eyes, without letting it touch the inside of your eyes. If it is your chest that hurts, anoint it; if your kidneys, anoint them with it, and you will be better.

However, if its wood is burned in a fire, and its smoke touches someone, it harms him a bit, so that it weakens him. If someone carries in his hand a staff made from that wood, it diminishes his strength.

The fruit of this tree is not good for a person who is physically healthy to eat, since it affords him pleasure and gives him a swelled mind. He will seek honors and tend toward greed, and will have changeable morals, so that he does not remain in one state of mind. Eating it is not beneficial for his body, since it renders flacid flesh and withstands all the person's humors. It irritates his humors to evil, as if it were their enemy. It delights one who has an infirm body, and is good to eat. One who is deficient in mind and body should eat it until he is better and then avoid it. If a healthy person wishes to eat it, he should first soak it in wine or vinegar, so that its inconstancy is tempered. He should then eat it, but in moderation. It is not necessary for a sick person to temper it in this way.

xv. Laurel Tree

The laurel tree *(laurus)* is hot and has a bit of dryness. It signifies constancy. Take the bark and leaves of laurel, pound them, and express their juice. Make small cakes with that juice and wheat flour. Grind these, reducing them to a powder. Then make hydromel with honey and water, put a bit of this powder in it, and drink it. Or, drink the powder in wine. Do this as often as you want. It will purge your stomach from all filth and will not hurt it much.

Also, cook the root, bark, and leaves of this tree in water, and make an ointment with it, using goat tallow. If you have pain in your head, chest, side, back, or kidneys, anoint the place, and you will be better.

The fruit of this tree is very hot and a bit dry and is useful for medicine. If anyone often eats it raw, it checks all fevers in him. If you are troubled with gicht and fevers, you should reduce these berries to a powder, and add half as much of the powder of the fruit which grows on pine cones. If you do not have pine nuts, mix in half as much powdered fenugreek. Warm it in wine, and drink it hot. The gicht and fever will cease.

Also, express the oil from these berries and anoint your body where it is troubled with gicht, and you will be better. If you add to this oil a third part of savin sap, or that of the box tree, it will be a much stronger oil, and it will penetrate your skin more quickly for healing, and the gicht will go from you.

If you have pain in your head, pound these berries, infused with a bit of wine, in a mortar. Then smear this wine over the top of your head, your forehead, temples, and entire head. When this is done, cover your head, so that it becomes warm, and put yourself to bed. Although you have great pain, that pain will go away.

If you are sick in your lungs, so that they are putrescent, pulverize these berries and frequently eat this powder with bread, and you will be cured. If you have pain in your stomach, cook these berries in wine, and drink the wine warm. It will carry mucus away from your stomach and purge it, and will even expel fever from it.

When these berries are raw, express the oil from them. When you touch the inside of your eyes with it, it will remove the fogginess from them. Or, if you have pain in your heart, or in your side, or if your back is feeble, rub the place with this, and you will be better. If you have a fetid stomach, so that you even produce unclean saliva, make little cakes with this oil and a bit of flour and eat them. They will clean your stomach, overcome the fetid humors, and bring forth good, correct humors.

XVI. Olive Tree

The olive tree *(oleybaum)* is more hot than cold. It signifies mercy. Cook the exterior bark and leaves of this tree in water, and make an ointment with this water and old fat. If anyone has pain in his head, back, side, or loins from gicht, anoint that place with this ointment. It will penetrate his skin, just as fat penetrates a new clay pot when placed near the fire, and will make him better.

And, for one whose stomach is cold, cook the bark and leaves of this tree in water. Strain the water through a cloth, and dissolve less pine resin, and even less myrrh than resin, in a small dish. Add it to the foresaid liquid, and make a plaster. Dip a hempen cloth in this, and place it over the stomach. The stomach will warm up, and will provide good digestion.

The oil of the fruit of this tree is not much good for eating. If eaten, it provokes nausea and makes some foods troublesome to eat. However, it is useful for many medicines. When its oil is first prepared, it is cooked on a fire, and then roses and violets are put into it. Thus it prevails against various fevers and, because it was cooked on a fire, it is not necessary to leave it in the sun anymore.

Whosoever is troubled by gicht should put roses in olive oil. He should anoint himself with this where the gicht moves his body, and he will be better. But, for one who ails in the head or loins, or on whose body a swelling has risen up somewhere from a fall or blow, he should place violets in the olive oil and anoint himself where it hurts. If there is a swelling, he should anoint himself near it, but not on it.

XVII. DATE PALM

The date palm tree *(datilbaum)* is hot. It has moisture in it which is as sticky as mucus. It signifies happiness. One who has pleurisy should cook some of the bark and wood, or blades of leaves of this tree, in water. Squeezing out the water, he should place the wood and leaves, so heated, around his head. If this is done often, he will recover his senses. Also, when they are green, dry the leaves in the sun. Then pound them, and reduce them to a powder. Add a bit of clear salt, and eat the powder with bread, often. It will prevent internal putrefaction, and neither bad nor great amounts of phlegm will increase in you. If someone cooks and eats the fruit of this tree, it will bring as much strength to his body as bread does. But, if he eats too much, it will easily congest him and weigh him down.

XVII. CITRON TREE

The citron tree *(bontziderbaum),* on which the great citron grows, is more hot than cold. It signifies chastity. A person who has daily fevers should cook the leaves of this tree in wine, strain the wine through a cloth, and drink it often, and he will be cured. The fruits of this tree, when eaten, also check fever in a person.

XVIII. CEDAR TREE

The cedar *(cedrus)* is hot and a bit dry, and it denotes encouragement. When the cedar is green and has sap, a splenetic person should pound some of the branches and wood of this tree, breaking it down into a powder. With cooked honey, he should make an electuary from it. He should eat it in moderation with a meal, and his spleen will recover its health. Once he is well, he should eat no more of this electuary.

One who ails internally, and who is putrescent inside, should place some of the same green wood in pure wine overnight, so that it takes its flavor. Having eaten, he should drink this wine in moderation. It will purge the illness and the rotten matter from inside his body, and he will be healed. After he has sensed his internal health he should drink no more of that wine. If a healthy person eats this electuary or drinks this wine, he will become internally rigid and as hard as wood, and he will die. The power of this tree is so great that it internally injures a person.

One who is troubled by gicht should eat the green fruits of the cedar. It will stop and prevent this disease. If you are not able to preserve that fruit through the year, pulverize the fruit, and put some of the powder in water. Frequently drink it, while fasting, and the gicht will cease.

XX. CYPRESS

The cypress *(cypressus)* is very hot and signifies "secret of God." One who has a stomachache should take some wood of this tree, either green or dry, cut it up, and cook it a moderate amount in wine. He should drink it often, without food, and he will be better. One who is ill, or indeed failing in his whole body, should cook the branches with their leaves in water, and should bathe in that water. He should do this often, and he will be cured and recuperate his strength. Also, take some of the wood from the middle of the tree, from what is called the heart of the tree, and always carry it with you. The devil will all the more avoid you since, having a strong nature, the tree holds more good fortune than the wood of other trees. The devil, disdaining all things which are virtuous, and having no virtue himself, will flee.

If a person is ensnared by the devil or by magic, take some of the wood from the middle of the tree and perforate it with a bore. Then take water from a living spring in an earthenware vessel. Pour the water through this hole, catching it in the earthenware vessel. While you pour it say, "I pour you, water, through this hole, and this virtuous strength, so that you may flow in this person, whose senses are ensnared. With the strength present in your nature, may you destroy all the misfortunes within him, and put him back into the rectitude in which God placed him, in his right sense and knowledge." Then, because this person had been troubled or ensnared by the devil, by phantasms, or by magic, this water should be given to him to drink, while fasting, for nine days. He will be better, and indeed he should be blessed in this way for nine days.

XXI. SAVIN

Savin *(sybenbaum)* is more hot than cold. Its heat is so strong that it preserves its greenness throughout the year. It signifies severity. If worms are in a person, pound savin and express its juice. To this juice add a bit of vinegar. Pour this liquid into the wounds where the worms are eating the person's body. The worms will die and will be unable to live. Also, if one ails in his lungs, so that his lungs are putrescent and full of poison, take the sap of the savin tree. Add half as much powdered licorice as sap, and cook this in wine, with a bit of lard. Have him drink this frequently and, because of its bitterness, immediately afterward drink some hydromel. It will carry pus and poison away from his lungs, and he will be cured.

XXII. Box Tree

The box tree *(buxus)* is hot, so hot that it keeps its greenness throughout the year. Its heat exceeds that of the savin. Indeed, it is also dry, and that dryness overpowers its moistness. It signifies liberality.

A person who has a rash or eruption on his body should pound the bark and leaves of this tree and express the juice. He should add to this a little less licorice and heat it in pure wine. He should drink this often, warm, and it will send the pain and poison out of his body, so that it does not reenter the body. Then he should mix a bit more olive oil to the forenamed box tree juice and dip a feather in it. With that, he should gently anoint the area around the rash and its swelling. If he does this often, he will be cured. Before he anoints himself in this way, he should always drink the sap, which had been heated as already described in wine with licorice, lest the unction send the external fetidness into the body. This drink will expel the interior fetidness, so the person will be cured.

The juice of this tree is sound and strong. Therefore its wood is sound and firm. If someone makes of this wood a cup or goblet and pours wine into it, so that it takes the flavor from the wood, and drinks this wine often, it will remove fever from his stomach and clarify his eyes. Also, if one frequently touches his eyes with this wood, then his flesh, head, and eyes will become much healthier. [Also, one who makes a staff from it, often carrying it in his hand, and who even puts it by his nose, receiving its odor, and touches his eyes with it, will find that his skin, head, and eyes will become much better.]

XXIII. Fir Tree

The fir tree *(abies)* is more hot than cold and contains many powers. It signifies fortitude. Spirits of the air hate, and avoid more than in other areas, any place where there is fir tree wood. Magic thrives less and is less prevalent there than in other places.

When the tree is green and has not yet lost its sap, as in March or even May, take the bark and leaves of this tree, and even some of its wood, and cut it into tiny bits. Add half as much sage and boil this in water, until it thickens. Then add cow's butter, prepared in May, and strain it through a cloth, making an ointment. If someone ails in his head, so that he is *virgichtiget*, raving, or mad, and if his heart is failing in strength, first anoint his heart well with this ointment. Then, having shaved his hair, anoint his head with the same ointment. Repeat this on the second and third day, and his head will recover its health, and he will return to his senses.

If someone ails in his stomach or spleen, first anoint his heart with this ointment, because of the weakness of his heart. Soon afterward, anoint his stomach, if that is where the pain is, or his spleen, if he is ailing there. The ointment will pass through his skin with its strength, so that he will be cured quickly.

For one who is congested in his chest, who coughs, and who even ails in his lungs so that they are swollen and are beginning to be putrescent, burn wood of the fir tree, when it is fresh and the sap is still in it, until it is ash. Let nothing else be added to this ash. Into these ashes put twice as much burnet saxifrage and the same amount of fennel, and half as much licorice as saxifrage. Cook this together in good wine with some honey. Strain it through a cloth to make a spiced wine. Drunk often, it will purge the chest, restore the lungs to health, and therefore cure the person.

When crabs eat a person, reduce to a powder, over a hot tile, the seed that grows at the top of the fir tree. Toss that powder over the wound where the crabs are eating the person, and the crabs will die. Again heat the tile, on which the seeds were crushed, with another hot tile and put the tile, so warmed, over the wound where the crabs are eating. They will die.

If your mouth and lips swell up from some infirmity, warm the seed or fruit of the fir tree on a hot tile. Do not reduce the seed to a powder, but place it, so warmed, over your mouth. The swelling will cease.

The fir has a strong heat, and its odor inflames the humors in a person, causing them to rush out in a flood. A person should not take in the odor of the fir, unless some spices and other odoriferous herbs of some kind are added. Otherwise the humors in his body are excited beyond moderation, and are stirred up in the storm of the inundation, rather than being retained and strengthened.

XXIV. LINDEN

The linden *(tilia)* has a great heat. Its whole heat is in its root and ascends into its branches and leaves. It signifies frailty. A person who ails in his heart should take the interior of the linden root and reduce it to a powder. He should often eat this powder with bread, and his heart will be better. In the summer, when the tree is green, take the bark away from the rootstock, not the branches, until you come to white wood. Then cut a sliver from the wood, and place it into a hole bored into a golden ring. Over this wood splinter place a green glass, and no other stone. Put a spider web, cotton, or wool between the splinter and glass lest the power of that splinter penetrate the glass. Always wear the ring on your finger, so that the heat of your finger rises to the splinter, and the power of that splinter touches your finger and its veins. This is a very strong power against all diseases most dangerous to the human being. Even if the diseases inundate him a bit, it keeps them from him, just as a weir keeps an oncoming flood of waters from making a wrong course.

In summer, place fresh leaves of linden on your eyes when you go to sleep, and cover your whole face with them. This will clarify your eyes and make them clean.

If you are virgichtiget, you should take the earth which lies around the root of the linden, and put it on the fire. Pour water over it when it is hot, and so bathe in a sauna. Do this for nine days, and you will be cured.

XXV. OAK

Oak *(quercus)* is cold, hard, and bitter. However, something in it is fully strong. It signifies worthlessness. It is hard and bitter, and it is not possible for softness to be in it. Even its fruit is not good for a human being to eat. Neither do worms eat its wood freely. If they begin to eat it, they quickly stop, forsaking it altogether. Nevertheless, some strong animals, such as pigs, eat its fruit and become fat. Neither the wood nor the fruit is good for medicine.

XXVI. BEECH TREE

The beech tree *(fagus)* has correct balance, with equal heat and cold, both of which are good. It denotes discipline. When the leaves of the beech begin to come out, but do not yet fully show, go to this tree, and take a branch of it in your left hand. With a small knife in your right hand, say, "I cut your natural vigor from you, because you correct all a person's humors which have been turned to the wrong path by yellow bile; by the living Word, which makes a person without contrition." Hold the branch in your left hand while you say all these words. Then cut the branch off with the steel knife. Save that branch for a year, and repeat this each year. If anyone in that year has jaundice, cut a small piece from that branch. Place it in a metallic jar, and pour it over a moderate amount of wine. Whenever you pour the wine over these bits, say these words, "By the holy spark of the holy incarnation, by which God became human, draw from this person, N., the sickness of jaundice." Then heat the wine, with the bits of wood which you had cut off, in a small crucible. For three days, give it as a warm drink to the one with jaundice. He will be cured, unless God forbids it.

If someone has ague, take some of the fruit of the beech tree when it first comes out and mix it with pure spring water. Say these words, "By the holy spark of the holy incarnation, by which God became human, you, ague, and you, fevers, forsake this person, N., with your heat and cold." Then give him this water to drink. Offer it for five days, and he will be quickly freed from quotidian or quartan fevers, unless God does not wish to free him.

Also, when the root of the beech tree appears above the earth, take away its outer bark. Take as much as you are able to cut with one incision and say, "By the first vision, when God saw a human being at the root of Mamre, break the waves of this person's poison, without his death."* Again, cut as much as you can from a second incision, and say the same words. In a similar way, cut a third incision in the root, so that you cut the root three times, lest it run short during the year. Save these bits for a year, and repeat this each year. During the year, whenever anyone has freislich on his body, cut off a bit from one of these cuttings of wood, place it in a metallic jar, and pour over it pure spring water, saying these words each time, "By the first vision, when God was baptized in the Jordan, through this poison, without the death of this person, N., carry from him every snare of this disease, (so that he be) with pure life, just as Jesus was." Give this water to him to drink, while fasting, for three days. On each day offer it to him to drink in this way. He will be freed from freislich, unless God prohibits it.

———

*Translator's note: According to the Old Testament (Gen. 18:1) the Lord appeared to Abraham at the Oak of Mamre and announced that Sarah would have a child within a year.

Anyone who prepares and eats a puree from the leaves of the beech, when they are new and fresh, will not be harmed by it. If someone eats its fruit, he will not be harmed, but will become fat.

XXVII. ASH TREE

The ash tree *(asch)* is more hot than cold. It denotes counsel. If anyone is troubled by gicht in his side or other part of his body, as if all his limbs were broken and bruised, cook the leaves of the ash tree in water. Place the sick person, nude, on a linen cloth. Having poured off the water, place the warm, cooked leaves all around him, particularly on the place where he is ailing. Do this often, and he will be better.

If you want to prepare beer from oats, without hops, cook it only with groats, with many ash leaves added. This beer, when drunk, will purge the stomach and make the chest light and pleasant. [If goats are ill in some way, they should be given ash leaves to eat, and they will be cured.]

XXVIII. ASPEN

The aspen *(aspa)* is hot and designates excess. When an infant lying in his cradle is wounded and suffused with blood between his skin and flesh, so that he is in much pain, take new, fresh aspen leaves. Put them on an unfolded linen cloth and wrap the infant with these leaves in the cloth. Place him for sleeping and cover him with clothing, so that he emits perspiration. The power of the leaves will draw it out, and he will get well.

But, if one is virgichtiget, or has a cold stomach, he should take the bark of this tree, when it is green, and wood from the exterior, down to but not including the inner heart. He should cut it into minute bits and cook them in water. Then he should pour this water, with the wood, into a cask and take a bath in it. If he does this often, the gicht will leave him, or his stomach will be warm, and each malady will be better.

Also, in May, take the bark of this tree and the wood from the outside, into the heart, and cut it into small bits. Pound this in a mortar, and express the juice. Add this juice to other ointments which you prepare. They will be much better against all diseases that trouble a person in his head, torso, loins, stomach, and other parts, and these unguents will check bad humors to a greater degree.

XXIX. ALDER

The alder *(arla)* is more cold than hot. It denotes uselessness and is not much use in medicine. But, if someone is a bit ulcerous on his skin, place new, fresh leaves of this tree on the ulcers. During that time it will become smoother.

XXX. PLANE TREE

The plane tree *(ahorn)* is cold and dry. It signifies that which has been frightened. One who has quotidian or diurnal fevers should cook branches of this tree, with its leaves, in water. Then he should bathe frequently in this water. When he comes out of the bath, he should pound some of the inner bark, and express the juice. He should pour it into pure wine, and drink this cold. If he does this often, the diurnal fevers will cease, and the fetidness and tempests in him will vanish.

Anyone who is troubled by gicht in any of his body parts should take wood of this tree and warm it well on a fire. He should place it, so warmed, on the place which hurts, and the pain will be chased away. If he cannot endure the whole piece of wood, he should shave off some of the heated wood and place it where it hurts. He should tie it on with a bandage, and he will be better.

But, if someone's nose is swollen by some illness, he should heat the earth which is around the roots of this tree. He should place it on his nose at night, and tie it on with a bandage. He should lie in this way for a little while. If he does this often, the swelling will vanish, and he will be better.

XXXI. YEW

The yew *(ybenbaum)* is more cold than hot, and it is dry. It signifies happiness. When its wood is burned in a fire, neither the moisture nor the smoke that come out of it is harmful. If someone has a defect in his nose or chest, from bad humors, he should inhale the smoke of that wood into his nose and mouth. Those bad humors will be gently and smoothly dissolved, and will vanish without danger to his body. If one prepares a staff of this wood and carries it in his hands, it will be good and useful for the prosperity and health of his body.

XXXII. WHITE BIRCH

White birch *(bircka)* is more hot than cold. It denotes felicity. If someone's skin is beginning to redden and to have swollen pustules, whence a tumor rises up or worms begin to bubble up, he should take some of the shoots of this tree. He should heat them in the sun, or on a fire, and place them on the spot where he is ailing. He should tie it with a cloth and should do this often, and the tumor will go away.

XXXIII. Sea Fir

Sea fir *(fornhaff)* is more hot than cold. It is also moist, so it signifies mourning, and has no happiness in its nature. But its sap is very valuable for ointments and eye lotions. If someone prepares ointments, they will be stronger and better if juice from its twigs is added. If a person makes eye lotions, he should add a bit of this juice. It makes the eyes sparkle with light and gives very clear sight. By itself it is not good as medicine. Its juice is too strong unless it is tempered with other ingredients.

But if pestilence torments and kills herd animals, place fresh branches of this tree in front of these animals, so that they receive its odor. Lead them to a place where these trees are growing, so that the odor passes into their nostrils. Because of it, they will begin to cough, ejecting the putrid matter from their nostrils and heads, so that the pestilence vexing them shall vanish. But take care that the animals taste no part of these trees, lest they be harmed and suffer.

XXXIV. Spindle Tree

The spindle tree *(spynelbaum)* is more cold than hot. It designates generosity. It holds some happiness in its nature. A person who has dropsy should remove the bark of this tree and burn the inner wood in a fire. He should make ashes from this, with no other ashes added. He should tie the ashes in a cloth, and put them in pure, good wine. He should frequently drink this, while fasting, from morning to noon. It will consume the illness within him.

One who has pain in his spleen should cook the fruit that grows on this tree in pure wine. He should strain it through a cloth and drink it frequently, with a meal. His spleen will be better. One whose stomach is being eaten by worms, or who suffers a stitch in his stomach, should often drink this same potion, and he will be better.

XXXV. English Elm

The English elm *(hagenbucha)* is more cold than hot, and it displays prosperity in its nature. Take twigs with leaves, when they are green, and cook them in milk from cows or sheep, but not from goats. Throwing out the twigs and leaves, prepare this milk with flour or eggs, so that it can be eaten. Women who are fecund—not sterile, but in whom the fetus usually dies—should frequently eat milk prepared this way. It will greatly benefit their fecundity so that they may retain the fetus.

Also, cook the twigs and leaves of this tree in water, and make a bath. Place one who is out of his mind in this bath. Having shaved his hair, dip a linen cloth in the water, so that it is wet and warm, and carefully warm his head while he is in the bath. After he comes out of the bath, put him in bed. Then cook the fruit of this tree in water. Pour off the water, and place the cooked, warm fruit on his head. Tie it with a cloth, so that he may sleep with it on. Do this often, and he will be better and recover his senses.

For one who has bad spots on his body, cut a chip of this wood from under the bark. Heat it on a fire, and place it, so warmed, over these spots, and they will vanish.

It is good and useful for a person to always have with him wood from this tree. For if English elm, or another kind of wood in which good fortune is shown, is burned in the fire in a house, spirits of the air and diabolical deceptions go away, fleeing in disdain, because they sense some prosperity there. If a person sleeps in the forest, or wishes to rest there in the afternoon, he should lie under the shadow of an English elm. There the evil spirits show their deceptions and horrors so much less. To avoid devilish horrors, one can rest under other trees which display prosperity, but the English elm is the best.

XXXVI. WILLOW

The willow *(wida)* is cold, and it designates vices, since it seems to be beautiful. It is not useful for people, except in serving external uses, and is not good for medicine. Its fruit and juice is bitter, and not good for human use. If one wishes to eat it, it stirs up and augments melancholy in him, makes him bitter inside, and diminishes his health and happiness.

XXXVII. SALLOW OR GOAT WILLOW

The sallow *(salewida)* has the same nature and use as the willow.

XXXVIII. FOLBAUM

The *folbaum* has neither correct heat nor correct cold. It is useful for no medicine. Neither it, nor its fruit, has any other use. Just as a weed, it is useless.

XXXIX. FELBAUM

The *felbaum* is more cold than hot. It is not good for medicine or for any other human use. If a person eats its fruit, it harms him and diminishes his health. The cold in it augments the bad humors in him, because of the injuriousness in it.

XL. CORNEL CHERRY TREE

The cornel cherry tree *(erlizbaum)* is hot, and its heat is gentle. It has an agreeable moisture in it. Take some of the bark, wood, and leaves of this tree, cook them in water, and make a bath. One who is virgichtiget, whether infant, youth, or old person, should bathe often in it, and submerge himself in these baths. He should do this in summer, when the tree is green. It helps the infant and youth the most, but benefits the old person enough. The fruit of this tree does not harm the person eating it. It purges and strengthens the sick and healthy stomach, and is useful for a person's good health.

XLI. MASCEL

The *mascel* has a useless and harmful heat. Its wood, sap, and leaves are of no use for a person, and are harmful to his health and dangerous for his libido, since it excites lust in a person. If a person eats its fruit, he will become sick from it. Its fire and smoke are not good for a person's health.

XLII. MYRTLE

The myrtle *(mirtelbaum)* is more hot than cold. If scrofula rises up on a person, before it ruptures place warm myrtle leaves, which have been cooked in water, on it, and it will disappear. If the scrofula wants to rupture, heat wood of this tree in the fire, and place it over the affected area often, so warmed, in the shape of a cross, and the scrofula will disappear. If it has already ruptured, pulverize twigs and leaves, and often place this powder over it, and it will dry out.

If someone wishes to make beer, he should cook the leaves and fruit of this tree, and it will be healthful and not harm the person drinking it.

XLIII. JUNIPER

The juniper *(wacholderbaum)* is more hot than cold, and signifies excess. Take its fruit, cook it in water, strain this water through a cloth. To this water add honey and a bit of vinegar and licorice, and less ginger than licorice. Cook it again, and place it in a little bag, and make a spiced wine. Drink it often, whether fasting, or having eaten. It diminishes and mitigates pain in the chest, lungs, or liver. Also, take the green twigs and cook them in water. Make a sauna bath with that water. Often bathe in it, and it diminishes various bad fevers in you.

XLIV. Elder

The elder *(holderbaum)* is more hot than cold, and is of little value for human use, except its fruit does serve the human being. Nevertheless, one who has jaundice should enter a sauna bath and place the leaves of this tree on the hot rocks. He should pour water over them, and then place a twig in pure wine, so that it takes its flavor. While in that bath, he should drink this in moderation. After he comes out of the bath, he should lie in bed, so that he sweats. He should do this often, and he will be better.

XLV. Gall Oak

Gall oak *(gelbaum)* is more cold than hot, and it has much vital power. It signifies combat. It is contrary to the nature of the human, so that, were a person to taste its sap or fruit in any way, it would create much violence within him. Because of the coldness of its sap, it would pervert the heat of his stomach, so that he would be nauseous and spit up his food. It is of no use to man or beast. It is not much good as medicine, but only for burning in a fire.

One who has scrofula on his body should take the first fruits which come from the gall oak and crush them in a bit of wine. He should mix this with a third as much powder of a mole, which had been pulverized, and cook it in a small dish, making an unguent. He should frequently anoint his scrofula with this before it ruptures, and it will disappear. If the scrofula has ruptured, he should pulverize the shoot, that is the first fruit which comes out of the gall oak, and put this powder on the broken scrofula, and it will dry up.

XLVI. Hartbrogelbaum

Hartbrogelbaum is more cold than hot, and it denotes small skill. It is not of much value for the human being, since from it a person neither grows, nor is strengthened, nor is fed. Nor is it beneficial for medicine.

XLVII. Elm

Elm *(iffa)* has a summerlike heat. It is not very hot, nor very cold, but temperate. One who is troubled by gicht should burn a fire with its wood only. Soon he should warm himself by that fire, and the gicht will cease immediately. But, for one who is virgichtiget, so that his tongue fails to speak, fresh new leaves of this tree should be placed in cold water, and this should be given to him to drink. The gicht in his tongue will cease, and he will recover his speech. One who has freislich on his body should often drink the same water, tempered with those leaves, and the freislich will disappear. If someone burns this wood alone, heats water with it, and takes a bath in this water, it will take away malignity and bad will, give him benevolence, and make his mind happy. That tree has a certain prosperity in its nature, so that spirits of the air are unable to move their phantasms, wrongs, and illusions through it with their many wrathful confrontations.

XLVIII. HARBAUM

Harbaum has a summerlike heat balanced in it, and it designates audacity. A person who has large or small scabies should pound the leaves of this tree with fresh pork fat and then dissolve it in a small dish. If he frequently anoints himself with this, the scabies will diminish, and he will be healed.

Also, the twigs with their leaves can be cooked in water, adding rue, and more sage than rue, and more fennel than sage. This should be strained through a cloth and drunk. Very often it purges fevers and bad conditions of filth from a person, making him healthy.

XLIX. SCHULBAUM

Schulbaum is cold, is like a weed, and is not valuable for medicine. Its sap and fruit are useless for the human being. If someone eats its seed or fruit, it would be just like a poison for him.

L. TAMARISK

Tamarisk *(pruma)* is very hot. One who is leprous should rub tamarisk in his hands and express the juice. He should smear this juice frequently where he is leprous. It will lessen the leprosy and make it smoother. One may also cook the flowers of the tamarisk in cow's butter, and so make an unguent. If he often anoints himself with this, the leprosy will be diminished. One whose eyes are fogged up and infirm should stare at tamarisk flowers for a long time, until his eyes become moist. Then he should place those flowers on his eyes, and sleep thus. If he does this often, it will clarify his eyes. If people are well, it is good and healthful; if they are sick, it is good and useful, and does make them well.

LI. AGENBAUM

Agenbaum has neither correct heat nor correct coldness. It is like a weed, so that neither its sap nor its fruit is good for medicine or any other human use.

LII. ROSE HIP

The rose hip *(hyffa)* is very hot. It signifies affection. One who has pain in his lungs should crush rose hips with their leaves. Then he should add raw honey and cook these together. He should frequently remove the froth, then strain it through a cloth and make spiced wine. He should drink this often, and it will carry off the rotten matter from his lungs, purging and healing him.

One who burns this wood by itself, thus making ashes from it, should make lye from these ashes. If he often washes his head with this, he will be healthy and strong from the good heat of its juice. Someone who is healthy in body, yet sick in stomach only, should cook the fruit of the Tribulus, and eat it often. It will cleanse his stomach and take away the mucus. For one whose entire body is sick, it is not good to eat this cooked. It harms his stomach, since his stomach is flacid. But if he wishes to eat it, it is better for him to eat raw and moderately soft than cooked, or hard and raw. Eating it raw or cooked does not harm one whose entire body is healthy.

LIII. BLACKTHORN

Blackthorns *(spina)* are more hot than cold and are even dry. A person who is virgichtiget, so that his senses are failing, and he is made crazy because he is beginning to become lame, should take green or aged black-thorns and burn them by themselves in the fire. Then he should add to their ashes some powdered cloves and twice as much powdered cinnamon as cloves. He should add pure, cooked honey to wine, and so prepare a spiced wine, with the ashes exceeding a third part of the cloves. He should drink this moderately while fasting, and a sufficient amount with a meal. He should do this often, and the gicht will go from him. Since this potion is better than gold, he will recover his senses and recuperate the health of his limbs. He should also mix its fruit, namely sloes, with honey and eat this frequently, and the gicht in him will cease.

One who is sick in his stomach should roast the sloes in the fire, or cook them in water. He should often eat them to rid the filth and mucus from his stomach. If he eats their kernels, they will not harm him.

If crabs, but no other worms, are eating a person's body, he should take the inner kernels of blackthorn and dry them in an earthenware vessel near the fire. Then he should reduce them to a powder and put this powder where the crabs are eating him. Afterward he should pour a few drops of wine on top, and the crabs will die.

LIV. GRAPEVINE

A grapevine *(vitis)* has fiery heat and moisture in it. The fire is so strong as to change its sap to a flavor that other trees and herbs do not have. That great fire makes its wood so dry that it is unlike other wood. The grapevine is a wood twisted from the earth, very like trees. Before the flood the earth was fragile, and it did not produce wine. When it had been moistened and strengthened by the flood, it produced wine. The earth now is to the earth before the flood as gravel is to the present earth.

If one's flesh is rotting around his teeth, or his teeth are weak, he should put warm ashes of grapevine in wine, as if he wanted to make lye. He should then wash his teeth and the flesh around them with that wine. He should do this often, and his gums will be cured and his teeth will be strong. Even if one's teeth are healthy, this washing benefits them, and they become beautiful.

If someone has ulcers on his body or has been struck with a wound, he should add a third part of olive oil to pure, good wine. He should gently heat this oily wine, when the ulcer or wound is large, when it shows blackness or pus on the second or third day. He should dip a linen cloth in it, and rub the ulcer or wound with it until the pus diminishes. If the wound or ulcer is small, he should dip a feather in the oily wine, when it is cold, not heated. He should gently clean the ulcer or wound with it until the pus diminishes.

LV. GICHTBAUM

Gichtbaum* is very hot, and its natural power and sap are not much use alone, unless added to other ingredients. If added to other herbs or spices, they are better as medicine. Trees grow strong from the marrow, just as man does from his marrow. If the marrow of a tree is injured, the tree will feel its weakness.

---

*Translator's note: *Gichtbaum* may be black currant.

LVI. SMOKE

Smoke *(fumus)* from wood is wood's moisture, since when wood is burned in the fire the moisture in it comes out as smoke. The smoke from certain trees is harmful and hurts a person. It makes the flesh of his eyes ulcerous and induces much fogginess. The smoke which ascends from the oak congests a person's chest, making him dry inside. The smoke from a beech tree is not as harmful as that from the oak, although this smoke is injurious. The smoke of the aspen tightens the flesh around a person's eyes and makes his head ache.

LVII. MOSS

When trees grow old, they begin to lose their inner greenness, and if they are young, yet weakened internally by some accident, they send the greenness and health, which they ought to have inside, to the exterior bark. Thus moss *(mose)* grows on the bark because these trees do not have inner greenness. Some mosses, which grow on certain trees, have medicinal value in them. Others, such as those that grow on rotten wood, have almost no medicinal power, because the rotten matter—which is in the fetid humors of roofs, rotten wood, and stones—breaks out and grows into moss, and so lack nearly all usefulness.

If someone is tormented by gicht in any part of his body, he should take the moss which grows on the pear tree, the apple tree, and the beech tree. He should mix a third of each, cook them gently in water and, having squeezed out the water, place them, so warmed, over the part of the body where the gicht is. He should do this often, and the gicht in him will cease.

If someone who suffers fever from ague places on himself moss from roofs or rotten wood while he is suffering a bit, he will feel the heat briefly, yet he will not be cured of the ague.

LVIII. THE UNGUENT OF HILARION

The unguent which Hilarion the Egyptian made known *(unguentum hilarii)* is a remedy for pain of either side that hurts for any reason, as well as for pain of the chest, and for palsy. Take the leaves of the peach tree, and an equal weight of sysemera, and one-third as much basil as sysemera, and as much plantain as basil. Cook this gently in water, then strain it by forcibly twisting these herbs in a cloth. After this, take laurel oil, and twice as much deer tallow, and a third as much old fat. Dissolve this all with the foresaid water in a small dish. Then let it cool down, and make an unguent. With it anoint the person who has pain on either side, or who ails in his chest, or where someone has gicht. Do this often, and he will be better.

LIX. SYSEMERA*

When the sun rises toward summer in spring, or when it inclines toward winter, the air is sour like wine and gives a certain whiteness. Therefore, from *sysemera,* gather as much as you can, and often tie it over the eye where leucoma or *herbrado* is increasing, and it will be cured. And, where worms eat or are beginning to eat the flesh of a person, place there some of the same whiteness of the air. The worms will not progress any further and will die.

LX. AGAINST SCROFULA

Against scrofula *(contra orfimas),* which has not yet ruptured, take dung, a little dry and hard, which has come from a human being who is healthy and strong, whether male or female. Smear it on a linen cloth, and place it on the scrofula. Over that little cloth tie a linen bandage smeared with goat tallow. Keep it bound for three days, or two days and nights. Then, renew the human dung. Do this often, and the scrofula will vanish. Or, frequently place the dried blood of a leech or the dried liver of a vulture over the scrofula, and it will vanish.

LXI. PALM TREE

The palm tree *(palma)* is hot and moist. A person who has pleurisy should pound some of the bark, wood, and leaves of this tree and express the sap. He should drink this frequently in warm wine, and he will be cured. He should also often eat the fruit of this tree. It will check his pleurisy.

One who is mad, however, should cook some of its wood and leaves in water and place them, thus warmed, around his head. He should do this often, and he will recover his senses.

If anyone cooks the fruit of this tree and eats it, it will give his body almost as much strength as bread does, but it will easily aggravate his chest.

---

*See also Sysemera entry on pp. 25–26.

XLII. RED FIR

The red fir *(picea)* is hot and moist. If a pestilence is vexing and killing herd animals, fresh branches of this tree should be placed in front of them, so that they receive their odor. Or, the animals should be led under these trees. They will begin to cough and eject pus. But care should be taken that they taste no part of the tree, lest they be injured by it.

LXIII. TRIBULUS

Tribulus *(tribulus)* is very hot. One should prepare lye from the ashes of this wood, by itself, and with it wash his head, which if healthy will become more healthy and firm. One who is healthy in his body, and only sick in his stomach, should cook fruit of the Tribulus and eat it frequently. It will purge his stomach. For one who is sick in his entire body, this fruit is not good to eat.

STONES

BOOK FOUR
Stones

EVERY STONE CONTAINS FIRE AND MOISTURE. The devil abhors, detests, and disdains precious stones. This is because he remembers that their beauty was manifest on him before he fell from the glory God had given him, and because some precious stones are engendered from fire, in which he receives his punishment. By the will of God, the devil was vanquished by the fire into which he fell, just as he is vanquished by the fire of the Holy Spirit when humans are snatched from his jaws by the first breath of the Holy Spirit.

Precious stones and gems arise in the Orient, in areas where the sun's heat is very great. From the hot sun, mountains there have heat as powerful as fire. The rivers in those areas always boil from the sun's great heat. Whence at times an inundation of those rivers bursts forth and ascends those scorching mountains. The mountains, burning with the sun's heat, are touched by those rivers. Froth, similar to that produced by hot iron or a hot stone when water is poured over it, exudes from the places where the water touches the fire. This froth adheres to that place and, in three or four days, hardens into stone.

Once the inundation has ceased and the waters have returned to the river bed, the pieces of froth dry up. They dry from the sun's heat and take their colors and powers in accordance with the time of day and the temperature. Drying and hardening, they become precious stones and fall onto the sand, just like flaking fish scales. When they flood again the rivers lift up many of the stones, carrying them to other countries where they are later discovered by human beings. The mountains, where so many and such large stones have sprung up in this way, shine like the light of day.

And so, precious stones are born from fire and water; whence they have fire and moisture in them. They contain many powers and are effective for many needs. Many things can be done with them—but only good, honest actions, which are beneficial to human beings; not activities of seduction, fornication, adultery, enmity, homicide, and the like, which tend toward vice and which are injurious to people. The nature of these precious stones seeks honest and useful effects and rejects people's depraved and evil uses, in the same way virtues cast off vices and vices are unable to engage with virtues.

Some stones do not originate from these mountains and are not of the same nature, but arise from other, useless things. Through them, with God's permission, it is possible for good and bad things to happen.

God had decorated the first angel as if with precious stones. Lucifer, upon seeing them shine in the mirror of the Divinity, took knowledge from them and recognized that God wished to do many wondrous things. His mind was exalted with pride, since the beauty of the stones which covered him shone in God. He thought that he could do deeds both equal to and greater than God's. And so his splendor was extinguished. But, just as God restored Adam to a better part, He sent neither the beauty nor the powers of those precious stones to perdition, but willed that they would be held in honor and blessing on earth and used for medicine.

I. EMERALD

The emerald *(smaragdus)* grows in the wee hours of morning at sunrise, when the sun is powerfully placed in its orbit, traversing its route. Then the natural vigor of the earth and grasses is especially lively, the air still cold, the sun hot. The herbs vigorously imbibe vitality, as a lamb sucking milk. The heat of the day is scarcely sufficient to dry that day's vital energy, and it gives nourishment so the plants become fertile and produce fruit. Therefore, the emerald is powerful against all human weakness and sickness, since the sun readys it, and since all its matter is of the vitality of the air.

Whence, one who ails in his heart, stomach, or side should have an emerald with him. It will heat up his flesh, making him better. If this person is so beset by pestilences which cannot restrain their commotions, he should place an emerald in his mouth, so it becomes wet from his saliva and the saliva heats up from the stone. He should repeatedly place it on, and take it from, his body. The sudden pestilential attacks will cease, without a doubt.

When someone tormented by epilepsy falls, put an emerald in his mouth while he is lying prostrate. It will revive his spirit. After he gets up and takes the stone from his mouth, he should look at it intently, and say, "Just as the breath of the Lord filled the whole earth, so may his grace fill the house of my body, so that it can never be moved." He should do this in the morning for the next nine days, and he will be cured. He should always have that stone with him and look at it every morning while saying the those words, and he will be healed.

One who has great pain in his head should hold it near his mouth and warm it by his breath, so that it becomes damp from his breath. He should rub it, so dampened, on his temples and forehead. Then he should put it in his mouth and, holding it in his mouth for a little while, he will be better.

Someone who has much phlegm and saliva in him should heat good wine and then put a linen cloth over a metallic vessel. He should rest an emerald on that cloth and pour the warm wine over the stone, so the wine passes through the cloth. He should do this again and again, as if preparing lye. Then he should frequently eat this wine, mixed with ground broad beans, and drink the wine itself. It will purge his head and diminish the phlegm and saliva.

If someone is being eaten by worms, he should place a linen cloth, with an emerald on top, over the wound. He should tie over it other small pieces of cloth, so that the stone grows warm. If this is done for three days, the worms will die.

II. JACINTH

Jacinth *(jacinctus)* is born from fire at the first hour of the day, when the air holds a gentle heat. More airy than fiery, it senses the air and its heat, in proportion to the air it holds. Nevertheless, it is fiery because it is engendered by fire. A person who suffers fogginess in his eyes, or whose eyes are agitated or suppurative, should hold a jacinth in the sun. It immediately remembers that it was born from fire and quickly heats up. He should then dampen it with his saliva and quickly place it on his eyes, so that it warms them. He should do this often, and his eyes will become clear and healthy.

If someone is bewitched by delusions or magic words, so that he is becoming crazy, take warm rye bread, and cut the shape of the cross in the top crust, not breaking it totally. Drawing a jacinth down through the cut, say, "May God, who threw off every precious stone from the devil when the devil contravened his command, now throw off from you, N., every delusion and all magic words; and may he free you from the pain of this madness." Then, drawing the same stone across the warm bread, say, "Just as the splendor which the devil had in him was taken from him because of his transgression, so also let this madness which torments you, N., by various delusions and magic words, be taken from you, and disappear." The bread from around the area through which you drew the jacinth should be given to the afflicted person to eat. If he cannot eat the rye bread because of the debility of his body, then, using the jacinth and the same words, bless warm, unleavened bread in the same way, and give it to him to eat. In addition, draw the same shape of the cross through all foods which he will eat, namely through meats, vegetable purees, and the rest of his food. If you frequently make crosses on them and bless them with those words, he will be cured. One who has pain in his heart should make the sign of the cross over his heart and say the same words, and he will be better.

III. ONYX

Onyx *(onychinus)* is hot. It is formed around the third hour of the day, in a thick cloud, when the sun is very hot but when various clouds rise over the sun, so that it does not show through the abundance of water. Therefore, onyx does not have the great heat of fire, yet it holds the heat of air. It originates from a ray of the sun, is congealed by various clouds, and has great power against infirmities that arise from the air.

One whose eyes are foggy, or ailing in some other way, should pour good, pure wine into a bronze, copper, or steel vessel. He should place an onyx in that wine and let it soak for fifteen or thirty days. Then he should take out the stone and leave the wine in the vessel. Every night he should gently touch his eyes with the wine. They will become clear and healthy.

For an ailment of the heart or side, one should warm an onyx in his hands or against his skin. He should heat wine on the fire in a metallic vessel and, after taking the vessel from the fire, hold the stone over the steaming wine. The sweat coming out of it will mix with the wine. He should then put the onyx in the wine, and drink it right away. The pain of his heart and side will disappear.

One who has pain in his stomach should prepare wine with onyx, as already described. Then he should make a broth with that wine, hens' eggs, and flour and eat it often. It will purge his stomach and heal him. But, one who ails in his spleen should cook goat meat or that of young sheep. He should eat the cooked meat, dipping it in the wine prepared with onyx, just as one customarily dips certain foods in vinegar. He should do this often, and his spleen will be better and swell up fully.

One who has strong fevers should place onyx in vinegar for five days. Then, having removed the onyx, he should prepare and season all his foods with that vinegar, and so eat them. The fever will cease and swiftly vanish, because the good heat of onyx, mixed with the heat of vinegar, chases away the noxious humors which give rise to fevers.

If you are oppressed with sadness, look at an onyx intently, then place it in your mouth. The oppression of your mind will cease.

If pestilence should infest and kill cattle, heat water in a vessel over the fire. Take it from the fire and hold an onyx over that steaming water, so that the sweat coming out of it mixes with the water. Then place the onyx in that water for three days. After taking out the onyx, frequently give the water to the cows to drink. Sprinkle their fodder with the water, and mix bran with the same water, and set it out for them to eat. Do this often, and they will be better.

IV. BERYL

Beryl *(beryllus)* is hot and develops every day, between the third hour and midday, from foam of water, which the sun inflames mightily. Its power is more from air and water than from fire, although it is a little bit fiery.

If a person eats or drinks poison, grate a moderate amount of beryl into spring water, or any other kind of water. He should drink this immediately, and do the same thing for five days, drinking once a day on an empty stomach. The poison will either foam out through nausea or pass through his posterior.

One who always has beryl with him, who often holds it in his hand and looks at it frequently, is not easily at odds with other people, nor does he dispute, but rather he remains tranquil.

V. SARDONYX

Sardonyx *(sardonix)* is hot and develops every day when the sixth hour has already passed, (until) just past one line of the ninth hour of the day. Then it is warmed by the sun, which is shining in its purity. Because the air then begins to grow cold, sardonyx is more fiery than from air or water. It holds strong powers in its nature and furnishes strength to a person's five senses. It is a particular remedy for each of the senses, since it is born in the purity of the sun, when nothing soils its clarity.

When a person places it against his bare skin, and even frequently places it to his mouth, so that his breath touches it as he breathes in and out, he strengthens his understanding, his knowledge, and all the senses of his body. Great wrath, stupidity, and illiterateness are removed from that person. The devil hates this purity and flees.

If a man or woman has a nature strongly burning for the works of the flesh, then he should place sardonyx on his loins and she should place it on her umbilicus, and they will have relief from that lust.

After someone has sweated from an acute disease and considers himself better, he should soon place sardonyx on his finger, on a ring. He will not again fall into this sickness.

VI. SAPPHIRE

Sapphire *(sapphirus)* is hot and develops after noontime, when the sun burns ardently and the air is a bit obstructed by its heat. The splendor of the sun, from the extreme heat that it then has, pierces through the air. The splendor is not as full as it is when the air is a bit cool. Sapphire is turbid, indeed more fiery than airy or watery. It symbolizes a complete love of wisdom.

A person who has a sty in his eye should hold a sapphire in his hand and warm it, by holding it either closed in his hand or near a fire. He should touch the sty in his eye with the damp stone in the morning and at night, for three days, and the sty will grow smaller and disappear.

One whose eyes are red and painfully inflamed, or whose vision is obscured, should place a sapphire in his mouth before breakfast. It should become damp from his saliva. Then, taking on his finger the saliva which dampened the stone, he should smear it around his eyes, so that it even touches the inside of his eyes, which will be healed and will become clear.

One who is completely virgichtiget and unable to endure the great oppression in his head and the rest of his body should place a sapphire in his mouth, and the gicht will stop.

A person who desires to have good understanding and knowledge should place a sapphire in his mouth every morning, upon getting out of bed and while fasting. He should hold it in his mouth long enough for it to absorb the saliva which moistens it. He should take it from his mouth, then warm a bit of wine in a metallic vessel over the fire. He should hold the stone in the vapor of that wine so that, by sweating, it becomes damp. Then he should lick off some of that moisture and the saliva, which had heated the stone, and swallow it, and he will have pure understanding and knowledge. Even his stomach will be healed by this.

Also, for one who is a fool, in whom all knowledge is lacking, and who nevertheless desires but is unable to be wise: If he neither contemplates malice nor reaches out toward it, he should often rub his tongue, while fasting, with a sapphire. Its heat and strength, with the moisture of his saliva, will chase off noxious humors which oppress the person's understanding, and the person will receive good understanding.

One who is much moved with wrath should immediately place a sapphire in his mouth. The wrath will be extinguished and will go from him. If this stone is placed on a ring of the purest gold, without tin, and there is nothing but gold under the stone, then a person may place the stone in his mouth as medicine, and it will not harm him. If anything but pure gold is in it, then it is of no use, and one should not place it in his mouth, because that ring is harmful.

If a person is in the power of an evil spirit, another person should place a sapphire on some earth, then sew that earth into a leather sack, and hang it from his neck. He should say, "O you, most wicked spirit, quickly go from this person, just as, in your first fall, the glory of your splendor very quickly fell from you." The evil spirit will be greatly tortured. He will depart from that person, who will be better, unless it is a very cruel and most good-for-nothing spirit.

If the devil should incite a man to love a woman so that, without magic or invocations of demons, he begins to be insane with this love, and if this is an annoyance to the woman, she should pour a bit of wine over a sapphire three times and each time say, "I pour this wine, in its ardent powers, over you; just as God drew off your splendor, wayward angel, so may you draw away from me the lust of this ardent man." If the woman is unwilling to do this, then another person for whom that love is a problem should do it for her. He should give the wine to the man to drink for three or more days, whether he's eating or not, and whether he knows about it or not. If a woman burns with love for some man, and this is an annoyance to the man, he should do the same thing with the sapphire and the wine, and the burning passion will go away.

VII. SARD

Sard *(sardius)* develops after midday from an inundation of showers, when the leaves of deciduous trees fall in autumn. The sun is very hot, the air is cold, and the sun's redness warms the sard. Therefore, it is purely from air and water, and it is well balanced in a good moderation of heat. It averts adverse pestilences with its power.

If a person ails in his head from many diseases and illnesses, so that he is almost out of his mind from it, he should tie sard on top of his head, in either a hat, some cloth, or a leather sack. He should say, "Just as God threw the first angel into the abyss, so may he cut this illness from you, N., and restore good knowledge." He will be cured.

One whose hearing has been hardened through some illness should dip the sard in pure wine. When it is thus dampened, he should put it in a thin linen cloth and fasten it over the deaf ear, with a very thin string or piece of material over the cloth. The heat of the sard will enter the ear. If he does this often, he will recover his hearing.

One who has jaundice should do a similar thing, using urine and sard at night. He should say the words as described above. After doing this for three nights, he will be cured.

If a pregnant woman is oppressed by pain but unable to give birth, rub sard around both her thighs and say, "Just as you, stone, by the order of God, shone on the first angel, so you, child, come forth a shining person, who dwells with God." Immediately hold the stone at the exit for the child, that is at the female member, and say, "Open you, roads and door, in that epiphany by which Christ appeared both human and God, and opened the gates of hell. Just so, child, may you also come out from this door without dying, and without the death of your mother." Then tie the same stone in a belt, and cinch it around her, and she will be cured.

VIII. TOPAZ

Topaz *(topazius)* develops just before the ninth hour of the day, in the heat of the sun. The sun, from the day's heat and the variations of air, is then its purest. Topaz is hot and has a bit of air and water in it. It is clear, and that clarity is similar to water. Its color is more like gold than yellow. It resists heat and poison, and does not tolerate them, just as the sea is unable to bear any depravities in it.

If poison is present in bread, meat, fish, or any food, or in water, wine, or other drink, and there is topaz nearby, it will immediately sweat, just as the sea foams when there is filth in it. Therefore, when a person eats and drinks, he should hold his finger, with a topaz on it, next to the food and drink. He should frequently look at it. If there is anything poisonous in the food or drink, it will immediately sweat.

One whose vision is obscured should put topaz in pure wine for three days and nights. Then, at night when he goes to bed, he should rub his eyes with that topaz, so moistened. The liquid should touch the inside of his eyes a little bit. When the stone has been removed from the wine, it is possible to keep that wine for five days. Then, as often as he wishes to streak his eyes at night, he should dip the same stone in that wine and rub it, so moistened, around his eyes. He should do this often, always renewing the wine with the topaz after five days. Just as the best eye salve, it will clarify the eyes.

If a person has fevers, he should make with topaz three moderately sized trenches in soft bread, and pour pure wine in them. If the wine disappears, he should pour in more wine. He should look at his face in the wine which he poured into the trenches, as if he's looking in a mirror. He should say, "I look at myself, just as the cherubim and seraphim look at God in a mirror, so that these fevers might be cast from me." He should do this often, and he will be cured.

One who is leprous should heat a tile well, and place oat chaff on it, so that it smokes. He should hold the topaz over the smoke, so that it sweats, then smear the sweat over the leprous place. When he has done this, he should take olive oil and mix with it a third part of the juice of violets. He should rub it on the place which had been moistened with the topaz sweat. If he does this often the lesions will be broken, and the person will be better, unless he dies.

One who ails in his spleen or who has rotten matter inside himself, as if he is rotting internally, should place topaz in straight morach (wine) for five days. Then he should remove the topaz and boil the wine so that it steams. He should hold the topaz over the steam, so that it sweats and its sweat mixes with the wine. Then he should place the stone in the warm wine for a little while. Then he should take it out and prepare, without lard, a broth or beverage from that wine. He should do this often and sip it. His spleen will be healed, and his interior rot will diminish.

Also, every day, in the morning, place topaz over your heart and say, "May God, who is magnified above all things and in all ways, not reject me from his honor, but may he preserve, strengthen, and establish me with his blessing." For as long as you do this, evil will abhor you. The very strong topaz stone has in it this virtue from God: Because it grows while the sun is sinking, it deflects assaults from a person.

IX. CHRYSOLITE

Chrysolite *(chrysolithus)* develops from the heat of the sun and the humidity of the air, after noon, at the ninth hour of the day. It is almost as if it contains living strength. If it is near when the offspring of a sheep or other beast is born, its strength fortifies the animal so that it begins to move sooner than usual.

A person who has fever should heat up some wine and hold chrysolite over the vapor of that wine. Its sweat should be mixed with the wine, and he should drink the warmed wine. He should also place the chrysolite in his mouth for a little while. If he does this ofen, he will be well.

One who ails in his heart should dip chrysolite in olive oil and then smear it over the place that hurts, and he will be better.

This stone strengthens knowledge in a person who always carries it with him. One with good knowledge and skill should place this stone over his heart. As long as it lies there, his knowledge and skill shall not fail him. Chrysolite has the powers which are in the day's seven hours. Airy spirits shrink back from this stone a bit.

X. JASPER

Jasper *(jaspis)* develops when the sun is beginning to set, after the ninth hour of the day, and it is warmed by the fire of the sun. It is more from air than from water or fire. It has a varying heat because, when the sun is and setting, its heat is often in a cloud.

A person who is deaf should hold a jasper to his mouth and breathe on it with his warm breath, so that it becomes warm and moist. Then he should put it in his ear, and place thin fabric over the stone, thus closing the ear, until its heat transfers to the ear. This stone develops from fresh air, so it breaks up various illnesses of the humors, and the person recovers his hearing.

One who has thick nasal discharge should put jasper near his mouth and breathe on it with his warm breath, so that it becomes warm and moist. Then he should set it in his nostril and press his nose with his hand. This makes its heat enter his head, so the humors in his head are loosened more quickly and gently, and he will be better.

The person in whom commotions of the humors, that is gicht, are rising, whether in his heart, kidneys, or any other bodily part, should place jasper on that area, and press until that area warms up. The torment will cease, since the good heat and strength of the jasper heals and calms humors which are too hot or too cold.

When thunder and lightning appear in dreams, it is good for a person to have jasper with him. Phantasms and menaces are dispersed and disappear.

When a woman brings forth an infant, from the time she gives birth through all the days of its infancy, she should keep a jasper on her hand. Malign spirits of the air will be much less able to harm her or the child. The tongue of the ancient serpent stretches out toward the sweat of the infant as it emerges from its mother's vulva. At that time he is trying to ensnare the child as well as the mother. Also, if a serpent sends out its breath in any spot, place a jasper there. The breath will be weakened, so that it will be less harmful, and the serpent will stop breathing in that place.

XI. PRASINE

Prasine *(prasius)* develops around eventide, when the sun withdraws its rays from the upper parts of the earth, and when the dew is approaching. The sun gradually falls over the stone of the mountain and heats it up greatly. From the heat of the sun, the humidity of the air and water, and the vigor of the dew, the prasine is born.

One who has a burning fever should roll a prasine in a bit of rye bread dough, and tie it with a cloth. For three days and nights he should keep it tied over his umbilicus, and the fever will go from him.

But, if someone is bruised on any part of his body from a blow or a fall, he should take old fat, and mix with it equal amounts of sage and tansy. He should press prasine into it, then heat it in the sun or near the fire. Then he should place all this, with the stone, so heated, over the place where it hurts, and it will be better.

XII. CHALCEDONY

Chalcedony *(calcedonius)* develops when it is past eventide, when the sun is almost gone and the air is still a bit warm. It draws its heat more from the air than from the sun, and it has good powers. If a person carries this stone, and he always has it with him, touching his skin, so that it is placed over a vein, the vein and its blood will receive its heat and strength and carry these to the other veins and the rest of the blood. That stone turns infirmities away from a human being and gives him a mind which is very strong against wrath. He will be so tranquil in his ways that almost no one will be able to find a way to provoke him to wrath which is justified or harm him unjustly.

One who wishes to have a consistent way of speaking, and to bring forth wisely the things he says, should hold chalcedony in his hand. He should warm it with his breath, so that it becomes moist. He should then lick it with his tongue, and he will be able to speak more firmly to people.

XIII. CHRYSOPRASE

Chrysoprase *(chrysoprasus)* develops at the hour when the sun is totally withdrawn. Then the air and water are very turbid and colored green. When the moon receives the strongest power from the sun—that is when it is not yet full, but middle-sized, this stone has nocturnal power. Its great strengths have temperate and balanced heat, so that it is not too hot.

On whatever part of the body gicht is afflicting a person, he should place chrysoprase there, on his bare skin, and the gicht will cease.

If a person is very enraged, chrysoprase should be placed near his throat until it warms up. He will be unable to bring forth wrathful words while his ire is quieted.

Wherever this stone is, any death-bearing poison loses its strength, becoming powerless and as weak as water. It loses heat in its debility, becoming less noxious.

A person who has epilepsy should always have chrysoprase with him and that nocturnal disease will harm him less. The airy spirits around him will be unable to prepare their mockery, and the one suffering will expel the foam from his mouth.

For a person possessed by the devil, pour water over chrysoprase, and say, "O water, I pour you over this stone in that power by which God made the sun as well as the hastening moon." Give that water as a drink to the one possessed, in whatever way you are able, since he will be unwilling to drink it. For a whole day the devil will be tortured within him, will become weaker, and will not be able to manifest his powers in him, as he had done before. Do this for five days. On the fifth day prepare a bit of bread, with the same water poured over it, and give it to him to eat in whatever way you can. If the demon is not fierce, he will depart from that person.

Airy demons can be distinguished as gentle or bitter in the following way: If the person laughs readily and looks at people kindly while gnashing his teeth, the airy spirit is gentle. If the person speaks unwillingly, is willfully mute, and does not laugh readily, and if he strongly arches his hands and spits foam from his mouth, it is a bitter and fierce demon. Chrysoprase is not much use in expelling a bitter demon, but will torture the bitter and fierce demon in the person, making it weak, and the demon will be expelled in some way, when God wishes.

XIV. Carbuncle

Carbuncle *(carbunculus)* develops during an eclipse of the moon. Then the moon is weary and wishes to fade, as sometimes it shows itself failing when, by divine order, it shows that there will be famine, plague, or changes of kingdoms. At that time, the sun sinks all its powers into the firmament. It places its tongue in the other's mouth, so that it may resuscitate that which had died. It warms the moon with its heat, arousing and sustaining it with its fire, making the moon shine again. Carbuncle is born at this time. It has splendor from the sun's heat, while it enlarges the moon, so it shines more at night than during the day. It grows until the sun's heat casts it out. Since an eclipse of the moon is rare, this stone is rare. Its strength is unusual, and it should be feared and used with much reverence and concern.

If any illness has invaded a person, changing his humors, place a carbuncle on the sick person's umbilicus at midnight. Its strength then is particularly vigorous. As soon as the person either feels himself warmed by the stone or feels the slightest motion in his body, remove the carbuncle from him. If you permit it to lie on his umbilicus any longer, its power will penetrate his whole body, drying it up. More than is possible for any unguent, its heat will have penetrated the person and all his internal organs. And so, this stone checks and dispels from humans any disease.

If someone's head is ailing, place a carbuncle on the top of his head for a short time. When the flesh heats up, immediately take the stone away. The strength of the stone will penetrate his head better and more quickly than the most precious ointment or balsam. And so, his head will be better.

If you place this stone in clothing or any other thing, it will last longer and decay with difficulty. And, wherever there is a carbuncle, the airy spirits are unable to bring their phantasms to completion. They flee this stone, and turn away from it.

XV. Amethyst

Amethyst *(amethystus)* develops when the sun shows its circle, as though it were crowned, which it does when it prefigures some change in the vestment of the Lord, in the Church. Amethyst grows as a gum, and so there are many of them. It is hot and fiery and a bit airy, since the air is a bit cool when the sun shows its circle, as described.

A person who has spots on his face should dampen an amethyst with his saliva and rub it over his spots. Also, he should heat water over a fire and hold that stone over the water. The sweat coming out of it should be mixed with the water. Then he should place the stone in the water and wash his face with the water. If he does this often, his face will have smooth skin and beautiful color.

If a fresh tumor is swelling on one's body, he should dampen the amethyst with his saliva and touch the tumor all over with it. The tumor will grow smaller and disappear.

Pass that stone over the place where a spider has pierced a person's flesh, and it will be cured. Also, the serpent and adder flee this stone and avoid the place where they know amethysts to be.

XVI. AGATE

Agate *(achates)* is born from certain sand of water which extends from the east to the south. It is hot and fiery, but has greater power from the air and water than from fire. When the water abates, uncovering the sand, a certain area of the sand is suffused with the heat of the sun and the purity of the air, so that the stone begins to gleam. Abundant waters then flood over, lift the stone from the sand, and carry it to other lands.

If a spider or any other vermin pours its poison on a person, one may ensure it not enter his body by making an agate very hot, either in the sun or on a hot tile. Placing it on the painful spot will take away the poison. The person should again heat it in the same way and hold it over the steam of hot water, so that its sweat mixes with the water. He should then place the stone in the water for a little while and afterward dip a linen cloth in the water. With this cloth, he should cover the place where the spider bit, or where other poison was poured, and it will be healed.

If someone carries an agate with him, he should place it next to his bare skin, thus warming it. Its nature will make this person capable, judicious, and prudent in speech, because it is born from fire and air and water. Just as some bad herb, placed on a person's skin, sometimes makes a pustule or ulcer rise up, some precious stones, placed on his skin, make him healthy and sensible by their virtue.

A person who has epilepsy or is a lunatic will be better if he always has an agate next to his skin. People are often born with these infirmities; they even attract them from a superfluity of bad humors and pestilence. When the moon is full, an epileptic should place agate in water for three days. On the fourth day he should take it out and heat the water gently, so that it does not boil. He should save this and use it to cook all the food he eats while the moon is waning. He should also place agate in whatever he drinks during this time, whether wine or water. He should do this for ten months, and he will be cured, unless God is unwilling.

Also, a lunatic, when he knows his illness is impending, should, three days before, place this stone in water. On the fourth day, he should take it out and gently heat that water. He should cook in it all the foods which he will eat while he is in his senseless state. He should also put the stone in all the beverages he drinks. If he does this for five months, he will recover his sense and good health, unless God forbids it. He will be resuscitated by the virtue of this stone in gently heated water. Lest he be injured by the heat of this stone, his foods should be prepared with this water and his drinks prepared in the way described. By their moderation, and by the power of God, the humors which brought insanity to him will be sedated.

Also, every night before a person goes to bed, he should carry a clearly visible agate through the length and then the width of the house, in the pattern of a cross. Thieves are then less able to exercise their wills and so profit less in thievery.

XVII. DIAMOND

Diamond *(adamas)* is hot. It is born from mountains of southern shores, which are like glue and glassy as crystal. Like a heart of great strength, a lump arises from the viscous matter. It is so strong and hard that, before it becomes large, it splits from the mountain's viscous matter and falls into water, in the shape and size of a chrysolite, leaving the viscous area weaker than it was before. Then, when an inundation of rivers surges up, it carries that stone to other lands.

Certain people are malicious, either by nature or because of the devil, and express nothing willingly. When they speak they have a harsh look, and at times they nearly go out of their mind, as if propelled by madness. They then quickly return to themselves. These people should often, or indeed always, place a diamond in their mouth. It is of such virtue and of such great strength that it extinguishes the malice and evil in them. But, one who is frenetic, a liar, or wrathful should always keep a diamond in his mouth. By its power are these evils dispelled.

One who is unable to fast should place this stone in his mouth. It will diminish his hunger, enabling him to fast for a longer period.

One who is vexed by palsy or has apoplexy, the disease which takes hold of the middle of the body so that it is unable to move, should place diamond in wine or water for a full day and drink it. The gicht will cease, even if it is so strong that his limbs threaten to break, and the apoplexy will diminish. Also, one with jaundice should put this stone in wine or water and drink it, and he will be cured.

Diamond is of such great hardness that no other hardness is able to overcome it. It scratches and bores through iron. Neither iron nor steel is able to cut into its hardness. It is so strong that it neither gives way nor breaks before cutting into steel. Because this stone withstands his power, the devil is hostile to diamond, and so, at night as well as during the day, the devil disdains it.

XVIII. MAGNESIAN STONE OR MAGNET

Magnesian stone *(magnes)* is hot. It is born from the spume of certain poisonous worms that inhabit particular sand and water, but are in sand more than water. One kind of poisonous, sluglike worm lives around particular water and dwells in it. It sometimes ejects its spume onto land in a certain area where iron is customarily forged. When another venomous worm, living around and in that water or feeding on the earth where the iron is made, sees it, he runs eagerly to that spume. He pours out his poison, which is black, on the other worm's spume. The poison forcefully penetrates it, hardening it into stone. And so, Magnesian stone has the color of iron and naturally pulls iron after it, because it is coagulated by poison nourished by earth which produces iron. The water next to which the stone lies attenuates and diminishes most of the poison by washing over it in frequent inundation.

If a person is mad or in any way tortured by phantasms, smear the Magnesian stone with his saliva, then rub the top of his head and his forehead with the stone, and say, "You, raging evil, cede to that virtue by which God changed the strength of the devil who fell from heaven to human goodness." He will recover his senses. The fire of this stone is both useful and harmful: the fire it has from the iron-bearing earth is useful; the fire it has from the poison of the worms is harmful. When stirred up by warm, salubrious human saliva, it overthrows the noxious humors that disturb human understanding.

XIX. LIGURE

Ligure *(ligurius)* is hot. It is born from particular, but not all, urine of the lynx. The lynx is not a lascivious, libidinous, or unclean animal, but is even-tempered. Having such great power that it even penetrates stones, the lynx has sharp vision, which is rarely obscured. Ligure is not always born from its urine, but only when the sun is very hot and the breeze is light, gentle, and well moderated. This animal sometimes rejoices because of the heat and purity of the sun and the gentleness of the beautiful breeze. When it then emits urine, it digs up the earth with its foot and releases its urine into the hole. The ligure coagulates and develops in the sun's heat. Both the purity of the sun and gentle breeze, which touched and suffused this animal, and the happy mind of the lynx warm up this powerful urine, which when released congeals into this stone. This coagulation of stone in earth is more delicate than other stones.

A person who suffers greatly in his stomach should put ligure in wine, beer, or water for a little while and then remove it. The liquid will be suffused with the powers of this stone, thus receiving its powers. He should do this for fifteen days. Give it to him to drink in moderation, when he has eaten a little, but not while he is fasting. No fever or disease shall be powerful in his stomach. Rather, it will be purged, purified, and healed, unless death is present. No one else should drink this potion for any reason except stomach pain. He would not be able to live, since its power is so great as to damage his heart and split his head.

But one who is constricted by difficult urination, so that he is unable to make urine, should place ligure in milk for one day. It should be cow or sheep, but not goat, milk. On the second day he should take it out, warm the milk, and then sip it. He should repeat this for five days, and the urine in him will loosen.

XX. CRYSTAL

Crystal *(crystallus)* is born from certain cold waters, which are nearly black. Cold congeals it into a lump, when air has touched that water in some place. It coagulates into a solid, as if it were the heart of water. Then the heat of the air or sun touches it, bringing to the mass the thick whiteness which it now has. It now becomes somewhat pure and cannot be dissolved by heat. The cold again comes over the mass and makes it coagulate even more, and it becomes purer. It is of such great strength that heat cannot dissolve it, even though all the ice around it melts. And so, crystal emerges.

One whose eyes are blurry should heat crystal in the sun and place it often, so heated, over his eyes. Because it is of a watery nature, it draws bad humors from the eyes, which improves the vision.

If swellings or scrofula grow on someone's neck, he should heat a crystal in the sun and tie it over the place for a day or night. If he does this often, they will vanish. If the uvula enlarges or swells in the throat, one should heat crystal in the sun and pour wine over it. He should drink it frequently and often put the sun-warmed crystal to his throat over the uvula, and it will grow smaller.

If he ails in his heart, stomach, or belly, he should heat the crystal in the sun and pour water over it, leaving the crystal in the water for a little while. Then he should take it out and frequently drink the water. His heart, stomach, or belly will be better.

One who is troubled by *nesseden* should heat the crystal in the sun and place it so warmed on the place that hurts. The n*essia* will be chased away.

XXI. PEARLS

Pearls *(margaritae)* are born in certain salty river waters. The richness of these rivers falls, with saltiness, onto sand, so that the upper area of the water is purified. The richness congeals with the saltiness into pearls, and these pearls are pure.

Take these pearls and place them in water. All the slime in the water will gather around the pearls, and the top of the water will be purified and cleansed. A person who has fever should frequently drink the top of this water, and he will be better. One who ails in the head should heat pearls in the sun. He should place them around his temples, tying them with a cloth, and he will be cured.

XXII. MOTHER-OF-PEARL

Mother-of-pearl *(berlin)* comes from certain animals which lie in shells, and live in the sea and in certain large rivers. Some of these shell animals live at the bottom of these rivers and seek their food there. They draw into themselves some of the poisonous matter and the filth from the river bottom. When they spew this out, mother-of-pearl congeals from the poison. It is sometimes clouded, since these animals dwell at the water's bottom, and has practically no usefulness.

Certain of these shell animals are accustomed to dwell in the middle of these rivers, where the waters are pure. There the animals draw into themselves less dirt, but this includes a tiny bit of poison. The mother-of-pearl which comes from the waters these animals draw into themselves, and from the poison they spew out, becomes lucid, since there is some purity in these middle waters. Nevertheless, mother-of-pearl has no use in medicine, except for the more lucid ones, which have less poison than others.

Certain shell animals live near the surface of these rivers, where much foam and filth flows. Some mother-of-pearl is congealed with the poison of these animals, from the surface water's foam and filth. Even this type is a bit clouded, since it comes from the foam gathered with the dirt. It is not valuable as medicine, since it brings people more illness than good health.

If a person should place a piece in his mouth, he would attract such weakness to himself, and he would be as sick as if he had consumed poison. If he should place it on his skin, warming the flesh, he would draw its poison into himself. In this way, he would become weak and sick.

XXIII. CARNELIAN

Carnelian *(cornelion)* is more from hot air than from cold and is found in the sand. If blood flows from someone's nose, one should heat wine, place carnelian in it, and give it to him to drink. The blood will cease to flow.

XXIV. ALABASTER

Alabaster *(alabastrum)* has in it neither correct heat nor correct cold, but is tepid in both. Medicine is scarcely found in it.

XXV. LIMESTONE

Limestone *(calx)* is hot. When it is burned, lime, which is also hot, is made from it. When limestone is reduced to a powder by fire, it is strengthened, and with its fire it glues together earth and sand. But, if a person or animal should eat limestone, its powerful heat would weaken him and make him sick.

A person whom a worm is eating in some place should take lime and twice as much chalk and, with wine or water, make a thin cement. With a feather, he should apply it to the place where he suffers from the worm. He should do this every day, until the fifth day. Then he should take aloe and a third as much myrrh, crush them together, and with this and fresh wax prepare a plaster. It should be put on a hempen cloth and tied on the place of the distress for twelve days. Lime is hot, and chalk is cold. So the heat of the lime and the cold of the chalk, tempered by the heat and sharpness of the wine, will kill the worms. The heat of the aloe augments the myrrh. It draws the rotten matter out of the wounds and heals the area.

XXVI. OTHER STONES

Other stones *(ceteri lapides)* arise from a variety of earth and from various regions. From the lands in which they are born they draw into themselves diverse natures and varying colors. Among these are marble, sandstone, limestone *(calckstein)*, tufaceous limestone, and wacke. They are not very valuable as medicine, because they possess too much moisture, which is not balanced by correct dryness, or too much dryness, which is not moistened by correct humidity.

BOOK FIVE
Fish

CERTAIN FISH LIVE NATURALLY AT THE BOTTOM of the sea and rivers. They furrow the sea bottom, just as pigs furrow the earth, and there they eat roots of certain plants. They live a long time on these and other suitable foods which they seek out. They sometimes ascend almost to the middle of those waters and sometimes go down to the bottom, where they dwell. Their flesh is somewhat soft and flexible and, since they live at the bottom of waters, they are not good to eat. Some love the day and the splendor of the sun more than they like the night or the shining moon. Others love the night and the splendor of the moon more than daytime and sunshine. Certain fish pour out all their seed in a line, emptying all their roe and milt before stopping the effusion. Then, having hurried this pouring forth, they are a bit debilitated. Others keep intervals between their effusions, waiting until they are strengthened before again pouring forth. They pour forth their roe from March to autumn.

Other fish live especially in the purity of midsea or midriver, where they seek their food. They also eat very healthful plants which they find on prominent crags, such plants are so healthful that, if a person were able to ingest them, they would dispel any infirmity. These fish are healthful to eat, and their flesh is somewhat firm, since they are found in pure water. Sometimes they descend to the bottom, other times they ascend higher, but they are mostly in the middle of the rivers. Among these, there are smaller fish which dwell around the sea bottom. Some like the day and sun more than the night or moon. Others like the night and moon more than the day or sun. Some pour out all their roe before they stop, and therefrom, are a bit debilitated. Others keep intervals for this effusion, so they are strengthened for this work, as was said about the forenamed fish.

Still other fish customarily dwell around the surface of the sea and rivers. They seek their food in the foam and the great filth of the surface. More than others, they are suffused by the heat of the sun. Sometimes they hide in little caves, which contain fetid water that cannot flow out. Therefore, their flesh is soft and flexible and not healthful to eat. These fish descend a bit into the waters and are accustomed to live near shore. Some like the day and sun more than the night and moon. Others like the moon and night more. Indeed, certain of them pour out all their roe before they rest. Thence they become a bit weak. Others keep an interval in this work and recover their powers, as was said about the others.

All fish, according to their kind, eat plants suitable for them throughout the winter, and sometimes in the summer, whence the milt and the roe increase in them, which they gently bring forth. So, if a person, namely a woman who is infertile, should eat some of it, she will become fecund and conceive. These fish do not engage in coitus. But roe or milt is produced in them, and the desire they have for merely pouring it forth is as great as that which other animals have for coitus. Each one seeks a mate suitable for itself. When it is time for their effusion, they seek a place near the shore, where neither winds nor storms are able to harm them, but where the water has good, quiet, and tranquil constitution, and where the plants on which they feed are growing. Then the female fish proceeds in a straight line until, in accordance with her nature, she leaves off this effusion. Where she ends this outflowing, the male fish waits, ready to come in. The male then follows, pouring his milt in measure on the line of roe, where the female had preceded him. When he reaches her, he stops pouring forth his milt. Emptied, tired, and somewhat weak, they seek a quiet spot for themselves nearby, where they eat vegetation while recovering their strength.

From the time the seed is poured out until the time the little fish begin to grow, many sudden and diverse qualities and discomforts of the air come upon them. Many times, before the little fish have begun to live, the effusions of the fish are broken up by flood of rains or storms, or by ships. They do not come to completion and perish. If a person eats this effusion of the fish, it is almost like poison. Nets must be washed very carefully, lest it adhere to them, and care must be taken to not pull it up while catching fish. Since the fish are very fatigued after pouring forth their seed, they become weaker, as said above. Then their flesh is not healthful for humans to eat, as it is at other times. After the little fish which are poured out together have grown, they pour forth their seed in a similar manner. Should some be caught, the remaining ones seek others their own age.

And certain fish, as already said, are delighted by the day's clarity and the sun's brightness, and in them seek their food. Others are pleased by the night and the splendor of the moon and the stars, and seek their food then, since they consider the temperature of the water better at night than during the day. Just as a human forsakes his nature by mixing himself with animals, so even animals bring forth a different kind by mixing together. Sometimes fish turn away from their own kind in pouring out their seed onto another kind, producing a variety foreign to their nature, as we can notice in eels and other fish.

God has given certain knowledge to particular fish, according to their nature and kind, so that they recognize certain plants and roots in the water on which they can feed at times when they have no other food. Once they have recognized or tasted the strength or nature of these, they do not need food for four months to half a year, and their flesh does not become weak or diminished. Later, when they are hungry, if they have no other foods, they are again sustained by these plants and roots for a long time. If the human being were to know and recognize these plants and roots, and if he could have and eat them now and then, he would be able to exist for four or five months without other foods, after he had tasted them once. But his flesh would become hard and twisted, and not be as soft as it now is. When Adam was expelled from paradise, he recognized these plants and sought them in the water. He sometimes ate them when he had no other food. When he later had other foods, he avoided them. These plants neither grow nor perish easily. When fish or beasts have eaten a bit of them, they remain, undigested, in their stomachs for a long time, since they are digested with difficulty. Animals which eat them do not suffer hunger for a long time, as they are digested with other foods which they eat later.

I. WHALE

The whale *(cete)* has fiery heat and watery air in it. It has a certain relationship to the nature of fish as well as to the nature of beasts such as the lion and the bear. It lives in water in accordance with the nature of fish and, in accordance with the nature of beasts, it grows to a large size. It does not shun the human being, but, if beasts were able live in water and grow to an abnormal size, a human would not be able to stay in the water for horror of them. Both day and night, whales seek out the surface and the bottom of the sea. They feed on foods of fish as well as food of beasts, and they even eat fish. If the fish in the sea were not eaten and devoured, and so diminished, the multitude of fish would leave no passageway in the sea. When the whale has gulped down a lot, he is so thickened and fattened that he is scarcely able to move from place to place. Then he lifts himself up a bit and emits a spume from his mouth, spitting out a bit of what he has eaten, and in this way alleviating himself. When he has felt himself move, he gradually moves himself from place to place, thus losing his thickness and fatness a bit and becoming lighter. Then he rejoices, because it is possible to move. In his high spirit, he moves himself this way and that. Whatever then comes into his path he devastates and devours in a fury. Nevertheless, people very cleverly capture him at this time by snares.

When, as described, the whale has become lightened, he seeks those plants and roots by which he is able to endure a long time without other foods. When the sun climbs up and the day lengthens, the fish, both male and female, seek that land having sap from earth which is stronger than other earth, and where the dew is falling on the plants growing there. The fish lift themselves up on that land and are suffused with the dew. Their milt begins to increase, and they go away from that place. When they later send out the milt, they endeavor that it be suffused with the sap of that earth. The female sends out her seed where this land is high, and with her fins places the earth over them. The male follows and pours his milt over. Then they seek rest there, while they take in vital air. They do this once a year. One fish comes from these seeds, and the power of this earth is so great that he begins to grow quickly. After he has begun to live, they depart.

The strength in their flesh is so great that when eaten it resists all perverse and weak humors. In creating all animals, God made certain forms in which he shows his strength. He does this in the whale, so that this fish senses the iniquities of the devil and sends out his breath against him. The flesh of this fish is healthful and good for healthy and sick people to eat. Disdaining its strength, airy spirits flee. Wherever the whale senses anything diabolic around him, he contracts his skin, shows himself dreadful, and sends out horrible blasts against that phantasm.

A person who is delerious should frequently eat a sufficient amount of this meat, with only bread in addition, and he will recover his senses. One who is virgichtiget should often eat this meat, and the gicht will cease. Its brain is not of value for eating, just as any brain—whether of fish, bird, or animal. The brain of an animal weakens and harms the person who eats it. But, cook the brain of this fish in a new clay pot, boiling it in water while stirring it well with a spoon. Then pour it into another container and pound it well. Add the plant called goutweed and some olive oil. Cook it again in the clay pot, stirring well, so making an unguent. Someone who is tormented by strong gicht, or who has ague or ulcers, should anoint himself with this, and he will be healed.

One who suddenly becomes weak in his heart should pulverize whale's heart and drink it in water, and he will be better. But one who suffers from vicht should frequently drink this same powder in wine and water, and the vicht will go from him.

One who eats some of a whale's liver purges the inside of his stomach. It takes away all interior dirt from him, just as the best purgative. In any house or place where airy spirits are accustomed to produce their mockeries, burn the liver of this fish over live coals, and they will go away. They will not be able to remain in that place because of the powerful odor.

Whosoever has diurnal, nocturnal, or mutable fevers, which change in accordance with the temperature of the air, should cook whale's lung in water. He should often eat it, and the fevers will go away. Because the lung cannot be saved all year, one should pulverize it moderately and often drink this powder in water or wine. Fevers of any kind, even if ague has raged in him, will cease. One who has eaten or drunk poison should pulverize equal amounts of the lung and liver, adding as much horehound as there is of this powder. He should add a bit of honey, cook it with pure, good wine, and drink it warm in the morning, on an empty stomach, two or three times before day. He will spew out the poison he had consumed by nausea, or it will pass through him into the privy.

Someone may save the bladder for a year, and if [an ulcer grows on a person's body, the bladder is softened in water and placed over the ulcer]. The ulcer will break, and he will be cured. But, take away the bladder after the breaking of the ulcer and, if you have scrofula on your body, make it soft again in water and place it on the scrofula, and it will vanish. If there are swollen glands on someone's body, moisten the whale bladder with your saliva and place it over them, and they will disappear.

One who ails in his liver or is weak in his lungs should cook the small intestines of this fish with hyssop in water. From these, he should make a meat jelly and eat it frequently. The pain in his liver will cease, and his lungs will recover their health.

One who is troubled by gicht should place the eyelids of this fish in wine for a night, or a day, and then heat the wine on the fire. He should drink this often, and the gicht will go from him. If one is virgichtiget in his tongue and is unable to talk, shave some of the eyelid in water, and give it to him to drink. He will speak immediately, his tongue recovering its strength. Paralysis in talking is often impeded by cold humors, but is cured by the fiery heat of these eyelids.

Also, make a knife handle from the bone of this fish. Hold that handle in your hand until it warms up. There is no pain in your hand or arm that will not cease.

If cows, sheep, or pigs are dying from a pestilence, pulverize the bones of this fish and toss this powder into water. Give this frequently to them to drink, and the sickness will go from them.

Make shoes from whale skin and put them on. You will have healthy feet and legs. Also, make a belt from this skin. Gird yourself with it against your bare skin. Various infirmities will flee from you, and it will make you strong.

II. STURGEON

Sturgeon *(huso)* is more from hot air than from cold. It loves the nocturnal splendor of the moon and stars, and the night more than the day. It rests during the day. It grows in briskly moving waters, and loves them. It works so hard in swimming in them that its flesh becomes soft from the labor. It swims in the middle of the water, rarely seeking the bottom. It feeds on clean food, and therefore its flesh is good for healthy people to eat, though it harms sick people a bit.

It spawns as other fish. A person in whom dropsy is increasing should place the bladder of a sturgeon in water, so that the water takes its flavor. He should drink this frequently, and the dropsy will be lessened and disappear. The bladder of this fish is watery, harsh, and a bit bitter. When it is moderated by the smoothness of the water, it diminishes disease.

III. SEAL

The seal *(merswin)* is more from hot air than from cold. It has the nature of fish, and nearly that of pigs. It likes night more than day, and dwells willingly in caverns under the water. Sometimes it rises above the water. At times it eats unclean foods, and human flesh from people who have drowned, and the dirty foam which floats on the water. Therefore its flesh is not good for a person to eat. Both the male and the female eat certain plants, from which they become fecund. When it is time to release their spawn, the male and female join their necks together and rub, so they both warm up. Then the female sends out her seed. The male, seeing it, devours it. The female is indignant and releases another seed, lies over it, and rests. The male soon comes and sends out milt from his mouth, along with that which he had devoured. So, they both pour forth spawn and remain there until there is a beginning of life. There will be one fish. After it takes in vital air, they proceed to act in a similar fashion, since they send out all their spawn at one time.

A person who is virgichtiget should pulverize equal weights of the seal's liver and lung. He should put this powder in water and drink it often. The gicht will cease. The other parts of the seal are not of much value as medicine.

IV. TURBOT

Turbot *(storo)* is more cold than hot, and is more busy in the day than in the night. It seeks plants and roots at the bottom of waters, by which it is able to live for a long time with no other food. It freely moves back and forth in the water. It has healthy flesh, which does not harm a healthy person who eats it. It makes weak people a bit ill, since it is too strong. When the spawn ought to increase in it, it rises up above the water, and the dew from the air falls on it. Then the male as well as the female eat certain plants similar to clover and become fecund. When the time is right to spawn, it seeks certain black earth, and there sends out seed, over which the male pours nothing. This seed will be one fish. They rest next to the seed, until it takes in vital air. After it becomes alive, they go forth again and spawn with other seeds, and so on, until they have sent out all their spawn.

A person whom vicht troubles should frequently eat a sufficient amount of the liver of this fish. The vicht in him will cease. One whose flesh is swelling up around the eyes, or whose eyes are clouded, should take some bile of this fish and mix it with an equal amount of juice from rue, and less of chamomile, storing it in a copper jar. Rubbing it often above his eyes at night will cure his eyes, and he will see clearly, the cloudiness chased away. Also, if turbot bones are burned in a house, airy spirits will avoid it and not make their illusions there. Just as a person flees a fetid odor, so evil spirits flee this, since they do not like a clean animal.

V. SALMON

Salmon *(salmo)* is more from cold air than hot. It is more active in the night than during the day and likes the moon more than the sun. When the moon appears, it swims very much in its brightness, just as if it were the splendor of the sun. And so, its flesh is a bit like the moon and is soft and weak. It is not good for any person to eat, because it stirs up all the bad humors in a person. It seeks the bottom of waters, eating plants and roots there, which enable it to be sustained for a long time without other foods. It also eats the seed that grows on grain, which falls in the water. It takes its fecundity from that, and when it spawns, it seeks land. There it sends out its roe, and the male pours its milt over. From these seeds, one little fish is made. And so the salmon continue, until they are emptied of all their spawn. That is, they pour out at one time their spawn/milt at various places, and they rest there until (the little fish) take life from the air.

A person whose gums are rotting and whose teeth are weak and fragile should pulverize salmon bones and add a little roasted salt. He should frequently put this powder around his teeth at night and let saliva flow over his gums. It will clean and heal the flesh around his teeth. Other parts of the salmon are not of value as medicine.

VI. SHEATFISH

Sheatfish *(welca)* is more from hot air than from cold. It likes the day more than the night. It feeds on grain that falls into the water and on other good plants. It has healthy flesh and is good for sick as well as healthy people to eat. It spawns like other fish. A person whose eyes are cloudy should take its bile and add a bit of fennel juice and a few drops of wine. When they are mixed together, he should rub it around his eyes, gently, being careful that it not touch the eyes, and it will chase away the cloudiness from his eyes. And, if one eats its liver, cooked, it will collect all the mucus and poison in his stomach and draw it to itself. These get thrown off, with it, into the privy, and his stomach will be healed. Its heart, however, has no value either for eating or as medicine. It harms a person who eats it. Other parts of the sheatfish are of no value as medicine.

VII. PIKE

Pike *(lasz)* is more from hot air than from cold. It loves the day. It does not seek the bottom of waters, but looks for its food in the middle of the water, and for plants growing in certain muds and eats these. Its flesh is more healthful than that of the salmon. It is good for healthy people to eat, though it troubles sick people a bit. Because this fish is from hot air, its flesh is good for healthy people, who are warm, but is not of value for ill people, who are cold. It spawns as other fish. Its liver is soft and harms a human being. Other parts of it are not of much use.

VIII. COPPREA

Copprea is more from cold than from warm air. It likes the day and dwells always in fresh, cold water, near the bottom. It delights in clear waters, draws near to them, and seeks healthy foods there. Eating its flesh does not harm healthy people. Sick people can eat it in moderation, since it is from cold air. However, no one should eat its liver, unless it is jellied with dill and fennel, and then eaten. Its roe and milt are edible. They are a bit like the plants from which they take their fecundity—cattail. When its time is at hand, the female seeks mud and there sends out seed, from which there will be one fish. The male pours its milt over it and stays next to it until it takes in life from the air. They continue, and spawn as described, until both are emptied out.

If a person is hopeless—that is, he has a spirit that endures disagreeable things without desiring their termination—he should set the eye of this fish in a gold or silver ring, so that the eye touches the skin of the finger, and the skin is heated by that eye. He should also frequently put it near his mouth, and his understanding will awaken. If this eye is not able to last a long time in this ring, replace it with a fresh fish eye.

IX. NORTHERN PIKE

Northern pike *(hecht)* is more from hot air than from cold. It lives willingly in clearness, in the middle of waters, likes the day, and is fierce, like forest beasts. Wherever it dwells, it eats fish and empties those waters of other fish. It seeks clean food, and has hard, healthy flesh. It is good for sick as well as healthy people to eat and has a moderately tempered heat, so its flesh is healthy. The males and females eat certain plants which make their spawn grow, and they send it out, as other fish. If a person often eats this fish's liver, it gives him good, smooth digestion. If a worm is eating a person or an animal, pulverize the bones of this fish and put the powder over the place, and the worms will die.

X. EUROPEAN CATFISH

European catfish *(barbo)* is from hot air more than cold. It likes daytime and willingly holds its heat. When it feels something cold, it enters certain caves, in order to retain heat. It willingly chooses being in the sun, especially basking in it, so its flesh is soft and tender. It dwells in the middle of the water and seeks clean food. As other fish, it exposes its seed, which are spawned from certain herbs. In this endeavor it works especially hard, spawning quite diligently. It spawns in many places at a single time before stopping. If a healthy person eats it often, it gives him neither healthy flesh nor healthy blood. If anyone eats its head frequently, it rouses a pain in his head, and causes other fevers. One should not eat its snout, since it would make one sick. The head of this fish lacks airy natural vigor and so it draws muddy poison into itself. By it, one's brain and jaws will be infected and it will harm one who eats it. Its roe is like poison, since the seed is separated from it only with difficulty, and it is more damaging than healthful food.

XI. CARP

Carp *(carpo)* is more hot than cold. It likes day more than night and has in it the heat of marshes. From these marshes, it has soft, weak flesh. It seeks out its food in the marsh, and it willingly dwells in the foam of waters. Eating its flesh does not harm a healthy person, but does some damage to a sick person. A healthy person is able to eat its milt and roe, but a sick person should not eat them. This fish sometimes swims in clear water, often basking in it. There, it even eats clean foods. It draws in the sap of certain earth, eating plants there, from which it becomes fecund. When it is time to spawn, the female seeks solid rock and spawns there all at once, with the male following after. Unless driven away, they stay there for the vital air, in the same way other fish do.

A person who has a fever, so that he loathes eating and disdains food, should cook this fish. He should remove the head, then cut it in half. He should roast it on a spit on the fire, then place it in wine, and to this he should add a third part vinegar, pouring in a bit of honey. He should eat it, so prepared, often. The fever will cease, and he will set aside his loathing of eating. Other parts of the fish have not much value as medicine.

XII. SEA BREAM

Sea bream *(bresma)* is more hot than cold, and it has some sap of earth in it. It chooses to live at the bottom of waters, and it sometimes eats earth. Sea bream loves the night and basks in the moon's splendor. It is not much good for healthy or ill people to eat, but they can survive it. Around land this fish seeks out certain leaves of plants similar to thornbushes and eats them. From these they become fecund and, when their time arrives, they spawn. The male pours milt over it, and they watch it until it takes life from the air.

A person whose stomach is sick should cook this fish in water and preserve it in vinegar, with cumin added. He should eat this meat jelly, and mucus and fever will be purged from his stomach.

XIII. ELSUA

Elsua is from cold air and loves the night. It eats certain plants on the bottom of the waters or in dungy land and is fattened by them. It also seeks clean food. After it is troubled by the dung, it ascends to a clear part of the water and bathes itself. Eating it harms neither healthy nor sick people. Next to the shore it eats brambles and a prickly plant, by which it becomes pregnant. When it wishes to spawn, it seeks a cavern, where it spawns. Then it goes to other caverns, drawing the fluid with it, and spawns again. It goes from cavern to cavern in this way until it sends out all its fluid. The male pours over it, and so the seeds receive their vital air. This fish sometimes dies in the water. When the heat of summer is great, causing storms, high winds, and floods to arise, this fish becomes very frightened and is in turmoil, because it has soft flesh. When it hears thunder, it fixes itself in the caverns, where, unable to withdraw from them, it often dies. If a person eats its liver often, his heart will be strengthened, and his stomach will be well. Other parts of this fish do not have value as medicine.

XIV. PLAICE

Plaice *(kolbo)* is hot, likes night, and lives at the bottom of waters. It feeds on unclean foods and is not much good for a healthy or sick person to eat, since its juice is weak. When it spawns, it does so completely, but sends out its seed in a little sack. The male arrives there immediately, and sends foam from his mouth over them. It adheres to the seed, until the life-giving air moves them. Since, as described, these fish are congealed in the male's foam, they have weak flesh and do not sufficiently nourish the person who eats them. On the other side of their bodies they have almost no flesh, only skin stretched over their spines. If they had flesh there, it would be poisonous to eat and would be as harmful as poison. They carry poison in their heads, and so harm any person who eats the head of this fish. Plaice is not much value as medicine.

XV. SALMON TROUT

Salmon trout *(fornha)* is more from hot air than from cold. It likes the night and dwells at the bottom of brackish waters, though it does not feed uncleanly. It has not much value as food for sick people. It does not harm healthy people and has little value as medicine.

XVI. MONUWA

Monuwa is more from cold air than from hot. It likes the day, and it happily lives in caverns and in the foam of waters. It sometimes eats unclean little worms, so its flesh is not healthful. In food, it does not benefit sick or healthy people much, even though it does not harm them. It takes seed from small plants, and sends them out in its time. It contains no medicines.

XVII. PERCH

Perch *(bersich)* is from hot more than cold air. It likes the day, dwells freely in the sunshine, and lives happily in clear waters, seeking clean food there. It sometimes enters crags, rocks, and caverns, seeking good, salubrious food to eat. Its flesh is sound and is good for healthy and sick people to eat. It spawns like other fish.

XVIII. MEYSISCH

Meysisch is from cold and very humid air. Eaten, it does little harm to healthy or sick people. But, eaten very often, it makes a bit of mucus in a person's stomach.

XIX. A FISH HAVING A SHELL

There is a kind of fish having a shell over it *(piscis conchas habente)*. It is of no value for sick or healthy people to eat. [If cattle are ill from noxious blood or from hard labor, a person should pulverize these shells, put them in water with betony, and give this to the cattle, and they will be healed.] They like the night, dwell at the water's bottom, and eat unclean foods.

XX. GRAYLING

Grayling *(ascha)* is more from cold air than from hot. It likes day and lives in the middle of the waters, even resting on rocks and mud. It feeds on grass and small plants, and its flesh is good for healthy and sick people. It spawns like other fish. A person with leucoma in his eye should take its bile and add a drop of pure wine to it. He should anoint himself with this, so that it even touches the inside of his eye a bit. If he does this often, he will be cured. Other parts of this fish are not useful as medicine.

XXI. ROACH

Roach *(rotega)* is from hot more than cold air and likes the day. It lives up in the foam of the water, and it sometimes washes itself in the middle of the waters. It eats moss and small plants growing on crags, and also that which floats in the foam on the water. It is good for healthy and sick people to eat. It spawns as do other fish that are not too big or too small.

XXII. HERRING

Herring *(allec)* is from cold air, and it has an unstable and cold nature. It likes the day and lives at the surface as well as the bottom of the water. It seeks clean food. When it is caught and still fresh, it is not good for a person to eat. It easily causes him to swell up and poisons the inside of his body. So, when fresh it is harmful for a sick or healthy person to eat. If afterward it is suffused with a great deal of salt, the poisons in it are diminished by the salt, so that it is less harmful to the one eating it. A person who is well can survive eating it in this way, but it will harm a sick person, if he eats much of it. Herring is better baked than boiled for both healthy and sick people to eat. Its roe and milt can be eaten. However, if the herring is fresh, when it is cooked and still warm from the cooking, pour unfermented wine with vinegar over it and let it soak for a little while. It will be much less harmful to eat.

A person who has incrustations on his head, small scabies on his body, or leprosy should take herring which has been suffused with salt for a long time. He should clean it in water and wash his head, or the scabies, or the place where his leprosy is with the water. After a little while, he should wash himself with hot water in the same place. On the next day he should make harsh lye from the ashes of the beech tree, and again wash the place. On the third day, he should anoint himself with goat tallow. If he does this often, in this order, his incrustation, scabies, or leprosy will be better.

XXIII. Groundling

Groundling *(crasso)* is more from hot air than from cold. It likes the day and willingly dwells where waters are gushing, near small river banks. It eats clean foods and is good for both sick and healthy people to eat. Groundling milt as other fish do.

XXIV. Chub

Chub *(hasela)* is more from hot than from cold air. It likes daytime and heat. It spends its time at the surface of the water, seeks clean foods, is good for both sick and healthy people to eat, and spawns as other fish do.

XXV. Bleak

Bleak *(blicka)* is more from hot air than from cold. It likes daytime and heat, and it willingly stays in the foam at the the water's surface. It eats clean foods and is good for healthy people to eat. People who are ill should eat only a little of it, since it has soft flesh. Bleak fish spawn as other fish do.

XXVI. Pafenduno

More from hot than from cold air, *pafenduno* likes the day and the heat. It dwells near the shore, in the foam of the water, and eats small worms and plants. Good for healthy people to eat, it is not very good for sick people. It spawns as other fish, and there is no medicine in it.

XXVII. Tench

Tench *(slya)* is from the heat of marshes and enjoys the night. It dwells around the bottom and the shore and eats more unclean than clean foods. It is of no value for healthy or sick people to eat. When it spawns, the male and female draw moss, which grows on the crags, to the opening of a little cavern. They send out foam from their mouths into the hollow behind the moss which they stay near, moving their mouths and breath toward it, until the coagulated matter receives vital air. Then they depart. In this way tench are born. Also, they are not useful as medicine.

XXVIII. Grundula

Grundula is more from moist air than from dry, and it likes the night. It lives at the surface, as well as the bottom, of waters, and even in hollows of rocks. It feeds on certain plants and other things. Although its flesh is not good to eat, healthy people can survive if they eat it. It quickly harms sick people with great upset of humors, and it stirs up all illnesses in a person. This little fish is more of a female gender than male. They rub against rocks and sand, and from there roe is blown out, which the fish receives, becoming fertile. When it flows out, it is congealed by the mucus in the foam of the water, without the male's milky matter. Then it leads the seeds, from which a little fish is made, from one place to another, so that the seeds separately receive the vital air of the water, or are coagulated. After the little fish has divided its seeds in many outpourings, as described, it does not rest near them, but goes away before they are alive. It is also of little value as medicine.

XXIX. STECHELA

Stechela (an acanthopterygian fish) is from hot air more than cold. It likes the day, eats certain plants, and has healthy flesh. Eating it harms neither healthy nor sick people. It combines the nature of perch and northern pike: At times perch send out their roe, and the northern pike, seeing the male perch about to pour his milt over the seeds, chases him off. He pours his milt over them. Then, as do other little fish, they receive their vital air from this effusion. After the perch sees that they are alive, but not of her kind, she goes away.

XXX. LOACH

Loach *(steynbisza)* is more from cold air than from hot, and also from moistness. It dwells at the bottom of rivers. Loach likes the night, eats things which are unclean, is not healthful for a person to eat, and is almost like a maggot. It is born from fish. Various fish, gathered in one place, lie together. There they make certain foams and discharges, which stick together and coagulate. Finally, receiving its vital air, and just as little worms are born from dung of a horse or cow, the loach is born. Again, it is not good for a person to eat.

XXXI. RULHEUBT

Rulheubt is from cold more than from hot air. It likes the day, dwells in the middle—and at the surface—of waters, and eats clean and unclean foods. Whatever is unclean in its food ascends to its head, increasing in its brain. Both its head and its stomach are noxious, but the rest of its body grows from clean food and can be eaten. When it spawns, it goes into a little cavern, sending its roe out here and there. The male pours a little wetness, not milt, over it. This moisture is so strong that the seeds are congealed by it. After rulheubt have poured out their seeds, they immediately depart.

XXXII. CRAWFISH

Crawfish *(cancer)* is more hot than cold; it has its heat more from earth than from air. It likes day and night, for it walks forward with the sun before its face, and backward following the moon. It has healthful flesh. A sick person, as well as a healthy one, can eat it, with the exception of one whose stomach is cold and stopped up, for he can scarcely digest the foods he has eaten, and the crawfish is too strong a food. In the head of the crawfish is a certain green matter. Take this and add a greater amount of butter to it, and knead these together. If someone has tiny pustules on his face and around his nostrils, as if pain and ulcers wish to bubble out there, he should take this and anoint himself there often, at night. When he gets out of bed in the morning, he should wash the ointment from his face with wine. He will have beautiful skin, and the ulcers will not rise up there.

XXXIII. EEL

How is the eel *(anguilla)* made? Formerly, the eel was made in another way than now. When winter will have come upon it, the female aquatic snake separates herself from the male. She rubs herself either on stones or on sand, so losing her skin. She rests this way in a hole for the winter. Then, when summer has begun, she searches for a stone and with her mouth breathes over it. Then, over that same stone, she spits seeds the size of horse beans from her mouth. She carries out this job with great desire and endeavor. She is then clean, having lost her old skin, which had poison in it. Seeing her, the male eel hurries near and she chases him, leaving the seeds which she had spat out. Soon the eel sends out from his mouth something like milk over the seeds, covers them with his tail, and writhes over them, stretching out. The female aquatic snake sees this and is indignant. She comes closer and sends many breaths under the tail of the eel. Then they both lie there, the eel protecting the seeds with his tail, and the snake blowing under his tail, until the young receive vital air. After they have begun to live, and the eel has sensed that, he and the snake flee in horror, since they have overstepped their normal nature. Thus are eels made, and there are many from one seed. Once they start germinating, a multitude of them quickly surge forth.

An eel is more from hot air than from cold. It likes the day, and it has the nature of certain worms that live in little caverns but are not unclean. It also has the nature of fish and seeks foods which are not very unclean. Nevertheless, its flesh is a little bit unclean. Like the flesh of pigs, it is not good for a healthy person to eat. It does no great harm to healthy people, but does afflict ill people with all fevers, bad humors, and every illness. It makes those who eat it bitter in mind, crafty, and evil.

But its bile is rich, and one who uses it to anoint his eyes against their cloudiness will clear them up in a short time, but later they will become much worse because of it.

XXXIV. COD

Whence cod *(alroppa)* is made: The female eel sometimes emits from her mouth a coagulation—not seeds, as from other fish—over a stone. The male eel sees this and chases away the female. He folds himself over this and warms it with his tail until it takes vital air. So cods are born. A cod is from cold more than from hot air. It likes the day, dwells in the middle of the water, and seeks more unclean than clean foods. Except for its liver, it is not good for healthy or sick people to eat. But sick as well as healthy people can eat the liver, which is useful and good.

XXXV. PUNBELEN

Whence *punbelen* is made: Together, both male and female cods emit a certain coagulation, like filth, from their mouths, then go away. That thing from them, like a maggot, takes vital air, and punbelim are born. Like the *kulheuvlchen*, their nature is to be in swamps and dust. They are not useful for medicine.

XXXVI. LAMPREY

Whence comes the lamprey *(lampreda)*: A certain serpent, when it sees the eggs of an aquatic snake, soon chases off the snake, folds itself over the eggs, and warms them. And so from those eggs lampreys are born. The lamprey is from hot more than cold air. It has the nature of fish, and it also holds the nature of serpents, since it is poisonous, and in its tail is some poison. It has only two eyes. The openings on it which look like eyes are not eyes but only blind openings. It likes the night, willingly lives in caverns and swamps, it eats unclean foods, and is bad for healthy and sick people to eat. It gives bad digestion to a person's stomach, and it stirs up tempests in all his veins.

BIRDS

BOOK SIX
Birds

As long as it is in the body, the human soul, being airy, is lifted high and sustained by air, lest it suffocate in the body. It dwells in the human body with sensitive intelligence and stability. Since birds are lifted by their feathers into the air, and since they dwell everywhere in the air, they were thus created and positioned in order that the soul, with them, might feel and know the things which should be known. And so, while the soul is in the body it extends everywhere, elevated by its thoughts. Perfection is shown in the earth's moisture, so the human being is discerned to have been complete in his formation and physical being; and the human being recognizes himself, among the trees, as corporeal. By these two things, moisture and corporality, he ought to understand that, as long as the soul is in him, he cannot be added to.

I. GRIFFIN

The griffin (*griffo*) is very hot. It has some of the nature of birds and some of the nature of beasts. Having the nature of birds, it is swift, so that the mass of its body does not weigh it down; having the nature of beasts, it eats humans. When it flies in the air, it does not fly in the burning heat, but approaches it a bit. Its flesh is not good for a human to eat. If one should eat its flesh, he would be greatly harmed by it, since it holds fully within itself the nature of beasts. In both natures, it has imperfection.

When the time is at hand for laying its eggs, the griffin seeks a cave with a wide interior but a narrow opening, so that it is very difficult to enter. Inside the cave, because of her fear of lions, the griffin guards her eggs carefully. A lion can smell them from a long way off and, if able to come near, it would trample and break them. The griffin is always on guard against the lion and, despising its strength, does not allow herself to remain near one. Nevertheless, she allows a bear to be near, since a bear is weaker than a lion. She places her eggs in such a way that neither sunshine nor wind can touch them. Neither flesh nor the eggs, nor other parts of the griffin, are much use for medicines, since in its two natures it has more deficiency than perfection.

II. OSTRICH

The ostrich *(strusz)* is very hot and has in it the nature of beasts. It has the feathers of birds, but does not fly with them, since it runs quickly, just as a beast. It dwells on land, eating on pasture lands. She is of such great heat that, if she were to keep her eggs warm herself, they would be burned up, and her young would not come forth. And so she conceals them in sand, where they are warmed by its moisture and heat. After the chicks have come out of the eggs, they run, as other chicks do, after and along with their mother.

A person with epilepsy should often eat ostrich flesh. It will furnish him with powers and take away the madness of the epilepsy. This flesh is also healthy for fat and strong people to eat. It diminishes their superfluous flesh and makes them strong. It is not good for thin or sick people, since it would be too strong a food for them.

One who is melancholic, so that he has a heaviness and listlessness of the mind, should frequently eat ostrich liver. It will diminish his melancholy and, by lightening his mind, make it pleasant and charming. [Its eggs are not good to eat, since they are poisonous. But one who has dropsy should pulverize the shells from which the chicks have emerged, and place this in water. He should drink it often, either fasting or with meals, and he will be cured.] The heart and the lungs, and other parts of the ostrich, are not good for medicines, because the ostrich does not have the complete strength of birds or beasts.

III. PEACOCK

The peacock *(pavo)* is hot and moist, and it has the nature of both birds and beasts in it. Its voice is a mixture of that of birds and that of beasts, and so it sounds. Before there was a peacock, certain small animals capriciously mingled with certain birds in coitus; whence peacocks were born. The peacock is fierce and cunning and does not seek high altitudes in its flight. The male peacock has devious, unclean habits. It sometimes mixes in coitus with small animals and little beasts. Young which they have brought forth have the shape of their mother, not their father. Some young are colored with the color of the father's feathers or crest. When the peacock sees these little animals running, he recognizes them as his children and loves them.

When the peahen lays her eggs, she hides them so the male does not see them. It is as if she were ashamed to have brought forth eggs and to have generated a chick covered with an eggshell, rather than one with bare flesh. The male hates the eggs and breaks them if he finds them. And so, the female hides her eggs and the male does not see them until the chicks have hatched. She then hides her chicks until they have grown more and can run. After they are strengthened and are able to walk, she goes with them to the male. Seeing them approach, he knows they are his chicks; he strikes them with his feathers and shows himself joyful. Still, the female segregates the chicks, moving them away from him until they are stronger, fearing he might trample them with his feet.

The male seeks a certain altitude at which he knows the air is blowing, which will quickly bring forth his feathers in great numbers and length. When he sees these, he rejoices, as beasts rejoice in their leap. Later, other air blows on the feathers. This softens them and draws them out, and he is distressed until they grow again. The female does not seek that air in order that her feathers grow, but stays, as if constrained, in lower places.

The flesh of a peacock is good for neither a healthy nor a sick person to eat. One who is healthy is able to survive it, but it stirs up and violently moves all noxious humors in a sick person. However, dry and preserve the bladder of a peacock; if an ulcer or carbuncle boils up on a person, tie this over it, and it will gently rupture. After it ruptures, place this on it again. It will draw out the rotten matter, and the person will be healed much more quickly.

IV. CRANE

The crane *(grus)* is hot and has a clean nature. It can both fly and move about on land. It flies willingly with a multitude and can very easily avoid snares. It has great strength in its neck, is straightforward and cautious, and has an alert disposition, a skill which forewarns it so no bird or beast can easily harm it. Its flesh is good for sick and healthy people to eat, but its eggs are not good to eat.

A person who is troubled by gicht should frequently eat its meat, and the gicht will cease. One who has vicht should frequently eat its liver. If a pestilence is troubling and killing pigs, pulverize the bill of a crane, and give this powder to them to eat in a mush, or to drink in water. They will be better, and the pestilence will go from them.

Also dry and save crane's blood, as well as its right foot. If any woman labors with a difficult childbirth, crush some of the dried blood in a bit of water, and rub the top of the vulva with it. Make the woman look at herself in that water mixed with blood, as if in a mirror. Tie the right foot of the stork over her umbilicus. The power in these things is so great that the closed viscera and loins will more quickly be opened for childbirth. Other parts of the crane are of no value for medicines.

v. Swan

The swan *(cyngnus)* is cold and moist. It has some of the nature of a goose, some of the nature of a duck. It bathes itself freely in water, likes water and land more than flight, and sometimes forages for unclean things in water. Its flesh is good for healthy people to eat, but is of no value for sick people. A person who is congested should cook its liver and eat it often. It will take the rotten matter from his lungs, and he will be cured. One who ails in his spleen should often cook and eat the lung of the swan, and his spleen will be healed. One who has a rash on his body should fatten a swan and, when it is killed, take the fat and dissolve it in a small dish. Then he should add equal weights of mugwort and oak bark to the fat, so there is twice as much fat. He should cook it again in the dish, making an ointment. He should often anoint himself with this. The skin where he first anoints himself will become blistered, but will quickly heal afterward. The other parts of the swan are not of much value for medicines.

vi. Heron

The heron *(reyger)* is hot and dry. Its flesh is good for sick as well as healthy people to eat, since it does not make mucus in a person's stomach. A person who has a sad mind should often eat its heart, and it will make his mind happy. One whose eyes ache or are clouded should cook the head of a heron in water. Once this is cooked, he should take the eyes and dry them in the sun. He should then place them in cold water for a little while, so they become soft. Again he should dry them in the sun, and repeat this three times. After doing this, he should crush the eyes to a powder. Then, only when the person's eyes are clouded or painful, he should put this powder in good, pure wine and dip a feather in it. With this, he should smear it around his eyelids and eyelashes. If he should touch the inside of his eyes a bit, it will not injure them. He should do this often at night when he goes to sleep, and it will take the cloudiness and pain from his eyes. One whose stomach has hardened, so that he has constriction, should often eat heron's liver, and it will soften his stomach. One whose spleen is ailing should shave a sufficient amount of heron bones in water and frequently drink this, at night, while fasting, and he will be better.

VII. VULTURE

The vulture *(vultur)* is of a cold nature, and it knows the skills of both birds and beasts. It is a prophet among birds. It flies to such an altitude as to that which much of earth's humor ascends, that is, to the heat of the air. It does no harm to other birds, but warns them, lest they be harmed by another. It eats dead bodies and sometimes forages in earth which is suffused with blood of animals, that is, where animals were killed.

One ought not eat its flesh, because the coldness in it would be mortal for a human. The brain of the vulture has this nature: that if a person were able to have it, uninjured, it would dispel every infirmity, except death. But a human is not able to have it uncorrupted, because, when death invades the vulture in any way, so that its vital air leaves, the thin skin of the brain is broken, and soon the brain dissipates, so that it loses its power.

When you kill a vulture, remove its feathers while it is still warm, cut its body, and throw away only the intestines, in which there is dung. Cook the rest of its body—with the head and heart, liver and lungs—vigorously in water in a new clay pot. Then add a bit of olive oil, and less henbane oil, to the fat and make an unguent. With this oil, anoint the entire head of one who is insane and the whole body of one who is virgichtiget and whom gicht torments. Use it for one who has any infirmity in his back, loins, or any part of his body. He will be cured, unless God does not wish to cure him. This ointment is more precious than the most precious ointment, because it quickly penetrates the skin of the sick person, healing him. If the head of the vulture is cooked with the fat, as described, it is possible to have some juice of the brain, but not any other way.

Divide its heart in two, so that it can be dried more easily. Dry it gently over the fire, so that it does not burn, and then also dry it in the sun. Then sew it in a deer-hide belt, and gird yourself with it. If anyone wishes to kill you with poison while you are girded with this belt containing the vulture heart, you will soon sweat and your whole body will tremble. You will know that poison is nearby, and you will be able to avoid it. Since the vulture harms poison, every injury flees from it. The vulture naturally knows the times of winds and the seasons' winds, and avoids killing itself while flying. Whence its heart is placed in fire, so the humors in it might be dried up. It is placed in the sun so that its firmness might be strengthened by the heat of the sun. It is placed in a deer-hide belt because the deer is quicker and more sensible than other animals. When cinched around a person, as described, and when his body is warmed by it, it makes him avoid the dangers of poison. The air around the person dispels the approaching noxious air—sent forth by treachery—with the strength of the heart and the deer-hide belt, because that same air is around those things. Sensing that poison is present, the air alarms the person with trepidation. Just as places and people are led into holiness and prosperity from their good deeds, so they are turned toward traps and injury from their bad deeds.

But when the vulture is cooked, fix its eye on a ring. If you wear it on your finger, it will check paralysis and gicht. The lungs and feathers of the vulture are not useful for medicine.

VIII. EAGLE

The eagle *(aquila)* is very hot, just as if it were fiery. Having eyes more fiery than watery, it can boldly look at the sun. Since it is so fiery, it can withstand heat and cold and fly high because it endures heat well. Its flesh would be deadly for a person to eat. It would be too strong for one who eats it, because of the very great heat in it. Since it is suffused by the heat of the sun, and since it boldly looks at it, it is grim and has great sensibility in its heart. It seizes and carries off many things which it throws away and does not eat. It eats only things that are healthful and warm.

The eagle seeks a place where sun or air is the warmest to lay her eggs, so that they are greatly suffused by that heat and strengthened. If it happens that there is a lack in these, so that it is not possible for the heat to have been poured in, the chick that emerges will be weaker, more sickly, and less strong than it ought to be. For the eagle has a marvelous nature within it and in its heart. It contains such great knowledge, shining beyond the ordinary, that the human heart cannot endure it.

The instant an eagle is either killed or dies by itself, its whole strength is in its heart, so that the heart becomes as if it were weak, weaker than the hearts of other birds and animals. No person can have that heart as strong as it was when it was alive. The many varieties of eagles have the same nature, though one may be fiercer, another gentler, or one may fly higher, another slower; just as people differ in their illnesses, but have one nature—humanity.

IX. STORK

The stork *(odebero)* is hot and has the nature of foolish animals. It flies in the middle of the sky, because birds which spend time in the middle of the sky sense the earth and understand the seasons better than those that fly at a high altitude in the air. Those up high dwell in the heat and are often deceived by its strength, so that winter, and other seasons, are upon them before they become aware of it.

Its flesh is not good food for a human, since it harms him. Therefore, take the stork and its head, throw away the innards, and take off all the feathers. Place the whole cadaver in a new clay pot, perforated with small holes, and heat it, without water, over the fire. Under that pot, place another new clay pot to catch the fat that flows off. Add to this a third as much bear fat and the same amount of butter. Pound the plant called goutweed with an equal weight of herb Robert, and cook this with the fats in a new pot. Strain it through a cloth and make an unguent. If one is insane, or troubled by paralysis, or tormented by gicht in any of his parts, he should anoint himself with this ointment, and he will be better. Other parts of the stork have not much use as medicine.

X. GOOSE

The goose *(anser)* is hot and, also, from the air in which beasts live, and from watery air which brings out its feathers. It cannot fly high, since it has some of the air of beasts, but it gladly spends time in water, because of its watery air. It eats clean and unclean foods. Because of its double nature, its flesh is weak and not good to eat. Since it eats unclean foods, it often gives a person mucus or ulcers, which are like scabies or similar to those of leprosy. People who are healthy are able to somehow survive when they have eaten its flesh. One who wishes to eat a goose should allow it to go very hungry for two or three days, so that its bad humors vanish. Then it should be fed grain. When it is killed, it should be roasted on the fire. After it is roasted, sage and other herbs should be placed on it, so that their juice may penetrate the goose. It should continually be sprinkled with wine or vinegar, so the blood flows from it, since its fat ought not to be eaten. Because it is fattened by bad humors, it makes a person sick; but, when it has been roasted in this way, one who is healthy may eat it, in moderation. It is bad for a person to eat goose cooked in water, since the bad humors in it are not carried away by the water, as they are when it is roasted on the fire. No matter how they are prepared, goose eggs are bad for people to eat [since they bring about scrofula and many other illnesses].

XI. Wild Goose

Wild goose *(halegans)* is very hot and swift in flight. It works hard flying, so it is good for both sick and healthy people to eat.

It flies in the heat of the air, since it would perish in the cold. It flies with a flock, so it is not harmed as much by enemies. Not fearful in the day, at night it is a bit vigilant and afraid. It eats unclean foods.

A person whose eyes are clouded or painful should take its bile and add twice as much pure wine to it. He should place this in a copper jar and, at night, smear it around his eyes with a feather, so that it even touches the inside of his eyes. If he does this often, they will become clear and healthy, and neither leucoma nor scum nor abscess will easily grow there.

One who ails from vicht should cook the liver of this bird and eat it often, and he will be better. One who has a cough should frequently eat its lung, cooked, and the cough will cease. One whose stomach is ailing should take wild goose and boil it in water, having thrown away the head and intestines. When he takes it from the water, he should separate the flesh from the bones, pound the flesh in a mortar, and twist the juice out through a cloth. He should prepare a broth from that juice and a bit of flour. He should sip this, while fasting, and without his awareness it will gently remove the bad humors from his stomach. Other parts of the wild goose are not useful for medicine.

XII. Domestic Duck

The duck which has been domesticated *(aneta domestica)* has a deep heat. It naturally has a little bit of the air of beasts, but more of watery air. It eats unclean things, but the unclean things which it devours are cleaned by the water in which the duck swims and pass through it.

Those who are healthy are able to survive eating its flesh, but it is not good for sick people. All the other parts of the duck are not good. [If someone wishes to eat duck, he should not eat it cooked in water but— just as explained about the goose—should roast it in the fire. Its eggs are as poisonous to a person as a spider bite.]

XIII. Wild Duck

Wild duck *(aneta silvestris)* has the same nature as the domestic duck, but is more healthful for a person to eat, since it always lives in the water. Having thrown out its head, intestines, and feathers, completely burn the wild duck in a new clay pot. Frequently put this powder on broken pustules, and they will be healed. Duck feathers are better than chicken feathers for beds and pillows.

XIV. Cock and Hen

The cock and hen *(gallus et gallina)* both have a cold and dry nature and, because they are especially of the air of terrestrial animals, they do not fly high. Their flesh is good for humans to eat. When eaten, they do not make people fat, and they nourish sick people a bit. But, if someone is very ill and frequently eats the meat cold, it will make mucus in his stomach, thus making his stomach weak and scarcely able to digest any food he eats. If one who is very ill wants to eat chicken, he should have it cooked with other meats, so that its dryness is balanced by the others' juice. He should eat it this way and avoid roasted chicken, which he is scarcely able to digest. Hen is better than cock as food for sick people, since it is more tender. A person with a healthy body is able to eat both. The capon is also good for a healthy person to eat. It is not much good for a sick person, since the capon does not work enough but is always resting, and its meat is too strong. The liver of both the cock and the hen are good to eat often against infirmities that harm a person internally. Chicken liver is hard, not soft. The feathers of the cock are bad for pillows, since they stir up gicht in a person who lies on them. Other parts of chickens are not useful as medicine.

[Any eggs of birds are more of a cold than of a hot nature and are harmful to eat. People can eat domestic hens' eggs, but in moderation. If a sick person wishes to eat eggs, he should mix water and wine, boil it in a small dish, and, having thrown away the shells, cook eggs in this, and they will not harm him. For a person with dysentery, egg yolks should be beaten with cumin and a bit of pepper in a little platter. This should be put back into the shells and roasted over the fire. After the sick person is able to eat a little, these may be given to him to eat. Anything the sick person eats should be hot and soft, like hens' eggs, other soft meats, and fish—but he should avoid herring and salmon. He should not eat beef, cheese, raw or coarse vegetables, leeks, rye or barley bread, and anything roasted, except roasted pear. He should drink wine. If anyone has a flow of blood, he should mix two egg yolks with mithridate juice (as much as half of one yolk) and vinegar (as much as two egg shells hold). He should add powdered cinnamon and a bit less zedoary powder, making a slightly thick draft. He should sip this in moderation, on an empty stomach or with food, and he will be better.]

XV. CAPERCAILLIE

The capercaillie *(urhun)* is hot and a bit moist. Therefore it is good for sick as well as healthy people to eat. If maggots or other worms are eating a person, pulverize the bladder of the capercaillie and put this powder on the wounds. When the worms eat this powder, they will die.

XVI. PARTRIDGE

Partridge *(rephun)* is cold, though not as cold as the domestic hen. Partridge has a bit of imperfection in it, so it is more unstable than the domestic hen, since its flesh is not soft but fragile, as it is not fully of the earth. When eaten, it does not harm healthy people much. Since it makes mucus in the stomach, it is not good for sick people. One should take its bile and mix it with old fat and often anoint himself where lice grow on his skin from the sweat of his flesh. This goes through the skin, cleansing the sweat, so that lice no longer grow. [If they grow inside, from his fat, this ointment is not beneficial.]

XVII. GROUSE

The grouse *(birckhun)* has almost the same nature as the partridge, except the flesh of the grouse is better and more healthful than partridge for both sick and healthy people to eat. If a crab is eating a person, dry the bladder of a grouse in the sun, or on the fire, then moisten it with a bit of wine. Stretch it across the place of the wound, and press on it. Allow it to lie there for a while, and the crabs will die.

XVIII. FALCON

The falcon *(falco)* is hot and a bit dry. Its heart has great power, and it is swift in flight. It flies up high, and back down lower, and in the middle of the air. Its flesh is not eaten. If there is scrofula on a person, whether ruptured or not, anoint it with fat of the falcon, and it will dry up. The falcon has so much bitterness in it that it is not valuable for medicine. Other falcons, from any land, have the same nature as this one, and are useful for the same medicine, except—according to the regions in which they are nourished—one may be stronger or quicker than another.

XIX. HAWK

The hawk *(habich)* is hot and moist [and because of its wildness its flesh is not eaten]. It knows other birds and understands their nature. Following what it knows about them, it traps and seizes them. It flies high and spends time in the middle of the air. A person who has pain in his liver or right side should cook the lung of a hawk in water. He should add hemlock to this, and more comfrey than hemlock, as well as butter, from cows' milk, which was prepared in May. There should be more butter than the other three things. He should cook these together and strain it through a cloth, making an unguent. He should anoint himself with it around his liver, or on his right side, and he will be better. One who is leprous should take the hawk's bile and add twice as much wine to it. He should smear this on the area where there is leprosy, and afterward anoint the area with fat from the same hawk. He should do this often, and the leprosy will be healed. The feathers of the hawk are not good for beds or cushions. If anyone were to lie on them, he would sleep deeply only with difficulty.

XX. SPARROW HAWK

The sparrow hawk *(sperwere)* is hot, and happy, and quick in flight. It flies high into the sky and in the middle of the air. A man or woman who burns with lust should take a sparrow hawk and, when it is dead, remove the feathers and throw away the head and viscera. He should place the rest of its body, without water, in a new clay pot perforated with a small hole, and heat it over the fire. Under this pot he should place another new clay pot, and in it catch the fat that flows off. He should then crush *calandria* and less camphor and mix them with the fat. He should heat this again, moderately, on the fire, and make an unguent. The man should anoint his privy member and loins with it for five days. In a month the ardor of his lust will cease, with no danger to his body. The woman should anoint herself around the umbilicus, and in the opening of the belly button. Her ardor will cease within a month. When the month is finished, the person, man or the woman, should oil him- or herself, and thus have relief from lust. If calandria and camphor are not available, they should take the smallest feather of the sparrow hawk and put it in olive oil for five days, so that it warms up from the sun and gets very hot. They should anoint themselves with it, on the parts of the body already mentioned, and the ardor of the lust will vanish. Other parts of the sparrow hawk are not valuable as food or medicine.

XXI. KITE

The kite *(milvus)* is hot and loves heat. When the sun shines, it flies willingly in its heat, and it also stays in warm shadows. But, it avoids the heat of the air, flying not high in it, but in the middle and lower parts. It gladly seizes very small birds.

Nevertheless, it is not very savage. Its flesh is harmful to eat, since all birds which grab prey with their claws are harmful for people to eat. A person who has scrofula on his body should take the kite. When it is dead, he should pluck its feathers, and throw out the entrails which contain dung. He should heat the rest of it, including the head and claws, over the fire, without water, in a new clay pot perforated with a small hole. He should place another pot under this to catch the fat. He should burn any flesh remaining in the pot to a powder. He should often anoint the scrofula, if it has not ruptured, with the fat, and it will vanish. If it has ruptured, he should place some of that powder on the wounds, and they will dry up.

XXII. WEHO

Weho is cold and has thieving habits. It does not fly high and eats unclean, sometimes poisonous, foods. It is not valuable as medicine, but harms a person.

XXIII. RAVEN

The raven *(corvus)* is more hot than cold and flies in the middle of the air. It is clever and daring, is not fearful, and does not flee or fear the human being very much, so that it easily speaks with him, and would nearly acquire knowledge from this, if he weren't an irrational animal. Since the raven recognizes the human, it often seizes things from a person. Because it has the nature of robbers and thieves, its flesh is harmful for a person to eat. Other parts of the raven are not useful for medicine.

XXIV. CROWS AND JACKDAWS

Crows and jackdaws *(krewa et kraha)* are of a cold nature. They fly in the middle of the air, imitate human voices, and are of the raven family.

In the beginning, before there were crows and jackdaws, a magpie saw a raven's eggs and stole them. She placed herself over the eggs and warmed them. Thus crows and jackdaws emerged, and then, as now, they laid their own eggs, crow with crow, jackdaw with jackdaw, and thus they multiplied. They are not useful for medicine, because a bird or any animal that is with a person by means of its cleverness is not much use to anyone as a remedy. Just as a bad person is evil in his ways, so he would become evil from it.

XXV. Carrion Crow

The carrion crow *(nebelkraha)* is hot and has ostentatious ways. It recognizes air and seasons. It scarcely awaits various outcomes; where it knows there will be sadness, it hurries there. It uses clean and unclean foods. Its flesh is not very useful as medicine.

XXVI. Hooded Crow

The hooded crow *(mursar)* comes from the hot air of the sun. When it is young, it is hot and strong, and eats very strong foods. When it progresses in age, it becomes cold and weak, and then seeks weaker foods. Arriving at old age, it returns to its original heat and strength, and seeks stronger foods, as it did previously. Its flesh is good for healthy and sick people to eat.

If a person has consumed poison in any way, he should cook its heart, liver, lung, and cleansed intestines in water. Then, with wine and white pepper and a bit less cumin, he should prepare a meat jelly. If he has no white pepper, he should add a little bit of aloe, less than there is of cumin. He should place those meats in this, so they become infused with it. He should often eat this, while fasting. Even if the poison which he ate or drank were to have hardened in his stomach, it would removes it, purging it, and that person would be healed.

XXVII. Ordumel

Ordumel has in it a bad heat. It is not good to eat, since everything in it is contrary to a human. Neither is it useful as medicine.

XXVIII. Alkreya

More cold than hot, *alkreya* eats clean foods, as well as certain poisonous ones. Sometimes it eats sick fish. Its flesh is good for neither healthy nor sick people to eat. Those who are healthy are able to survive it, though it harms those who are ill. There is no medicine in it.

XXIX. SEAGULL

Seagull *(mewa)* is hot, of a correct balance of air and water, and moderately moist. It does not fly high and is good for healthy and sick people to eat.

XXX. DOVE

The dove *(columba)* is more cold than hot, and it loves the morning—when the frosty day first begins—more than it likes the heat. It is simple and timid, and so it flies with a flock. In this way it is harmed much less by other birds. Because it is cold, it is readily hungry. Food does not warm up in it, as happens in other birds, and so it is quickly hungry, and eats more than other birds of the same size. Its flesh is not firm. It is a bit dry and does not give much juice to a person. It is not beneficial as food for a healthy person, though it does not harm him. When eaten, it harms a sick person whose body is failing. Wood-pigeon and ring-dove have the same nature, except that they dwell in the forests, and thence are a little bit fiercer and larger, and eat foods from the forests. None of these have use as medicine.

XXXI. TURTLE DOVE

The turtle dove *(turtur)* is hot and dry. It has a virile stength, is not afraid, and always has a quasi servant.* Since it neither has moisture nor lives in diverse places, bile cannot increase in it, as it does in humans. In one who has good will, bile cannot increase but rather decreases; and when one has a wicked mind, his bile increases. The turtle dove's flesh is not good to eat, because it stirs up gicht in a person. Other parts of it are not useful.

XXXII. PARROT

The parrot *(psittacus)* is very hot and moist. It has some of the quality of the griffin's flight and part of the strength of a lion. It is not as daring as it could be in either flight or strength. It knows the times of the seasons and expresses its songs according to those events. It has some colors in its feathers in accordance with fire and bile. It is not useful as medicine,

---

*Translator's note: The Latin for this phrase reads, *et quasi servum semper habet,* suggesting that for the turtle dove there is another turtle dove who serves his needs.

since it holds no virtue fully within it, and is defective because of its diverse nature.

XXXIII. MAGPIE

The magpie *(pica)*, which has deep coloring, is mischievous. From air and earth it has variegated feathers. It naturally pursues a kind of boasting. When it sees strange people approach, it sends out its voice at their arrival. It seeks foods that are poisonous and harmful, whether small plants or cadavers. Its flesh is as harmful as poison for a person to eat. Like the devil, it is accustomed to dwell around humans. If a person has thick scabies on his head, he should take the fat of the magpie and anoint his head with it. He will be healed. Other parts of the magpie are not useful as medicine.

XXXIV. NUTCRACKER

The nutcracker *(hera)* is hot and a bit dry. It is able to fly well in various winds and storms, does not fly high, and has canine habits. It is unclean and eats foods that are noxious to humans. Whatever it sees, it imitates, as far as it is able, and it greets any person it sees approaching. Its flesh is poison to a person who eats it, since it is suffused with storms and has diverse habits. However, take the nutcracker, throw away its head and intestines, and remove its feathers. Then cut up the rest of the body, and place the cut pieces in a new clay pot. Add fenugreek and a little less mallow, and then cow butter prepared in May, with an equal amount of deer marrow and chicken fat (less chicken fat than deer marrow). Cook these together in water, and make an unguent from what floats on top. This is the best thing against pain of the head, shoulders, kidneys, and entrails. If you frequently anoint yourself with it, the pain, even if it is strong, will cease. It will make a person better. [And if cows or pigs or sheep are sick in any way, this bird should be cooked in water and given to them to eat. They will be cured from whatever disease held them.]

XXXV. SCREECH OWL

The screech owl *(ulula)* is hot and has the habits of a thief. Aware of the day, which it flees, it delights in the night. It hates other birds because it does not like their nature. It has knowledge of human death. It knows by the odor of the air where there will be mourning and grief, and it hurries to the cadaver before the lamentation has started; then it flees. It eats things that are contrary to the nature of a human being. If a person should eat its flesh, it would be like a poison to him, because of its bad nature. However, throw away its head and intestines and remove its feathers. Roast the rest of the body on the fire. Take the fat from it and, after cooking marshmallow and twice as much tansy in water, add the screech owl fat. Place it again on the fire and add olive oil—a fourth as much as the amount of fat. Having squeezed this through a cloth, make an unguent. If a person who has palsy or is virgichtiget is frequently anointed with it, he will be cured.

XXXVI. Great Horned Owl

The great horned owl *(huwo)* is hot and has almost the same nature as the screech owl, except this owl is stronger and more robust in its villainy; it has the habits of a thief. It knows the day, but flees it and prefers the night. It hates birds that fly in the daytime. Its flesh is injurious to a person's eyesight. If a person who has scrofula, whether whole or ruptured, anoints himself with the fat of this bird, heated in a small dish, it will dry up. Other parts of this bird are not useful for medicine.

XXXVII. Pelican

The pelican *(sisegonino)* is hot. It loves the night and the splendor of the moon more than daytime and sunshine (although it likes the day more than the screech owl does). It goes about at night because it abhors other birds and does not wish to be seen much. It has the habits of a thief a bit, as if it were sometimes mad, like as one who doesn't care what he does. When the pelican first sees her chicks hatch from their eggs, she thinks they are not related to her and kills them. When she sees that they do not move, she is sad and lacerates herself, resuscitating them with her blood. This bird also perceives and understands a person's sad and happy times. If they are happy, it rejoices by singing; if sad, it shows itself sad, by being quiet. Sometimes it hangs in the air, on its back and turned toward the earth. It looks in the air, and considers when times will be either joyful and happy or sad. If it foresees that people will die, it indicates this with a few sounds and is then quiet.

XXXVIII. Cuckoo

The cuckoo *(cuculus)* is hot and has in it some of the habits of beasts as well as birds. When it hears people, it greets them with its voice. it dwells in dull breezes. It is able to endure neither great heat nor great cold. When there is great heat in the summer, it seeks the shadows of the forests. The great summer heat disturbs its feathers, so they fall out in winter. When it senses that its feathers are dying, it gathers food in its nest and endeavors to drop its little feathers into the nest. It lies in these through the winter, so that it has heat from them. By the beginning of summer, its feathers have grown again. It cleanses its nest of the old feathers and goes forth.

Its flesh is not good for humans to eat, since it has mange and would be poisonous if one ate it. A person who has a rash on his body, so that his skin is split, or who is troubled by any pain, should throw away the head and intestines of the cuckoo. To the rest of its body he should add equal weights of mugwort and sage, a bit more dittany, and a little bear fat. He should cook all this in water in a new clay pot. He should take what floats on top, make an ointment from it, and frequently anoint himself with it. The rash will heal, and the pain which torments his body will cease.

XXXIX. Snipe

The snipe *(snepha)* is hot and is from the high air. Its flesh is good for healthy and sick people to eat. One whose eyes cloud up should take its bile and add a bit of wine to it, less than there is of the bile, and pour this in a copper jar. He should rub it around his eyes when he goes to bed at night. If it touches the eyes a bit, it will not harm them. If he does this often, it will diminish the cloudiness. Other parts of the snipe are not much use as medicine.

XL. Woodpecker

The woodpecker *(specht)* is hot. It is from clear air and flies in the middle of the air. It is speedy, and it loves heat and summertime. Its food is not poisonous. But the green woodpecker is better and more robust than the other kind. The other kind is strong enough, but not as strong as the one that is green.

A person who is leprous should roast the green woodpecker on the fire and eat it often; it will destroy the leprosy. Also, take the green woodpecker, throw away its head and intestines, and remove the feathers. Roast the rest of the body, then remove and save the outside skin which has been burned in the fire. Pound the rest of the body in a mortar and cook it vigorously in water, so it is in small bits. Then, remove it from the water, separate the bones from the flesh, and throw out the entrails. Pulverize the meat on a hot tile. Put this with the outside skin and some rue in the water in which the woodpecker was cooked. Add some vulture fat and a little deer tallow, and cook these together vigorously. Throwing the rest out, make an unguent from that which floats on top. Use this to frequently anoint the person's leprosy and, no matter how strong the leprosy is, he will be healed, unless the judgement of God does not allow it, or unless his death is in the leprosy.

Also, dry the woodpecker's heart. Set it in gold and silver, as if it were a ring. When you carry it with you, gicht will go from you. This bird's nature is clean, its heart simple and without any evil art. The power of its heart in pure metal sedates the diverse humors which bring forth the drops of paralysis. Other parts of the woodpecker are not useful for medicine.

XLI. SPARROW

The sparrow *(passer)* is cold and has great variety in its habits. Astute and deceitful, it flies with a flock, so it might not be harmed by larger birds. It often lives in thick air, so it has weak flesh, which is good for neither healthy nor sick people to eat. It is not even useful for medicine.

XLII. TITMOUSE

The titmouse *(meysa)* is hot and dry. It is tame, flies in clear air, has healthy flesh, and is good for both sick and well people to eat. A person who is troubled by palsy should cook titmouse in water, with butter, and make soup from it. He should eat this frequently, and he will be cured.

XLIII. BLACKBIRD

The blackbird *(amsla)* is hot and dry and tame. It flies in clear air; indeed, it grows from clear air and is good for healthy people to eat. Because it is dry it harms sick people. If you dry its liver and set it into whatever you want, then always carry it with you, the devil will torment you in neither horror nor deception, because it hates the blackbird on account of its cleanliness.

XLIV. THRUSH

The thrush *(drosela)* is hot, and it is tame in its habits. A person who has a pain inside his throat, or whose voice is hoarse, should cook a thrush in water. He should dip a linen cloth in the water and tie it loosely over his whole throat, up to his ears. From the rest of the water he should prepare a broth and eat this. His throat and voice will be better if he does this often. One who ails in his liver or lungs should often eat thrush cooked in water, and he will be cured.

XLV. LARK

Lark *(lercha)* is very hot and of a dry nature. It loves the summer and willingly flies in the sunshine. It thrives in heat, but in cold it easily perishes. It is cheerful and clever, and it seeks clean foods. It is not good for healthy or sick people to eat. If someone's throat is swollen, take a lark and discard the head, intestines, and feathers. Dry the rest of its body over a hot tile, so that you do not burn it. Add three pennyweights of the powder of the linden tree. Tie this, in a cloth, around the neck, and the swelling will go away. If you have a large ulcer anywhere on your body, tie this same powder on it. Because of its nature and strength, as already described, the ulcer will soften and rupture. And, if you have swollen glands, first moisten them with your saliva, then tie on the powder in a cloth, and they will vanish. If a dog is mad, cut off the head of a lark and feed it to the dog, who will lose its madness and become gentle.

XLVI. KINGFISHER

The kingfisher *(isenbrado)* is hot and is balanced in that heat. It is a bit moist and always seeks the purity of the air. In it there is good fortune. Sometimes it seeks those waters that are pure and clear of filth. If a person is near that air or that water by which it builds a nest, he is able to dwell there. No infirmity shall befall him there, because the kingfisher always seeks air where there is no filth. This bird eats clean foods.

Throw away the kingfisher's head, intestines, and feathers and wrap the rest of its body in oak leaves. Place this over coals, until the leaves are consumed by the fire. Repeat this three times, then place the little bird— in a new clay pot without water—on the fire. Burn it a moderate amount, so you can pulverize it. Gradually reduce it to a powder, then add a little less nutmeg. If someone has apoplexy, and already cannot move on one side, give him, while he is fasting, some of this powder in a bit of water to drink every day. It will cure the infirmity in him if he is young, but not if the infirmity has become old in him over a long period. If someone is so virgichtiget that he wishes to tear himself to pieces, when he suffers this evil he should drink some of this powder in water. He will be better because of the good virtues of this bird, as already mentioned.

XLVII. HOOPOE

The hoopoe *(vedehoppo)* is hot and moist [and not good as food for people]. It flies in the middle of the air, loves the day, and has an unclean nature. It always dwells in filth, or around filth, and makes progress in it. It always seeks the strongest filth, in which to make its house. Throw away its head and intestines, draw off the feathers, and reduce the rest of the body to a powder in a new clay pot. If scrofula has ruptured on a person, or if worms are eating him, put this powder in the wounds. The scrofula will be dried up, and the worms will die.

XLVIII. QUAIL

The quail *(wachtela)* is hot and moist. It seeks clean foods and is good for healthy people to eat, but it is not good for sick people inundated with bad humors. It stirs up the humors in them, since it has a sluggish moisture.

XLIX. NIGHTINGALE

The nightingale *(nachtgalla)* is hot and a bit dry. It has its life from nocturnal air, is clean, and, because it is from night air, it sings and is more joyful in the night than in the day. By day the sun gives too much brightness, which it abhors.

One whose eyes are clouded should seize a nightingale before sunrise. He should take its bile, pour it out, and add to this one drop of dew which he finds on clean grass. Then, when he goes to bed, he should smear this on his eyelids and eyelashes, and also around his eyes. If he should touch the inside of his eyes a bit, it will not harm him. It will wonderously take the cloudiness from his eyes, just as foam is purged and done away with by the heat of fire in the summer.

L. STARLING

The starling *(stara)* is hot and timid. It flies with a flock, is friendly to its own kind, and does not hate other birds. It flies a bit high. Remove its head, intestines, and feathers and reduce the rest of its body to a powder by burning it in a new clay pot. Place this powder on ruptured scrofula, and it will dry up. Hold a dead starling over anything you suspect is poison. If there is poison, the starling feathers will separate and be moved, even though it is dead. If the bird were alive, he would sense pain from this and fly away. If there is no poison, his feathers will neither separate nor be moved.

LI. CHAFFINCH

The chaffinch *(vynco)* is hot. It forages for herbs from the earth's viridity. Although not very harmful for a healthy person to eat, it harms one who is sick. It is of a dry nature and does not fly high in the air. Take a chaffinch and remove its head, intestines, and feathers. Place it over live coals and roast it moderately, until just warm. Where a child's skin is ulcerous, place it there thus warmed. Warm it again, and place it on another spot. Do this often anywhere on the child's body. It will draw out unclean and bad humors from his skin. Shortly after, anoint the area with goat tallow, and the ulcers will be cured. Other parts of the chaffinch are of little use.

LII. GOLDFINCH

The goldfinch *(distelwincke)* is hot and is from that air which first brings forth blooming flowers, and so it has a beautiful color. A person whose chest is wounded inside his body, who ails in his stomach or loins, or who has illness in his head should take a goldfinch and clean it, throwing its head and feathers away. He should gently roast its flesh with its liver and heart. He should draw off the flesh after it is roasted and break the bones into little pieces. He should take wheat flour, add a bit of lard to it, and place it on the meat. He should cook it again in a small dish and so prepare a condiment, which he should eat frequently. If he is young, it will heal him internally; if old, it will diminish the pains in him, because it is just like the best unguent which heals a person internally.

LIII. BUNTING

The bunting *(amera)* is hot and flies willingly in pure air. It is good for neither healthy nor sick people to eat, since its food is both clean and unclean, and it is bitter.

LIV. PIPIT

The pipit *(grasemucka)* is cold. It is from the air of foaming waters. Its food is clean and unclean, and it is not much use as medicine.

LV. SPECKLED MAGPIE

The speckled magpie *(wargkrengel)* is cold and from the air of noonday demons. It has no happiness until it sees sadness in other animals. It sometimes breaks its eggs, and is harsher and more hostile to its chicks than are other birds. It does not have the sort of powers that bring about good or evil in medicines.

LVI. BLACKBIRD

The blackbird *(merla)* is cold, and its food is unclean and injurious. It is not good for healthy or sick people to eat, and there is no medicine in it.

LVII. WHITE WAGTAIL

The white wagtail *(waszersteltza)* has a moderate heat in it and is from whirlwinds. It always moves its tail, and is able to endure whirlwinds and storms, because it comes from them. It willingly lives near stirred up waters, and it particularly seeks its food in water. It has soft flesh and is good for a healthy and sick person to eat, since it refreshes one who is ill. Dry and save the wagtail's throat. When someone has a pain in his heart, or when he is troubled by gicht, place that throat in water for a little while. Take it out and pour off the water the throat had been in. Give this to the person to drink. His heart will be better, and his gicht will cease. Also, dry its heart and always carry it with you. When gicht troubles you, place the heart in water for a little while. Then drink the water, and the vicht in you will cease. Also, have its dried bladder with you. If freislich rises up in a person, make it moderately damp with your saliva, then put the bladder next to, not over, the freislich. It will disperse it. Swollen glands will also vanish if, after dampening them with your saliva, you put the bladder over them.

LVIII. YELLOW WAGTAIL

The yellow wagtail *(beynstercza)* is hot and moist and also from whirlwinds. It moves its tail and seeks poisonous and harmful foods. Anyone who eats its flesh will have gicht stirred up in him.

LIX. SWALLOW

The swallow *(hirundo)* is hot. It seeks heat and calm air, and there builds its nest. It has warmth and is a bit fierce. It flies quickly and eats much unclean food. Though it is harmful for a person to eat, where there is scrofula on a person, whether whole or ruptured, anoint it with the fat of the swallow, and it will be healed. If a person ails in his testicles, he should burn a whole swallow's egg, with its shell, and reduce it to a powder. To this powder he should add a bit of chicken fat and mix it together. He should anoint the testicles, and he will be better. [For someone who has become leprous from gluttony and inebriation, one should make a powder from swallows' dung and four times as much of the plant called burdock, which has red flowers. He should fry some stork fat and a bit more vulture fat in a frying pan, mix the powder and a bit of sulphur with the fat, and make an unguent. He should order the person to anoint himself with it, in a steam bath, and to then go to bed. The person should repeat this for five days, or more.]

LX. GOLDEN-CRESTED KINGLET

The golden-crested kinglet *(cungelm)* is hot and from the air of the shining sun. Its flesh does not harm a person who eats it. By itself, it is not valuable as medicine, because it is small. But, when preparing unguents in May, take off its head and throw out the intestines. Reduce the rest of its body to a powder in a new clay pot. Add this powder to any good herbs with which unguents are made, and no other herb will be more precious in curing ailments.

LXI. BAT

The bat *(vespertilio)* is more hot than cold. It abhors heat and daytime, and it flies while airy spirits are particularly active, while people sleep. If someone has jaundice, strike a bat gently, so it does not die. Tie it over his loins, with the back of the bat turned toward the person's back. After a little while, take it off, and tie it over his stomach. Leave it there until it dies.

LXII. WIDDERWALO

The *widderwalo* is hot and unstable and has a sad nature. A person with jaundice should tie this little bird—feathers and all—when it is dead, over his stomach. The jaundice will pass into it, and he will be cured. Or, the person with jaundice should reduce the bird to a powder. Dip this powder a bit in olive oil, and tie it over his stomach for two or three days, and he will be cured. If someone is deaf in one ear, he should place the heart of this bird in the affected ear, which will warm up inside and recover its hearing. One who has catarrh should pulverize this bird's liver and place that powder at his nostrils. He will draw in its odor through his nose, and the bad humors of his head will gently dissolve, easily flowing out, and he will be cured very quickly.

LXIII. HONEY BEE

The honey bee *(apis)* is from the heat of the sun. It loves the summer, has a swift heat, and is unable to endure cold. For anyone on whom ganglia grow, or who has had some limb moved from its place, or who has any crushed limbs, take bees that are not alive, but which have died, in a metallic jar. Put a sufficient amount on a linen cloth, and sew it up. Soak this cloth, with the bees sewn within, in olive oil, and place it over the ailing limb. Do this often, and he will be better. And, if a worm eats the flesh of a person, he should take bees, which have died, in a metallic jar, and put this powder on the place of the wound, and the worm will die.

[The honey that bees make is very hot. If a fat person eats it often, it creates mucus and pus in him. If a dry and lean person eats cooked honey, he will not be harmed much. Honey which is cooked, and very well skimmed off, does not do much harm to a thin or fat, healthy or ill, person. But eating the honeycomb or wax can stir up melancholy in him.]

LXIV. HOUSE FLY

The house fly *(musca)* is cold. In summer, if a person is stung or hurt by some minute little worm [such as a spider], tie a crushed fly over the area. The heat the fly has in summer will debilitate the poison a bit. In winter, the fly is absolute poison and very dangerous for anyone, unless God is watching out for him. For a person who eats or drinks a fly, crush clary sage right away. He should put some of that juice in good wine, the wine exceeding the juice and should heat this over the fire and then drink it until he emits, by nausea, any poisons remaining in him from the fly.

[If a pustule which is called freislich has swollen up on someone, he should crush flies, with their heads thrown away. He should make a circle with these crushed flies, around the outside of the swelling. It will stop the poison from going further. He should then crush a red snail without its shell, and with it make the same circle as he had made with the crushed flies. Afterward, he should take sap from a lily and anoint the skin around the circle he made with the snail. He should then place a leaf of lady's-thistle over the pustule. Then, having made a little cake of pure wheat flour, he should put this on the leaf and tie the whole thing on with a cloth, until it softens and ruptures by itself. If it does not rupture on its own, it should be punctured with a dry wooden thorn, or other dry splinter, and not by any fiery or cold iron or needle. While the person is suffering from this pustule, he should keep himself away from fire, cold, wind, and moist air. He should abstain from hot, roasted, and fat food and from wine. He should also avoid raw vegetables and fruits.]

LXV. TREE CRICKET

The tree cricket *(cicada)* is more cold than warm. Whether it is alive or dead, it harms a person more than it benefits him, since it has mucus from bad things in it. A person who touches it suffers. A person who has ruptured scrofula should take a tree cricket which has died by itself and reduce it to a powder on a hot tile. He should often put this powder where the scrofula is, and it will dry up.

LXVI. GRASSHOPPER

The grasshopper *(locusta)* is as cold as dew and is neither very useful nor very dangerous. In areas where the land and breezes are cold, the grasshopper is a bit poisonous and dangerous to eat. Where the earth and breezes are warm, it is less dangerous, and it can be eaten very much like a crab. From the cold of the earth, the grasshopper collects poison in himself, but in warm earth the grasshopper lacks poison, because of the good heat. There is no medicine in it.

LXVII. GNAT

The gnat *(mugga)* is hot. Anyone who has thick scabies on his head should collect gnats in a metallic jar. He should set this afire from the top using straw and, in a clean place, place it on top of live coals so that, together with the coals, it turns to ashes. Then he should make lye from these ashes. He should use this to wash the head where the scabies are, and any other bad spots on his body. If he does this often, he will be cured.

LXVIII. BUMBLEBEES

Bumblebees *(humbelen)* are cold. A person whose eyes are cloudy should take the small bladder from between the head and stomach of the bumblebee. When he goes to bed, he should put a bit of the liquid from inside it in his eyes. Then he should anoint his eyelids and eyelashes with olive oil. He should do this once or twice a month, and he will see very clearly. One who has very ugly nails should smear them with liquid from the little bladder of the bumblebee and tie it with a band. He should do this until they become beautiful. One who has deep scabies on his head should often smear this same liquid over his head, and he will be cured.

LXIX. WASP

The wasp *(wespa)* is hot and clean. A person should pulverize hog's-fennel and add twice as much powdered wasp. He should then hold these powders over hot smoke, so they gradually and gently heat up. He should then hold it, so warmed, over food he wishes to eat. Any poison in the food is so weakened that it is unable to harm him.

LXX. GLOWWORM

The glowworm *(glimo)* is more cold than hot. When someone who suffers from epilepsy falls, as many live glowworms as possible should be tied in a cloth and placed over his umbilicus. He will immediately recover his strength.

LXXI. MEYGELANA

*Meygelana** is cold. If there is scrofula on a person, he should take this little worm and squeeze out its poison. To it he should add less powder of (the herb named) meygelana. He should drink this in moderation, in either wine or water. Immediately, just like an arrow, it will invade the rotten matter of the scrofula and consume it.

LXXII. WREN

The wren *(parix)* is hot, and its flesh is good for healthy and sick people to eat. A person who is tormented by palsy should cook this bird in water, adding lard, vinegar, and a bit of wine. He should eat this often, and he will be cured. One who has jaundice should tie the same little bird, without its feathers, on his stomach. The jaundice will pass into the little bird, causing it to become yellow colored.

*See also Meygelana entry on p. 76.

ANIMALS

BOOK SEVEN

Animals

 BIRDS, WHICH DWELL IN THE AIR, represent the virtue a person reveals in his thinking when, by his internal premeditation, he reckons many things before they come forth in an illustrious deed. Animals, which run around on land and live on the earth, represent the thoughts and meditations a person brings to completion in work. And—just as works follow thoughts—so too when good will, right desires, and pious sighs come forth the Maker of the world finishes them in heaven; they are not completed there unless they have come forth in this world, in thoughts with spiritual longing. Lions and similar animals show the will of a person, which he wants to bring forth in works. Panthers, and those similar to them, show the ardent desire in the already incipient work. Other forest animals represent full abundance and show that a person has the potential to complete both useful and useless works. The tame animals that walk on land show the gentleness of the human being, which he has through his correct ways. And so human rationality says to each person, "You are this or that animal," since animals have in them qualities similar to the nature of the human. Animals that eat each other, are nourished on bad foods, and bear multiple offspring (as the wolf, the dog, and the pig) are—like weeds—harmful to the nature of a human being, since he does not do those things. However, herd animals that eat clean foods, like hay and similar fodder, and bear no more than one offspring at a time are—like good and useful plants—beneficial for people to eat. In both kinds of animals certain medicines are found.

I. Elephant

The elephant (elephans) has the heat of the sun, rather than that of flesh. It also holds a large amount of sweat, sweat so strong it cooks the elephant's bones, just as fire cooks food; whence, those bones are beautiful. The sweat under its skin is very thick and keeps the outer skin within bounds by its strength. The elephant has more bones than flesh, so it does not alter in its various habits, for flesh is always changed by a variety of habits. Lacking a great amount of flesh, it has strong veins. Its umbilicus heads its internal organs, which are very hot. The elephant serves to embellish man, much as a leader serves as an embellishment to his city. The elephant is neither deceitful nor evil in rectitude. It is sometimes fierce, and it seeks the land that has the water of paradise and digs that land with its foot, until it smells in its nostrils the water of paradise. From that odor, it seeks to mingle in coitus. After the female conceives, she carries the young one inside herself for a long time. It cannot grow quickly, because it is more bone than flesh. After she gives birth, she does not seek intercourse again until she sees that the young one is as strong as she is.

One who ails in his lungs, so that he coughs and is congested, should heat the bone of an elephant in the sun and shave some of it into wine. He should cook it in a little dish, then strain it through a cloth, and discard the powder. He should drink that wine often, and he will be cured. The heart of an elephant and its liver, lungs, and other parts are not valuable as medicine.

II. Camel

The camel (camelus) has a precipitous heat in it, but it is a bit tepid. Whence it is also tepid in the vicissitudes of its unstable ways. In its humps, it has the strength of a lion, panther, and horse; in the rest of its body, it has the nature of an ass. The hump near its neck has the strength of a lion; the next hump has the strength of a panther; and the next hump has the strength of a horse. From these natures the camel grows large and tall, and from them it is of such great strength that, were it not tame, it would surpass the lion and other beasts in strength.

A person whose heart is ailing should shave, into water, some of the bone from the hump having the strength of a lion. He should drink it often, and the pain of his heart will cease. One whose spleen is ailing should shave some of the bone of the hump having the strength of a panther into water. He should drink it often, and his spleen will be healed. One who has scabies and various fevers, and who freely emits bad sweat, should shave into water some of the bone from the hump having the strength of a horse. If he drinks it often, he will be healed. Also, dry the hoof and callous skin of its foot. Save it in the house, or any place you wish. Airy spirits will not create their delusions in that place nor arrange many struggles, because the devil will flee, on account of the camel's strength and fortitude.

III. LION

The lion (leo) is very hot. If its bestial nature did not detain him, he would be able to penetrate stones. The lion recognizes a human being. If, in its fury, the lion injures a person, it grieves afterward. When the lion mingles with the lioness in coitus, it forgets its strength and beastial nature, mingling with her decently. When the lioness does not sense that the cubs in her are alive, she becomes sad, and she is hostile to the lion, because she does not know that she has conceived. After she has given birth to the cubs, she thinks they are dead, and goes away from them. The lion, seeing her, understands that she has given birth to the cubs, and immediately smells them. He runs to them, roaring, and regathers the powers he had lost in mingling with the lioness. He sends forth such loud roars that they waken the cubs. After the cubs are roused, they emit such loud roars that the lioness hears them and happily runs up to them. She chases the lion from them, warms them, and makes them get up. She does not allow the lion near them again while they are growing. Adam and Eve did not shout in lamentation before a person was born. After the first child was born, it immediately lamented by crying out to the height and depth of the many elements. Hearing it as an unknown sound, Adam ran up and shouted out with the same sound of lamentation, and Eve with him, just as the lion and lioness and the cub roar together when they awake.

Draw off the skin of the lion, from the neck, over the head and its crown. Save it. If someone is mad from any infirmity in his head, he should warm up from having that fleece over his head, and he will recover his senses. One who ails from any other infirmity of the head should place that same skin from the lion's head over his head, until his head warms up. He should soon take it off, and not let it lie on his head any longer, lest he be injured by its strength. He will be better. From the rest of its skin, do not make a belt, or gloves, or shoes, or anything you would carry with you. Its strength might harm you more than it would help.

If someone is deaf, cut off a lion's right ear. Another person should hold it on the ear of the deaf person, until the inside of his ear warms up from the ear of the lion, and no longer. He should say, "Hear adimacus, by the living God, and by the sharpness of the lion's strong hearing." Do this often, and he will recover his hearing. One who is foolish will become wise for a long time if he places the dried heart of a lion on his breast for a little while—only until that spot becomes warm from it. If he were to allow it to remain longer, he would become nonsensical. A woman who is having difficulty in childbirth, so that she is not able to bring forth the child, should place a lion's heart on her umbilicus for a short time, not long. The infant within will loosen and quickly come forth.

Also, dry and save the lion's liver. If someone is unable to digest food he has eaten, place that liver in water for a short time—not long, lest the water become too strong from the power of that liver. Then give the water, as a drink, to the one who cannot digest. He will immediately digest the food which he had eaten. Bury the heart of a lion in your house or anywhere you wish and, as long as it lies buried there, lightning will not cause fires in that place nor thunder crash there, for a lion is accustomed to roar when he hears thunder.

[A person should also dry the end of a lion's tail and keep it with him always. He will not easily be harmed by the hissings of airy spirits, or by magic. And, when he eats or drinks, he should hold it near his food or drink. If there is poison in these, they will be set in motion in their vessels. Also, the vessel which contains poison will sweat, and in this way the poison will be detected. If someone has eaten or drunk poison, he should put that end of the lion's tail in warm wine for a short time, then drink the warm wine. Immediately the poison he has consumed will pass through him with his digested food. A person should also dip steel in lion's blood, and it will be strong either against iron or for any other skill in which it is employed.] Other parts of the lion are not useful as medicine.

IV. BEAR

The bear (ursus) has nearly the heat of a human being and is sometimes cold. When it is hot, it has a deep voice and is gentle. When it is cold, it suppresses its voice and is wrathful. In its lust, it has gentle habits and is not easily angered; but, if held back in its lust, it is angry. In creating the human being, God made his framework, arranging the course of his veins and all the routes the soul has in his body. Earlier, God had made the birds, and fish, and animals, which did nothing until the human being worked. But they waited for the human being to begin work first. After the human ate the apple and sweated in difficulty, his blood changed its nature to the way it is now, and all other animals changed in their natures. And so the bear (changed) his love to lust with love. When a human is lustful or lascivious, how is it that a bear does not smell him from nearly a half mile away and run to him, if possible—that is, a male bear run to a woman, a female bear to a man—and mix with them in coitus? Because, if the human were tending toward rationality, and if he were not behaving like an irrational beast, the bear or female bear would tear the human apart.

When a bear conceives she is so impatient in childbirth that, in her impatience, she aborts before the cubs within her have come to maturity. Although they receive vital air in their mother, they do not move within her. When she gives birth, she pours out something like flesh that, though it has vital air within it, does not move; it does have all the exterior features of its shape. Seeing this, the mother grieving, licks it, passing her tongue over all its features until all its limbs are distinguished. She spreads herself over it, warming it. In five or six days, a cub large enough to rise grows from her warmth. Until the time she abandons her cubs, she does not leave them alone but, if disturbed by hunters, she will carry them in her claws and run on three feet. At that time, they are still immature.

The flesh of the bear is not good for a person to eat. If it is eaten, it will so fire up lust in a person, contrary to the way water extinguishes his thirst. Pig's flesh, and that of similar animals, acts in the same way, but not as much. They create lust in a person, with a force that would make a wheel roll, and they render him unclean in another way. But herd animals, which are ruminants, do not quickly rest from lust.

[When the hair of an adolescent human first starts to fall out, he should mix bear fat with a bit of ashes made from wheat or rye straw. He should dip his whole head in this, especially where the hair is beginning to shed. He should not wash this ointment from his head for a long time. He should do this often, and the hair that has not yet fallen out will be so moistened and strengthened by this ointment that it will not fall out for a long time.]

If someone is timid and terrified, trembling and anxious, so that he is always in a panic, he should take the fleece from between the ears of a bear, dry it a bit, and then place it on his chest, over his heart, until he warms up from it. He will immediately be still, and the terror, tremor, and anxiety will leave him. Also, make that fleece dry, just as with other skins, so that its sweat is removed. If a person is warmed by the skin of a bear—which is without flesh, so that its sweat does not touch his bare skin—he will not be harmed by its lust. Bear fat added to certain ointments and medicines makes these medicines more precious. By itself it is not valuable as medicine, since the bear has unstable ways.

V. UNICORN

The unicorn (unicornus) is more hot than cold. Its strength is greater than its heat. It eats clean plants. In moving it has a leap, and it flees humans and other animals, except those that are of its kind, and so it cannot be captured. It especially fears a man, and shuns him. Just as the serpent in the first fall shunned the man and got to know the woman, so this animal avoids a man but follows a woman. There was a certain philosopher who scrutinized the natures of animals, and he marveled greatly that capturing this animal, by any skill, was impossible. One day he went hunting, as he usually did, and was accompanied by men, women, and girls. The girls walked separately from the others, and played among the flowers. Seeing the girls, a unicorn shortened its leaps and gradually drew near. It sat on its hind legs, diligently gazing at them from afar. The philosopher, seeing this, thought hard about it; he understood that a unicorn could be captured by girls. He approached it from the back and caught it by means of the girls. A unicorn, seeing a girl from afar, wonders that she has no beard but does have the shape of a person. If two or three girls are together, it is more amazed, and it is caught more quickly when its eyes are fixed on them. The girls by whose means the unicorn is captured must be nobles, not country girls. They should be neither completely grown nor entirely small, but in the midst of adolescence. The unicorn loves them, because it knows they are gentle and sweet.

Once a year it goes to the land that has the water of paradise. There it seeks the best plants, which it digs up with its hooves and eats. From them, it has great powers, but it still flees other animals. It has beneath its horn something as clear as glass, so that, in it, a person can look at his own face, as if looking in a mirror. Nevertheless, it is not very valuable.

Pulverize the liver of a unicorn and put this powder in fat prepared from the yolk of an egg, making an ointment. There is no leprosy, of any kind, that will not be cured if you often anoint it with this ointment, unless death is present for the one who has it, or God does not wish to cure it. The liver of this animal has good heat and cleanliness in it, and the fat in the egg yolks is the most precious thing in an egg and is just like an unguent. Leprosy very often is from black bile, and from overabundant black blood.

From unicorn skin, make a belt. Gird yourself with it against your skin, and no strong disease or fever will harm your insides. Also, make shoes from its skin and wear them. You will always have healthy feet, legs, and loins. No disease will harm you in these places. [A person who fears being killed by poison should put unicorn hoof under the dish where his food is, or under the cup containing his drink. If they are hot and there is poison in them, it will make them boil in their vessel; if they are cold, it will make them smoke, and he will be able to tell there is poison in them.] Other parts of the unicorn are not suitable for medicine.

VI. TIGER

The tiger (tigris) is hot. It walks through mountains and valleys, having a bit of the nature of an ibex. From its long journeying, pustules come out of it, like gum, which it wipes off. They have a sweet odor and are valuable for medicines. Its flesh is slimy and, because of the tiger's strength and quickness, it is not good for a person to eat. If someone has recent, not long-standing, leprosy, he should take the heart of a tiger, when it is freshly killed, and place it, warm, over the place of the leprosy. The leprosy will pass into the heart, and the person will be healed. If the leprosy is old, it is not beneficial to place this heart on it. If the heart is fresh and warm and placed on old leprosy, or old and cold and placed on fresh leprosy, the disease does not pass into the tiger heart, but into the flesh of the person. It would harm him, because the person's heart would easily burst.

VII. PANTHER

The panther (panthera) is very hot in its nature. It is as if it were striving toward vainglory, since it freely imitates all animals in its doings. It does not value other animals because of love of them, but because it willingly does their deeds, in accordance with its nature. It does not eat clean foods, whence its breath is not clean. It is a bit poisonous, although sometimes it seems to have a good odor. Parts of the panther are not much use as medicine.

VIII. HORSE

The horse (equus) is more hot than cold and has a good nature. It has such a great strength that it does not know it has it. It always wants to walk in front, eats clean things, and has flesh which is firm and is heavy to eat. It is harmful for a person, since, because of its strength, it can scarcely be digested. Flesh of ruminant animals is tempered, as if it had been placed in a press: it can easily be eaten and digested. Flesh of non-ruminant animals is heavier and not easily digested.

A person who has scabies, however strong, should take goat tallow and mix in blood from a horse's ear. He should often anoint himself with this near the fire, and he will be healed. [But a person who has contracted leprosy from anger should go where a bit of horse blood flows into the ground, when blood diminishes in their veins, where clean animals are killed. He should take the blood and with it the earth it has tainted. He should boil it in a caldron, being careful that there is enough water to remove the powers from the blood. Afterward, he should sit up to his throat in this bath. He should also put some of the same blood and earth in a small sack, which he should place on his face if he has pain there. When he comes out of the bath, he should lie in bed and put the sack with the blood and earth over his heart, lest it be weakened. He should do this four or five times, or more.] Other parts in a horse are not useful for medicine.

ix. Ass

The ass (asinus) is more hot than cold. It is stupid and is almost blind from the superfluous nature of its lust. It does not have anger, nor does it flee either subjection or human beings. It is willingly with people, because some part of its nature nears that of the human. Its flesh, which is not good for people to eat, is fetid from the ass's stupidity. If a person troubled by palsy has those changeable diseases in him that, as in madmen, increase and decrease in accordance with the moon, look for a place where an ass has been killed, or has died by itself, or where it rolls on the earth. There, whether on grass or on earth, with a cloth or, if the patient is very sick, a thin bubicio placed over it, make the patient lie. He should sleep, if he can. Later, take his right hand and say, "Lazarus slept and rested, then rose. Just as he was roused by Christ from stinking foulness, so rise from this dangerous disease and changeable ways of these fevers, in conjunction with those things which Christ who sits above conjoined to himself when, foresignaling that he would redeem people from their sins, he awakened Lazarus." Then, with short intervals, do this three times on the same day. On the next two days do it similarly, three times in the same place, and he will be cured.

x. Deer

The deer (cervus) has a hasty heat in it and cools off less, so it is more hot. It is gentle and eats clean foods. Its flesh is good for healthy and sick people to eat. When it perceives that the branches on its horns are not coming out further, it knows that it is beginning to dry up inside and becoming slow. It then enters a river and draws into itself the dampness that rises from the river. Leaving the river, it eats small herbs on shore, which are suitable for it. Then it seeks a place where it finds a basilisk and, when it has found it, it lows loudly, greatly troubling the basilisk, which also breathes on the deer. The deer raises its voice again and again; it lows and whinnies. At last the basilisk, as if out of wrath from its fatigue, twists itself into the deer's mouth and enters its stomach. The deer hurries to a spring it knows as having the nature of carrying off rotten matter and poison, and it drinks excessively from it, so that the basilisk is submerged in that water. Having done this, it seeks out herbs that cause purgation and eats them. It emits the serpent, as if in a potion, through its rear. If that serpent were to not pass through, the deer would die from its poison. But then, it begins to be ill, and so it seeks a valley where the best, health-giving herbs grow. It eats them and stays quietly in that place for almost a month. Its horns and hair fall off, and then the deer begins to get a little better. Later, it again goes into the spring, drinking a little from it, so that any remaining foulness is gently purged. It then eats more of the above-mentioned herbs and begins to be healed. Its horns grow, and its hair comes out again. Afterward its flesh, and everything in the deer, is more healthy than it had been before. If a person eats the flesh of the deer when it is a bit hot, but not burning, it will purge his stomach, making it light. Shave some of its horn, add frankincense, and burn them together over a fire. The horn's power gives off an odor that chases off airy spirits, spells, and bad worms and checks magic. If a person eats deer liver, it will restrain his gicht and purge his stomach, making it light.

xi. Roe Deer

The roe deer (rech) is of a moderate temperature. It is gentle and has a clean nature. It gladly climbs mountains and seeks air that is not too hot and not too cold, but temperate. In the mountains it forages for herbs that grow from this sort of air. They are good, healthy foods. Its flesh is good for healthy and sick people. A person who is troubled by vicht should often eat its liver. It will check the vicht. If anyone frequently eats its flesh, it will purge mucus and foul matter from him. One who is tortured by gicht between his shoulder blades should dry and save the heart of the roe deer. When he has pain between his shoulder blades, dip that heart in olive oil and tie it over the place of his pain, and he will be better. One who has pain in his stomach, so that his stomach has pus in it or is cold or hardened because it cannot digest the foods he has eaten, should take the roe deer's tallow. He should add a third part of the oil from the fruit of an elm, or beech tree, and mix them together. He should smear this on a hempen cloth and place the cloth over his stomach. He should wear it and, even if the pain in his stomach is great, he will be better. If neither oil is available, he should place tallow from the roe deer on the cloth as described and place it around his stomach. However, for making this plaster, the oil from the elm is better than rue oil.

XII. IBEX

The ibex (steynbock) is more cold than hot, and it is complicated in its ways. It willingly dwells in mountains and clouds, and in dosste and in dauwe, and its strength is very sudden, because it often labors. Its flesh is slimy, weak, and not good for a healthy or sick person to eat. Nevertheless, a healthy person is able to survive eating it. From its skin, make a belt and shoes. Wear them and they will preserve health in your body. Dry the ibex's tail, along with the tail's skin and flesh. Carry it in your hand, and you will not be able to be led unwillingly by magic. If you have consumed poison in your food or drink, immediately put this tail in wine, or any drink whatsoever, for an hour. Then drink it, and the poison will pass through you in nausea, or in emptying your bowels, and you will be cured. From its horn, make a knife handle. Always keep this with you, in your hand or elsewhere, and it will give you health. Other parts of the ibex are not useful as medicine.

XIII. BISON

The bison (wisant) is hot. It has the habits of a deer, but is faster and a bit more healthy than a deer. Its flesh is healthful to eat and good for a person. If a pestilence is troubling horses or asses, oxen and sheep, goats and pigs, or any other animals, shave some bison horn into water and give it to them to drink for nine days. The pestilence will go from them. Other parts of the bison are not suitable for making medicine.

XIV. OX

The ox (bos) is cold and dry in temperament. Where there is an ox, airy spirits do not make emnity for a human being, nor can they create their various illusions. The ox is clean, and in ancient days was often given to God as a whole burnt offering. Its flesh, because of the coldness in it, is not good for a cold person to eat. But for one who is warm by nature, it is good to eat, because of the coldness in its flesh. If someone has a stabbing pain in his limbs and joints, and also has pain in his stomach, he should cook the feet of an ox, that is the callous skin and tallow, and eat a sufficient amount. It will check the piercing disease in his joints and the pain in his stomach. One who frequently eats the liver of an ox will be strengthened because of its good nature. Its heart and lungs are not much good for eating. You will experience the same nature in a cow. Other parts of the ox are not very beneficial as medicine.

XV. SHEEP

The sheep (ovis), whether ram or lamb, is cold, but warmer than the ox. It is also moist and simple, has no bitterness or sharpness in it, and has flesh that is good for both healthy and sick people to eat. One who is failing in his whole body, and whose veins are withered, should, if he wishes, frequently sip juice from the flesh of the sheep, drink the broth in which it was cooked, and eat a bit of the meat. When he is stronger, he should eat more of this if he wishes. The meat is good to eat in summer, because the summer warms it up. In winter, it is not good to eat, because the winter makes it cold. The skins of sheep are good for people's clothing, since they carry no pride, or lust, or disease, as skins of other animals do. Whence, God gave Adam sheepskin clothing.

If someone is troubled by quotidian, tertian, or quartan fevers of any kind, take the fleece of a ram, without the skin. Sprinkle a bit of sheep tallow, which had been heated on a fire, onto the area of that fleece that had been next to the skin of the ram. Warm them together on the fire, and when the ague is tormenting the person with a chill, place the fleece on his stomach, chest, and around his shoulders. It will warm him up and enable him to sleep. Do this as often as the ague torments him, and he will quickly be cured.

XVI. GOAT

The goat (hircus) has a very rapid heat and unstable ways. Its flesh is good for both healthy and sick people to eat; eaten often, it heals weak and worn out intestines. It also strengthens the stomach of the person who eats it. The she-goat can be eaten by a strong person until August, but the he-goat is good to eat in August. Kids, whether males or females, are good for people to eat until autumn.

A person with stomach pain should roast the liver of a goat and eat it often until the middle of August. Like a good potion, it will cleanse and heal his stomach. [The tallow of the goat is good and healthful, and suitable for many medicines. The she-goat has the same nature as the male, except the male is stronger. If someone ails in his lungs, he should frequently drink goat's milk, and he will be cured.] Other parts of the goat are not useful as medicine.

XVII. PIG

The pig (porcus) is hot and has an ardent nature. It is full of mucus, since no coldness purges it. It is also a bit pussy. The pig is always an avid eater, not caring what it eats, so sometimes it eats unclean things. In its avidity it has wolflike habits, since it tears other animals apart; it also has canine habits, since it willingly lives with humans, just as a dog does. But it is an unclean animal, so its flesh is neither healthy nor good for either a healthy or sick person to eat. It does not diminish phlegm or other infirmities in a person, but augments them. Its heat joins with a person's heat, and stirs up in him tempests which are bad in their ways and workings. But, a person who is very sick, so that he is failing and dry in his entire body, should eat young piglets in moderation while he is sick. He will receive heat from them. After he has gotten better, he should not eat them anymore, for to do so would bring back his illness. A person whose body is nearly failing should often eat the cooked liver of a pig. It will nourish and strengthen him. Wild pig has the same nature, except it is cleaner than the domestic pig. Other parts of the pig do not have much use as medicine.

XVIII. HARE

The hare (lepus) is more hot than cold, and it has the gentleness and leap of a roe deer. Sometimes it appears to change sex, that is, the male at times draws its virile parts within, so that he is like a female; the female sometimes emits something like a bone, just like an intestine, from near her umbilicus, so she is thought to be like a male, but she is not. The male will not be a female, and the female will not be a male. The male does not bring forth young, and the female does not have semen. Pour the hare's bile, mixed with nothing else, over a person's leprosy, anointing it often. The ruse of the leprosy will fall off, and the person will be healed. The hare's bile is very useful for this. The other parts of the hare are not much use as medicine.

XIX. WOLF

The wolf (lupus) is very hot, has some of the ways of airy spirits, and has some of the habits of a lion. The airy spirits in its nature are often delighted by it, and accompany it. The wolf always lies in wait for a human, and will gladly tear him apart if possible, even if it is not hungry. In accordance with its lion's nature, it knows and understands the human being, and smells him from afar. When a wolf first sees a person, the airy spirits accompanying it weaken the person's powers, so he does not know that the wolf sees him. If the person sees the wolf first, he holds God in his heart, and by that effort both the wolf and the airy spirits flee. A person who is much troubled by gicht should take equal weights of the leaves of gicht-baum and southernwood and pound them in a mortar. He should add a greater amount of wolf fat and mix these together, making an unguent. He should anoint himself with this where it hurts and, one or two days later, enter a sauna, and the gicht will sweat off him along with the ointment. He should wash himself vigorously in that bath. He should not leave the ointment on his skin, but should wash it off. It is so strong that gicht will in no way be able to remain in any place oiled by it.

If someone, because of weakness of diseases, should be mad in the head and insane, shave the hair from his head and cook a wolf in water, having thrown away its head and intestines. Wash the head of the mad one in a broth of this water, with his eyes, ears, and mouth tied with a cloth, lest any of it enter these places. If any of the broth enters his body, he would be more crazy, since it would be as a poison to him. Do this for three days. Although the madness is great, he will recover his senses. If he does not allow you to bind his eyes, ears, and nose with a cloth, then dip a linen cloth in the broth, and dampen his head with the warm cloth. Allow it to lie on his head for a little while. After doing this for three days, he will return to his senses. When he is better, wash his head in warm wine, so the richness will be washed and removed from his head.

In any house where there is pelt, hair, or bones of a wolf, people are prone to quarrel and cause fights, and, because of the wolf's very bad nature, airy spirits freely run about there.

XX. DOG

The dog (canis) is very hot and has a common and natural affinity with human ways. It senses and understands the human being, loves him, willingly dwells with him, and is faithful. The devil hates and abhors the dog because of its loyalty to humans. A dog, recognizing hatred, wrath, and perfidy in a person, often howls at him. If it knows there is hatred and wrath in a house, it quietly growls and gnashes its teeth. If a person has treachery in him, the dog gnashes its teeth at him, even though the person loves that dog, since it recognizes and understands this in a person. If there is a thief in the house, or someone who wants to steal, it growls and gnashes its teeth. It will go after him testing his odor with its nose and stalking him. In this way the thief can be recognized. The dog sometimes has a foreboding of happy or sad events to come in the future or already present. In accordance with its understanding, it sends out its voice, revealing this. When the future events are happy, it is happy, and wags its tail; when they are sad, he is sad and howls.

The heat in its tongue confers healing to wounds and ulcers if it it touches them. If shoes are made from its pelt, feet become weak and painful. It has filth in it, since its flesh is often transfused with unclean sweat. Its flesh is of no value to humans. Its liver and intestines are almost poisonous, and therefore its breath is harmful. If a dog bites into some bread or other food, or if it imbibes some drink, a person should not eat or drink from what remains. Sometimes a dog can taste food or drink and send poison into the rest. If, later, a person eats or drinks some of it, he will comsume poison. A dog has a soft and weak brain, which is sometimes touched by bad clouds. At times it can smell a certain watery, putrid odor of the air, in which airy spirits create their delusions and evil whisperings. It sometimes becomes mad from this. Other parts of the dog are not useful for medicine.

XXI. Fox

The fox (vulpus) is very hot. It has some of the ways of a panther and some of the understanding of a lion: From the latter it knows many things; from the former, it has a diversity of habits and understands the human being a bit. Sometimes it eats unclean foods. Because of the diversity in it, its flesh is not good for humans to eat. But its pelt is healthy, and the heat of its pelt is good for clothing. A person who has scrofula increasing on his body should take the fat of a fox, and add to it less of the fat of egg yolks. He should anoint the scrofula with this often. He should then mix chamomile in these fats and heat it in a small dish. Then he should tie the chamomile over the scrofula with a cloth. When these leaves have dried up, he should heat others in the same way and place them on the area. He should do this for three days and nights, then anoint the scrofula with the fats (having discarded the chamomile), and it will vanish.

XXII. BEAVER

The beaver (biber) is very hot, and it has air from water in it. It has its nature from both earth and water, and it is unable to remain in the water, away from land. When its body grows dry, it runs to the water, takes moisture from it, and is strengthened. Its hair grows from water, and its pelt is thick. Its flesh is good as food for both healthy and sick people. If a person ails in his spleen, he should often eat cooked beaver tongue, and his spleen will be cured. Or, he should reduce that tongue to a powder, put the powder in honey, and eat the honey. His spleen will be better. One who has fever should dry the beaver liver and reduce it to a powder. He should put a bit of it in warm wine and drink it often, and he will be better. [The testicles, drunk the same way in warm wine, will check fever in a person.]

XXIII. OTTER

The otter (otther) is hot, has a clean nature, and eats both clean and unclean foods. Its head and tail and flesh would be like poison for a person if he were to eat them. The heat of its pelt is healthful for humans. Other parts of it are not useful as medicine.

XXIV. MONKEY

The monkey (simea) is hot and, since it is somewhat like a human being, it watches a person and does what he does. It also has the habits of beasts, but is deficient in both natures. Unable to do completely what a man or beast does, it is unstable. Sometimes, when it sees a bird flying, it goes up high and leaps, attempting to fly. When it is unable to carry through with what it wants, it becomes angry. Because it is similar to a human, it has monthly cycles, in accordance with the moon. Because it is weak and unstable in both its natures, it is not valuable as medicine.

XXV. MARMOSET

The marmoset (merkacza) is more cold than hot and, being from air and water, is sometimes able to live in water. It even has a bit of the natures of the fox and the cat. But it licks neither earth nor serpent. The marmoset has a certain poison in it, which makes it sick and which it spits out and buries under the earth, in disdain. It knows it is bad and buries it just as it buries the dung it emits. If a person should touch what the marmoset spat out in this way, it would act like a poison. Many times, certain serpents and bad worms are born from what the marmoset spat out.

XXVI. CAT

The cat (cattus) is more cold than hot, and it draws bad humors to itself. It does not abhor airy spirits, nor do they abhor it. It has some natural affinity with the toad and the serpent. In the strong summer months, when it is very hot, the cat is dry and cold. It thirsts, and it licks toads or serpents—in the same way a person gladly tastes salt to have good flavor from it. From their moisture the cat strengthens its own vital fluid and is refreshed. Otherwise it would be unable to live and would perish. That moisture which it takes from the toad or serpent is almost like poison inside the cat. Its brain and all its flesh are poisonous. The cat is not willingly with a person, except the one who feeds it. At the time when it licks toads and serpents, its heat is harmful and poisonous for a person. When it carries its young within, its heat stirs up lust in a person; at other times, its heat is not harmful for a healthy person.

XXVII. LYNX

The lynx (luchs) is hot. It follows its own volition, doing what it wishes. It is happy in beautiful, bright breezes and in the summer sun, as well as is in winter's beautiful breezes and snow. It has almost no stability in it, except in what it does in accordance with the mildness of the breeze. Since it follows its own will, its eyes shine like the night's stars. If a pestilence is devastating and killing horses, asses, oxen, and pigs, mix lynx blood with water. When you see they are sick, give it to them to drink, once a day for three days. They will immediately get well. If the animals are not sick, this blood, tempered as described, should not be given to them, lest they be harmed. The pestilence has not found a place in them to display its strength. You should not give this to sheep or goats to drink, even if they are sick. It would be too strong for them, because of their debility and because they are weak animals. Except for the ligure, other parts of the lynx are not much use in medicine.*

---

*Translator's note: Here "ligure" refers to the precious stone made from the lynx's urine. See Ligure entry on p. 153.

XXVIII. BADGER

The badger (dasch) is hot and has quiet ways. It is mischievous, but not malicious. It has strong powers in itself, but thinks its power is nothing. It shows it suddenly and quickly stops it. If it were to always show it, it would be nearly comparable to the powers of a lion. It is loathe to display its strengths, unless it shows them in happiness and exultation. Take its heart and cook it vigorously in water. Add to it fat from this same animal, and gichtbaum and southernwood, less southernwood than gichtbaum. Cook them together in the same water, and make an unguent. This is the best thing against gicht, and for limbs which gicht has worn out. A person who suffers from this should anoint himself with this where it hurts, and he will be healed. If someone has a headache, he should anoint his neck and temples and forehead with the same ointment. Or, if someone has pain in his side or back, he should anoint himself there, and he will be better. One who has weak flesh with black spots should anoint himself there with the same ointment. His skin will become clear, because this will check all infirmities in a person. There is also great power in its pelt. Make a belt from it, and cinch it against your bare skin. All disease will go from you, just as a great storm is checked in good, mild, tranquil air. Dangerous illness will not fall upon you. Also, make shoes and boots from badger skin. Wear them, and your feet and legs will be healthy.

XXIX. POLECAT

The polecat (illediso) is cold and smelly. It has the ways of a thief, the nature of a wolf. It often eats things which are unclean. Its pelt is not healthful for people's clothing, because it brings cold into a person. Other things which are in it are not suitable for medicine.

XXX. HEDGEHOG

The hedgehog (ericius) is cold and of an unclean nature. It eats wild fruits and berries. It is similar to a pig, but the filth that would be in its body ascends into its quills, and so it is cleaner than a pig. Just has its quills injure a person's hands, so the flesh of a pig diminishes a person's health and cleanliness. If a person who is physically healthy wishes to eat hedgehog, he should cook it in water, as he cooks a hare. He should pulverize equal weights of cinnamon, feverfew, and pimpernel and heat this in wine. When the hedgehog is cooked, and removed from the pot, he should pour the wine with the powders over it, just as he customarily pours pepper over meat. If he eats it this way, it will not harm him, but will make him strong, and he will retain his health.

Another hedgehog is cold, has some of the nature of a dog in it, and sometimes eats earth. The clean and unclean things in it rise into its quills. Just as a dog's, its flesh is not good for a person to eat. If scrofula has erupted on a person, he should throw out the viscera of the hedgehog and reduce the rest of its body to a powder. He should put this powder into the ruptured scrofula, and it will dry up. Other parts of the hedgehog are not useful as medicine.

XXXI. SQUIRREL

The squirrel (eichorn) is hot. It has in it some of the nature of both beasts and birds. From its bird nature, it is windy. Its skin is good for human clothing. If a horrible gicht lies in the joints of a person's limbs, and the limbs seem to contract and loosen, he should take squirrel. With the head and viscera thrown away, and the skin drawn off, he should roast the rest of the body on the fire. When it is roasted, it should be smeared with bear fat, so that fat flows from it. He should place the fat which flows from it with the bear fat on a cloth and twist all the liquid and fat through the cloth. With it, he should anoint the limbs which are in pain from gicht, and he will be cured.

XXXII. HAMSTER

The hamster (hamstra) is cold and fierce, and it is a bit like a bear. Its nature is somewhat clean, and its pelt is good for clothing. A person who has scrofula or swellings on his body should pulverize the liver of a hamster, and eat this powder with bread or drink it in a broth. The scrofula and swellings will vanish more than they do from mole's flesh. If someone is troubled with gicht between the shoulder blades, he should dry a hamster's right shoulder as well as its right foot and tie these between his shoulder blades. This will make him better.

XXXIII. MARTEN

The marten (marth) of the forest is hot and has gentle habits. Many live together, as if having a common life. The marten has bad sweat in its flesh, which makes its flesh harmful for a person to eat. That sweat remains in the flesh and does not pass into the pelt, so the pelt is good and healthful for people's clothing. If any person has scrofula on his body, he should skin the marten and dissolve its fat in a small dish. With the head and viscera thrown out, he should cook the rest of its body in a bit of water. The fat which he gets from that he should add to the other fat. He should add a lesser amount of the fat of egg yolks and mix these together, making an unguent. With it, he should anoint the scrofula, before it ruptures, and it will disappear. If it has already ruptured, he should smear this around it, and the scrofula will be healed.

xxxiv. Water Marten

The water marten (wasser marth) is cold. It dwells near water, in caves. It is fiercer than the forest marten, but the pelt of the forest marten is better. Make an unguent of its fat, and the fat of egg yolks, as described for the forest marten. If anyone is troubled by gicht, you should anoint him with this. It will check the gicht because of its cold nature.

xxxv. Sable

The sable (zobel) is hot. Its nature is similar to that of the squirrel, but it is cleaner and more pleasant than the squirrel. Its pelt is not good for human clothing, because if it heats up on a person it will stir up bad humors in him. Because it is weak, things in the sable are not valuable for medicine.

xxxvi. Ermine

The ermine (harmini) is cold. It has a bit of the nature of a cat. It does not have clean flesh. It is foamy and mucusy, like poison. When it ejects its froth, it often sends out short pieces of hair as well. Its skin is not good for human clothing, because it is cold. Those things which are in the ermine are not suitable for medicine, since its flesh is a bit poisonous.

xxxvii. Mole

The mole (talpa) is cold. It willingly dwells in rich, muddy earth and avoids thin soil. It rejects soil that is bad, depleted, and useless and instead lives in soil that is good and healthy. It cannot see, since it does not live in the air, but it has much knowledge within. By smelling it understands where it ought to go, and it eats earth. Its flesh is not good for a person to eat, because it is nourished by moisture. Nor should anyone eat it as medicine. A person who is putrescent inside or who has scrofula on his body should cook a mole in water and eat it, or he should pulverize it and eat that powder in whatever way he can. The inside of his body will be healthy, and the scrofula, if it had not yet ruptured, will be healed. Just as the mole throws out bad earth, so it sends away the rotten matter from inside a person's body. The person should also eat the mole's liver when he eats the rest of its body. It will remove the putrid matter from his body. He should not eat the heart or lungs.

[One who is tormented by epilepsy should pulverize the blood of a mole, the beak of a female duck, and the feet of a female goose, so there is twice as much duck beak as goose feet, and twice as much mole blood as duck beak. He should place this powder, tied in a cloth, in a place where a mole is currently throwing out earth, for three days. After removing it, he should put it in a place where there is ice, so it congeals. Then he should make it dry out in the sun. Then he should take as much as he can of the edible liver of this animal, and that of a bird. He should prepare little cakes from these things with a bit of wheat flour. He should add a bit less of the forenamed powder, and a bit of cumin, and eat it. The person suffering from epilepsy should eat these cakes for five days. If he is not yet well, he should eat them for another five days. If it is still not beneficial, he should repeat this five-day regimen seven times. He should meanwhile eat bread and goat meat cooked with celery and parsley. He may also eat lamb. He should avoid pork, beef, eel, cheese, eggs, and raw fruits and vegetables. He may drink sweet wine, mixed with water, and beer.]

XXXVIII. WEASEL

The weasel (wisela) is hot. In its speed, it has something of the power of a griffin when it raises its wings. It has a rotten and insensitive nature. It knows of a certain herb containing vital health. If it sees its young or another weasel in pain, it quickly seeks this herb, which is small and tender. It digs in the earth for it and, after it finds it, blows on it and urinates over it, mixing its strength with that of the herb. It waits for a short time, until that herb is fully suffused with the urine. Then, taking it in its mouth, it places it in the mouth of the weasel that is about to die, the vital air now being in its throat; thus it is healed, rises, and walks away. This herb is unknown to humans and other animals. If they did know it, their breath and urine would not be strong enough to suffuse it. This herb has no life-giving properties in itself. It has to receive its power from the weasel's breath and urine. Also, weasels always eat such good, strong herbs that they scarcely get diseases. Its flesh is not good for a person to eat, since it would be less strong in his stomach. But, draw off the little skin of a weasel and hold it over balsam, so it does not become damp from the balsam but only takes the odor from it. If you do not have balsam, place it on moss, so it takes its odor. Then, often place that skin on your eyes and nose, and they will stay healthy.

Also, dry the weasel's heart, set it in thin wax, and when you have a headache place the wax with the heart in it in your ear for a little while, so its heat might enter your head. Your head will be better. And, if you begin to go deaf in one ear, put the wax-encased heart on that ear until its heat reaches the inside of the ear, and you will recover your hearing. Also, cut the weasel's head off and dry the rest of its body, in two pieces, in the sun or over the fire. Then sew them separately into a belt made of any kind of leather, so the first piece is placed over your umbilicus, the other piece over both your sides. Always gird yourself with that belt against your bare skin. It will strengthen you and make you safe and robust, so that gicht will not trouble you.

xxxix. Mouse

A mouse (mus) is hot and has insidious habits and devilish skills. Since it always flees, its flesh is harmful to humans and not much use as medicine. But, if someone having epilepsy falls on the ground, after he gets up, place a mouse in a vessel (of water). Give that water to the person to drink, and wash his forehead and feet in that water. This should be done each time he falls and he will be cured. Since a mouse flees all things, it will chase off the epilepsy. When a mouse has to give birth, she has difficulty in bringing forth the young. She goes, in pain, to the edge of some water and seeks very small stones there. She eats as many as she can hold in her throat, runs to her hole, and spits them out there. She breathes on them and gets on top of them. She warms them up and immediately gives birth. As soon as she has given birth she hates the stones and kicks them away. She then lies over her young, warming them. If it is possible to find those stones within the same month that she has rejected them, one can tie them over the umbilicus of a pregnant woman who is already in labor but not able to give birth. She will then give birth and, as soon as she does, they should be removed. If one has the ague, take a mouse and give it a blow so it cannot run away. Before it dies, tie the back of the mouse between the shoulder blades of the person when the ague is tormenting him. Let the mouse die between the person's shoulder blades, and that person will be cured, and ague will invade him no more.

xl. Dormouse

The dormouse (lira) is hot, and it has the same nature as the other mouse, except that it is wilder and stronger than mice. It is just as valuable against the same dangers as the other mouse, as described.

XLI. SHREW

The shrew (spiczmus) has nearly the same nature as a mole, except the shrew is able to remain under the earth and in the air more than the mole, and so does not remain fully under the earth. The things in it are not suitable for medicine.

XLII. FLEA

The flea (pulex) is hot and grows from the dust of the earth. In the winter, when the earth is moist and warm inside, fleas lie in the earth and hide. When the upper earth is dried up by summer heat, they come out of the earth and invade the human being, bothering him. Therefore, take some earth, but not its dust, and heat it in on an earthenware tile. Dry it until no moisture remains in it. Sprinkle it in your bed. When fleas sense its aridity, they cannot bear it. They will flee and perish, and the person will have some relief from them.

XLIII. ANT

The ant (formica) is hot. It grows from that moisture which brings forth aromas. In accordance with the nature of birds, they produce eggs. A person who has much phlegm in his head, chest, or stomach should take an ant hill, with the ants inside, and cook it in water. He should pour that water over a hot stone and draw the steam into his nose and mouth, ten or fifteen times. The phlegm will diminish. But one who has a superfluity of bad humors in him, that is gicht, should take the ant hill, with the ants, and cook it in water, preparing a bath. He should get into that bath, and keep his whole body in it, exposing only his head covered with a cloth moistened in that same water. If his head were to touch the water in the bath, it would be easily hurt by its strength. He should do this often, and the gicht will go from him. If someone has leprosy of any kind, he should take the earth where there is a hill of ants, so that it is possible to know how much the ants had dampened that earth. He should place it among burning embers of beech wood and let it flare up from these embers, so the earth exceeds the quantity of embers. He should then let hot water pass through the hot earth nine times, as if making lye. Then he should mix goat tallow with a little more old pork fat and put it in the lye-water. After it congeals, it should be removed from the water. He should add powdered violet and chamomile, less chamomile than violet, to make an ointment. He should anoint the area of the leprosy with this ointment, while he is near the fire, for nine months or more. He will be healed, if the leprosy is not the death of him, or unless God does not want him to be cured. When he is applying this ointment, he should take care not to get near another person or a pig. The strong vapor of the leprosy, going out of him would infect them, and they would easily get leprosy from him.

A person who has swellings and scrofula should smear ant eggs on a green oak leaf, spread rooster dung over that, and often place it over the swellings or scrofula, and they will disappear. But, if a person is angry, or mentally oppressed, or sad, he should take young ants, when they still adhere to their eggs, with a bit of the nest in which they lie, and tie them in a linen cloth. Afterward, when he senses the heaviness in his mind, he should loosen the cloth that holds the ants and place them on his heart until it receives their sweat. He will have a calm mind, will be happy, and will receive a good understanding of the matters with which he is occupied.

XLIV. HELIM

Helim is hot and of great fortitude. It is daring and its flesh, because of its fortitude, is useless as food for humans. Its liver may be pulverized and mixed with bear fat, or with butter from cows. One who is out of his mind, or whose head is effected by palsy, should be anointed with this frequently, and he will be better.

XLV. DROMEDARY

The dromedary (dromeda) has the ardor of fire and the moderation of water in it. It has the quick flight of large, strong birds. If a person or other animal should eat some of its flesh, the strength of the fire and the powerful velocity in it would destroy all the powers of the one eating it. But, if someone has some of its pelt or hoof, phantasms and any magic thing will shun him.

REPTILES

BOOK EIGHT

Reptiles

 IN THE BEGINNING, every creature God made was good. Then, by means of the serpent, the devil deceived the human being so that he was thrown out of paradise. After that, in revenge, creatures testing divine will were made worse with humans. Whence, seeds of cruel and poisonous vermin rose up for this revenge, revealing infernal punishments with their death-bearing cruelty. Striking hellish terror in people, with divine permission the vermin used their poison to kill. Before the fall of man, they had in them not deadly but delectable liquid. Also, when the earth was corrupted with the spilling of Abel's blood, a new fire blazed in the underworld. Murderers were punished in it. And soon by divine will a certain cloud, bubbling out of the underworld, stretched over the earth. It infused the earth with a very bad humor. The worst, poisonous, deadly worms bubbled out repeatedly from that soil, so that the people's flesh might be punished by them, since one human killed another. When human beings were later wiped out in a flood of waters, in divine vengeance, these vermin, unable to live in water, were suffocated by it. The flood scattered their cadavers over all the earth and, when the flood subsided, these cadavers, full of poison, putrified. From the putrifaction, other worms of the same kind were born and were spread throughout the world. Certain vermin kill people or animals with their poisons, others kill only humans. Vermin that are a bit like diabolic arts in their nature kill other animals, as well as humans, with their poisons. Those that do not

imitate the diabolic arts have in them poisons which are a bit weak. Through their poisons, they bring to humans many diseases and dangers along with death, but they are unable to kill other animals.

I. DRAGON

The dragon (draco) has dryness, alien heat, and a certain fiery imbalance in it, but its flesh is not fiery inside. Its breath is so strong and sharp that it immediately ignites when it comes out, just as fire does when it is lured from a stone. It has a strong hatred for human beings and, according to its nature, has diabolic arts in it. Sometimes when it sends out its breath, airy spirits from this breath stir up the air. Everything in its flesh and bones is harmful for human medicine, except its fat. When the dragon sends out its breath, its blood is dried up and not fluid. When its breath is within it, its blood is moist and flows. Whence there is not even any medicine found in its blood.

A person who has a stone in him should take some dragon blood and put it in a damp place so that it gets a bit moist. He should then place the blood in pure water for a short time, until the water takes some heat from it. Having removed the blood, he should drink a moderate amount of that water on an empty stomach. He should soon eat some food. He should do this with the blood and water for nine days, and the stone in him will be broken up by the strength of the blood, and he will be liberated. No one should eat or drink any of this blood pure and simple. If anyone were to do this, he would immediately die.

II. A CERTAIN SERPENT

A certain kind of serpent (quoddam genus serpentis) is very hot and is able to live on land and water. It has diabolic arts for ambushing people. This serpent is hostile toward human beings. It sends out its breath, which is full of deadly poison, toward a person. Even its skin is thickened by the poison within it, so that the skin contracts into wrinkles and the outer layer is split from the heat of the sun. When it feels this, it is as if it were oppressed by ulcers. It seeks a narrow opening in a rock, which it rubs against until it throws off foam. It is then less savage than it had been when it was burdened by the foam. When it has thrown off the foam, its skin becomes delicate and clear, as if new. The serpent rejoices greatly and is then a bit less fierce in its poison and ambushes. A person who finds the snake in this condition should kill it and carefully remove its tail. He should dry the tail in the sun and preserve it in thin metal. When he is oppressed by some great sadness and trouble, he should hold it in his right hand. He will be made happy from it and, as long as he holds it in his hand, he cannot be harmed, internally, by poison. If he eats or drinks poison, it will pass through him in sweat, nausea, or in evacuating his bowels. The liver and other parts of the serpent are deadly and thus suitable for no remedies.

There is another kind of serpent that is hot but lives only on land, not in water. Its poison, being a bit weak, harms a person less if he touches or tastes it. This kind of snake sometimes lives with people in their homes or in dry places. It sets fewer ambushes for people. When it sees that a person wants to strike it, it sticks out its tongue and moves it in supplication. It is of the kind that seduced Adam, and therefore seeks human habitations.

III. Slowworm

The slowworm (blintsleich) is cold, and while alive it does not harm people. It has no utility and is not valuable for medicine. After it is dead, people will be injured by its poison if they have touched or eaten it.

IV. Toad

The toad (credda) has in it some great heat and some bitterness. Just as dangerous winds come forth with lightning and thunder and hail, it has some diabolic art in it. It seeks its home on land, under the earth. It has some association with humans and is sometimes dangerous. A person who has scrofula should take the liver of the toad, wrap it in moist earth, and then bury it in other earth for nine days. On the tenth day, he should throw the liver away and heat the moist earth, which had been around it, on a piece of pottery. For three days, he should put it on scrofula that has not ruptured. It will vanish without a doubt, unless it holds the death of the person, or unless God does not will it. If the scrofula has ruptured, he should heat the same earth, as already described, on the fire, and place it on an old linen cloth, which sometimes takes in a person's sweat. First, he should place a spiderweb over the ulcers, then this cloth with the warm earth within it. When it has lost its heat, he should reheat it and put it on again. He should do this two or three times a night, for three nights, and the scrofula will vanish. The earth is put in the linen cloth because of the cleanliness of the linen, since linen attracts mucus to itself. The cloth is old, because it ought to be suffused more than a new cloth with human sweat. There ought to be human sweat in it so that rotten matter flees the sweat, which is stinky. Something bad often dispels another bad thing.

V. FROG

The frog (frosch) is cold and a bit watery. Therefore, its powers are not as bad as the toad's. For one who is troubled by gicht in any part of his body, except the head, he should take a frog and suffocate him over grass or under any herb. Place a warm cloth over the place where gicht is raging, and then place the frog, now dying, on that cloth for a little while. The gicht in that place will stop for a year, or at least half a year.

VI. TREE FROG

The tree frog (laubfrosch) is more hot than cold. It grows from the air through which trees bring forth their greenness and flowers. At the time when trees are producing this greenness and their flowers, airy spirits attack humans more than at any other time. At that time people's minds are bursting with the vanity of joking and ridiculing. Just as the viridity of the tree is increasing, humans create idolatry and many empty things with the tree frog, through diabolic arts. If someone wishes to ensnare this reptile, so that diabolic deeds are not created though it, he should throw it in a spring of living water so that it becomes wet. Then no one can bring about diabolic happenings with it. It is not useful as medicine.

VII. HARUMNA

The harumna is cold, and mucus and poison are its hot components. The poison is not hot enough to harm a person very much. There is no medicine in it.

VIII. MOLL

The moll is more hot than cold, but its heat quickly grows cold. Its poison is deadly. The moll itself does not harm people much while it is alive, but people are killed by its poison if they taste it. Other parts of it are not useful as medicine.

IX. LIZARD

The lizard (lacerta) is hot and dry. Its poison is a bit weak and not very harmful to people. The lizard is harsh and fierce in its nature. Things in it are not useful as medicine.

X. SPIDER

The spider (aranea) is more hot than cold, and it is very like a scorpion in the danger of its poison. The scorpion's heart is large and fat, and the spider's is small and weak. Its poison is dangerous to humans if it touches the outside of their flesh. If a person eats or drinks its poison, he will either die or scarcely escape death.

XI. VIPER

The viper (vipera) is as hot as fire, and everthing in it is deadly. It does not allow anything it is able to conquer to live near it. It is of such great malice that a viper flees other vipers until the time when it is necessary to conceive. If anyone finds a dead viper in an area where vipers live (since it is impossible to get a live one), he should burn a great fire, with strong wood, in a secret place, and throw the viper in. He should hurriedly leave that place, lest the poison or bad vapors touch him. After it has been reduced to ashes, the person should leave any part of it that remains, but he should take its ashes, and the ashes of the charcoals in which it was burned, and keep them in a linen cloth. Then, if someone swells up on some part of his body, he should place that cloth, with the ashes, over the swelling. The swelling will immediately go away.

XII. BASILISK

The basilisk (basiliscus) is born from certain vermin that are somewhat diabolical, that is, from toads. Sometimes, when the toad has been impregnated and is going to bring forth young, if she sees the egg of a serpent or hen, she loves it and lies over it. She warms it until she gives birth to her naturally conceived young.

These die as soon as they are born. Seeing them dead, she again places herself over the egg and warms it until the young in that egg has begun to live. Soon, a particular power of the diabolic art of the ancient serpent touches it. This power rests in the Antichrist, and just as he resists all heavenly beings, so this animal fights against all mortals, killing them. After the toad senses that the thing in the egg is alive, she is immediately astounded by this unusual occurrence and flees. The animal breaks through its shell and emerges. It naturally sends out very strong breath, similar to thunder and lightning. The fire within it can be very fierce and strong, without the torments of Tartarus. It comes from its shell and with its breath it splits the earth almost to the depth of five cubits. It then lies in this split of moist earth until it grows to maturity. Then it climbs back up to earth, killing with its breath all the living things it finds. Nothing living desires, nor is able, to endure it. When it sees something that is alive, in its displeasure it sends cold and then its breath, so killing the creature it blew on. It falls immediately, as if struck by thunder and lightning. If a basilisk has died in any field or vineyard, and its cadaver has rotted there, that place will be unfruitful and sterile. If it dies and rots in any citadel or house, the people there will always be ill, and the animals in that place will frequently get disease and very often die from it.

XIII. SCORPION

The scorpion (scorpio) has in it a burning heat and passion, and also the harshness of infernal punishments. Whatever is in it is a totally deadly poison that is the death of a human, and sometimes of animals. Any person who wishes to prepare poisonous things with it would subject to death anyone to whom it was given to drink or touch. There is no medicine in it, only very certain death.

XIV. TARANTULA

The tarantula (darant) is very hot and poisonous. It sends all its poison into its tail, so that its tail is always full of poison, as beasts' udders are full of milk. It inflicts death on human beings and animals with the poison of its tail. There is nothing useful and no medicines in it.

XV. TYRIACA

The tyriacan vermin is very hot and naturally seeks dry air. It has a healthy moisture, which is not too hot or too cold, and purges itself from all its noxious humors at one time. Otherwise it would be very dangerous to humans. When sickly air or breezes are present, it seeks out sandy caverns and hides in them. While there, it eats certain herbs having a concern for good health, and from them it preserves its health. There are not many precious ointments in it, but it creates a certain terror, bringing out sweat when a person has tasted it in any way. However, it does not do much to expel inner illnesses of a person.

XVI. SCHERZBEDRA

Scherzbedra is hot and has moisture in it. A person who eats or drinks poison should reduce the whole scherzbedra to a powder and add a bit of whole wheat flour, so that there is five times as much powder as flour. He should mix water with it, make little cakes, and cook them in the sun, or in a somewhat cool oven. Then he should reduce the cakes again to a powder, and eat some of this powder in an egg. It will purge the poison from him through nausea or in evacuating his bowels.

XVII. EARTHWORM

The earthworm (ulwurm) is very hot. It grows in the same viridity in which grasses begin to sprout. It grows in that noisy greenness and, because of its clean nature, has no bones. It is good, and useful, like other useful things, such as cinnamon. Earth has moisture in it, which is contained in something like veins, so it does not flow out. When the rain is about to fall from the air, this moisture feels the coming rain, which will fill its veins. The earthworms understand this replenishing of the earth's veins and come forth.

A person who has scrofula should gather a sufficient amount of earthworms when they come out due to rainfall. He should place them on a shard, or in a clay pot, and expose them to the smoke of barley straw until they die. Then he should add wheat flour and vigorously mix it with oak wood. He should then add a little wine and vinegar, of equal measure, mix it, and make a paste. Before the scrofula has ruptured, he should put this paste over it for three days. The cleanliness of these clean worms will lessen the uncleanliness of his flesh, and the scrofula will be unable to stay there any longer. If the scrofula has already ruptured, dip the paste, prepared as mentioned, in very harsh lye and place it over the broken scrofula. This will heal it, carrying away the rotten matter. One who ails in his stomach should place the dung of the earthworm—heated over broken pottery as described—on his stomach. If he does this often, his stomach will be purged and lightened. If you are unable to have earthworms when you could have them easily, and if it does not rain, so they do not come out of the ground, then seek them, digging in a damp place, and make the above-mentioned medicines with them. These medicines are much more useful if the earthworms have come out on their own, in a rain shower.

XVIII. SNAIL OR SLUG

The snail (testudo) that is in a shell moves on top of the earth. It has a cold nature. The snail that does not have a shell is not much good for medicine. If vermin are eating a person, he should take the shell of the snail, reduce it to a powder, and throw this powder on the place where the vermin are eating him. They will die, and he will be healed. The snail that does not have a shell is cold and almost as useful for the same medicine, if you prepare it as described for the earthworm—although medicine made from earthworms is much better and stronger than that made from slugs. When you are unable to have earthworms, prepare the described medicines from the slugs, even though they will be weaker. The person who uses these as mentioned will be cured.

METALS

BOOK NINE
Metals

In the beginning, the spirit of the Lord was carried over the waters and the waters overflowed the earth. The water remained without wavering, but by breathing the Spirit made it flow. These waters poured across the land and strengthened it, lest it break apart. And where the fiery power that flows in water penetrated the earth, the fire of the water transformed the earth into gold. Where the purity of the flooding water penetrated the earth, that purity transformed itself and the earth which it suffused into silver. Where the fluctuation of the water penetrated the earth, moved by the wind, it and the earth it transfused were changed into steel and iron. Therefore, iron and steel are stronger than other metals, just as the fluctuation of water moved by winds is stronger than that moved by calm breezes. And, just as the spirit of the Lord first made the waters flood, so it also vivified the human being and gave plants, trees, and stones their vitality.

I. GOLD

Gold (aurum) is hot. Its nature is somewhat like the sun's, and it is almost like the element air. A person who is virgichtiget should take gold, cook it so there is no dirt in it, and reduce it to a powder. He should take a half handful of fine flour and knead it with water. He should then add to this paste a half pennyweight of the gold powder and eat it in the morning, before breakfast. On the next day, he should again make a little cake in the same way, with the same amount of gold, and eat it that day, before breakfast. This little cake, prepared and eaten in this way, will keep gicht from him for a year. The gold will lie in his stomach for two months, without irritating or ulcerating it. If the stomach is cold and full of mucus, it will warm it and purge it, without danger to the person. If a healthy person does this, he will retain his good health; if a sick person does it, he will get healthy. Again take pure gold, and heat it in a clay pot, or on a piece of pottery. So heated, place it in pure wine so it warms the wine. Drink it often, thus heated, and gicht will disappear. For one who has fever in his stomach, heat pure wine with hot gold in this way for him to drink, and the fever will abandon him. If a tumor rises up somewhere on a person's body, he should heat gold in the sun and rub it around the swelling, and the tumor will vanish. One who has deaf ears should prepare a paste with gold dust and fine flour, as described above, and stick a little of it in his ears. The heat will pass into his ear. If he does this often, he will recover his hearing.

II. SILVER

Silver (argentum) is cold [because it contains cold wind, which makes even the earth cold]. A person who has in him a superfluity of humors, which he often expels [by coughing them up], should heat very pure silver in fire and, thus heated, put it in good wine. He should do this three or four times, so that the wine gets hot from it. He should drink it often, heated this way, before breakfast and at night. It will diminish his superfluous humors.

[The strong natural cold of silver diminishes hot, cold, and moist humors by its sharpness, joined with the heat of the fire and the heat of the wine, altered as described. If someone takes food or drink in a silver vessel, it will not benefit him much, nor will it harm his physical health.]

If someone should eat silver reduced to a powder, it would be too cold and too heavy in his stomach, and he would be injured internally, even if it might be helpful against some illness at the time.

III. LEAD

Lead (plumbum) is cold. It would harm a person if taken into the body in any way [and it would do this because of the cold it contains and because it is indigestable and just like the scum and refuse of other metals]. If a dead person begins to swell up and lead is placed on top of him, the lead will restrict that swelling a bit [since he does not have vital breath in him]. If, however, it is placed on top of a living person who is beginning to swell, he would completely split and be unable to live [since its coldness, being like the scum of other metals, going through him, would split him. Neither food nor drink in a leaden vessel is beneficial, because of lead's coldness].

iv. Tin

Tin (stagnum) is more cold than warm. If a person puts tin on his skin, so that his skin and flesh warm up, it will carry illness into his body because of its coldness. If a person eats or drinks from a tin vessel, he will get sick, because tin is almost like poison. If the skin around a person's eyes droops, he should reduce tin to ashes and place them in pure wine. At night, when he goes to bed, he should smear this wine around his droopy eyelids. The eyelids will become healthy and beautiful, since the coldness of the tin, tempered with the heat of the wine, heals and sets right the flesh which hot humors shake up and let slip. However, this does not get rid of cloudiness in the eyes.

v. Copper

Copper (cuprum) is hot and quickly grows cold. It is somewhat like a golden spark—that is, like the sparks that fall from burning coals. If a person has fevers of the kind that arise in the stomach (but not quotidian, tertian, quartan, or ague), so that he yawns, is slow, and disdains food, he should take five pennyweight of pure copper. He should put this in a beaker of Franconian wine, boil the wine until it begins to be reduced, and then remove it from the fire. He should drink it moderately, while fasting, for nine days. The fevers will cease. But, if someone is virgichtiget, so that he is completely contracted and bent, take pure copper and throw it into the fire, until it is hot, twice. Take it from the fire, and let it cool down. Throw it into the fire a third time. When it is then hot, place it in good wine and cover the top of the vessel, so the heat and vapor do not escape. Then give it, moderately warm, to the person to drink, and the gicht in him will cease. [If someone eats or drinks poison, take good wine and a third as much vinegar and mix them with rue juice (half as much as the total amount of wine and vinegar). Place a bar of pure copper in fire and when it is hot place it in the wine so that it warms it up. Drink the warm wine, on an empty stomach, for three days. The poison will leave through nausea or evacuation of the bowels.]

Also, if horses, asses, oxen, goats, sheep, pigs, or any animals have a constriction of the throat or pain in the head, one should place a large piece of copper in a caldron, a clay pot, or a bucket. Pour water over it, and heat the water with the copper on a fire until it boils. Sprinkle this warm water on the animal feed whether oats or hay, so they eat it, so sprinkled, and the malady will go from them.

VI. BRASS

Brass (messing) is hot and made from something else, just as lime is made from a stone. Brass is not natural, but is made from other metal, just as a soldier is not a soldier from birth, but is made a soldier. Therefore it is not useful as medicine. It harms a person more than it helps him. If a person wears it as a ring on his finger, or if any of his flesh heats up from it, it will attract more illness than health [because that metal has no virtue in itself].

VII. IRON

Iron (ferrum) is naturally very hot and therefore is strong. Its strength is useful for many things. If someone has iron next to him, so that his flesh warms up, it is less harmful than tin [because iron is warm and correctly balanced. When its heat is roused by a fire and placed over a person's stomach, it chases off the cold humors that make his stomach sick]. If one's stomach is cold, so that he is in pain from it, he should take a thin sheet of iron and heat it on the fire. He should place it, thus warm, over his stomach, then remove it. He should heat it again, and place it on his stomach. If he does this often, he will be better.

VIII. STEEL

Steel (calybs) is very hot and is the very strongest form of iron. It nearly represents the divinity of God, whence the devil flees and avoids it. If you suspect there is poison in food or drink, secretly place a hot piece of steel in moist food, such as broth or vegetable puree. If there is poison present, the steel will weaken and disable it. If the food is dry, such as meat, fish, or eggs, place a hot piece of steel in wine and pour the wine over the food. If there is poison in it, it will suppress it, so that it does less harm to the person who eats it. Also, place the hot piece of steel in a drink—whether wine, beer, water, or any other beverage. Any poison present will immediately weaken. If steel, so heated in the fire, has been placed in poisoned food or drink, or if wine heated with the hot steel is poured over poisoned food—whether bread, meat, fish, or other foods of this kind—the power of the poison will be restricted and weakened. There is so much power in the steel that it dries up the poison, making it less able to harm the person who eats or drinks it. It will not be powerful enough to kill a person who tastes it, even though he may swell up or become sick for a little while. He will be able to evade death if the poison is weakened by the hot steel, as described.

Index